MW01113821

Bhagavad Gītā

Trans. by James E. Hall

ISBN-13: 978-0-578-40089-1 (Narasimha Publishing)
ISBN-10: 0-578-40089-8

Dedicated to Kimberly Cotton

Foreword

There are many misconceptions concerning the Sanātana Dharma (otherwise known as Hinduism, although the term does imply its universal and eternal nature) both within the West and India. Based on my research, these misconceptions were first introduced into Indian thought approximately around the year 500 BC with Sāṅkya philosophy and soon after, Buddhism. However, for the most part, the traditional current of Indian thought persisted within the country until at least Muslim rule, if not later, but was partially obscured with the influence of the British occupation.

Many terms that come from Sanskrit have been misunderstood by those in the West, which, due to the prevalence of the English language within India, have made their way into Indian culture, as well. For example, many assume that mokṣa is interpreted as escape from the cycle of saṃsāra, when the traditional definition (prior to Sāṅkhya) referred to self-realization (both in terms of the ātman and paramātman). Another example refers to dhyāna – many now believe this refers to either eliminating thought (a notion first popularized by Gautama Buddha) and in some very popular traditions, this concept is even associated with the negation of karma – when in fact the traditional Vedic viewpoint was related to concentration, either in an abstract or directed sense.

Missionary movements from India to the West first began in the late 19th to very early 20th centuries, with the Ramakrishna Order, the Theosophical society and later, in the mid to late 20th century, with ISKCON. All of these missionary movements were influenced by Christianity, specifically Roman Catholicism (despite a tradition of Syrian Christianity within India) – which included the Ramakrishna Order, Vivekananda and later, Śrīla Prabhupāda.

However, misconceptions concerning Vedic thought within the West do go back at least to the 19th century, with the advent of various European Sanskritists. Schopenhauer is well-known for citing Indian religion as being the product of a civilization that has known great suffering – when in fact, Vedic culture was quite joyful and celebrated life. Interestingly, Schopenhauer is regarded as one of the original sources of pessimism in German philosophy, and the traditional Germanic view (prior to Christianity), including that of, and even in particular the Scandinavians and Anglo-Saxons, embraced a traditional Vedic viewpoint.

Many in India believe that the original Vedic culture experienced its downfall when the Brahmins stopped performing the Aśvamedha. This was the ancient horse sacrifice – which celebrated the cycle of the sun and represented the fact that life is very short and should be enjoyed. One of the Sanskrit words for the horse refers to quickness, and this was a reference to the fact that each lifetime is extremely short and should be enjoyed. While no one should actually kill animals unnecessarily, the symbolism of this ritual is incredibly joyful and represents the value that Hindus placed on the celebration of each lifetime.

While there are many sampradayas within Hinduism, for the most part, all commentaries are consistent. Nearly all commentaries in the Hindu tradition say the same thing – they are all simultaneously monistic and dualistic. Even the Advaitins, who are commonly perceived as being pure monists, worshipped Īśvara. The ultimate distillation of Vedic thought from the perspective of commentary on the Vedas occurs with Rāmānuja, who is credited with the idea of qualified monism – the notion that God is simultaneously knowable and unknowable. This is the traditional Vedic point of view and is similar to other traditions within the area, such as Judaism and Islam.

The original point of commentary in India was related to explaining the concepts within the Vedas. They were originally written in Sanskrit and were part of the education of the youths within India, to educate them and to help them understand the language of the śāstras. While many traditions do encourage life-long celibacy, in the original system of varṇāśrama, this was only a practice for young men preparing for marriage. Some in the West (and even in India) believe that the final āśrama (saṃnyāsin) related to celibacy and solitude, but in fact the traditional interpretation related to what those in the modern era call retirement and or the notion of being freed from material concern. This also served as a means of divorce for those who had unhappy marriages for the select few who did actually leave their wives.

However, at least going back well before 800 BC, there has been a tradition in India associated with celibacy and the renunciation of life. This happened well before the introduction of Sāṅkhya philosophy, as evidenced by the language and message within the Bhagavad Gītā. India is well-known for the tradition of the fakir and the bum on the street who begs for alms, and in some cases, who seeks fame and to mislead the youth.

The Gītā is a portion of the Mahābhārata but is well-known by nearly all scholars as being part of a previous oral tradition which was added to this epic poem. It is incredibly obvious based on the language within this śruti śāstra that it is in fact part of a previous oral tradition and that it was first written down at the advent of the Classical period in the Sanskrit language, which occurred, more or less, with the invention of the Devanāgari script and is parallel with the evolution of most of the current written scripts in the East and Near East, with the exception of Chinese.

Based on the message of the Gītā, around the time period of 800 BC the original Vedic message was preserved (the Gītā is well-known as being both a summary and elaboration on the original Vedas and is considered by many to be part of the fifth Veda) – and it is incredibly obvious that the idea of those who did not understand the concept of a saṃnyāsin had emerged within society and was well-established, and that it had become the concept, instead, of the sannyāsin.

Hindus love women – it is my personal theory that the Vedas were originally authored by women, or by men who were inspired by their beauty and mystery. If one looks at the language of the Gītā and the tradition of the red bindu and the common term of phalam, then one will come to the conclusion that women were highly revered – and that Hindu society loves children and family. This is evident not only in the Gītā, but the original Vedas and traditional Hindu society and custom.

The traditional Vedic concept of "sin" is related to crime – it is the violation of dharma, discussion of which is part of the opening (and transition from the Mahābhārata) of the Gītā. This relates to violating God's law – and in the traditional view of karma, there is no way to undo one's actions. Instead, one can do good things in the future, and hope for the best (either in this lifetime, or the next). Unfortunately, most English translations confirm the Western notion of sin. Interestingly, both the Vedas and the Hebrew and Christian traditions associate sin with archery – however, in the Vedas, the concept of archery is related to successful aspiration towards the divine, and in the Judeo-Christian tradition, it is associated with missing the mark.

Modern interpretations of Hinduism seek to find ways to absolve sin. This is a Christian concept, mostly Roman Catholic, that has found its way into ISKCON. ISKCON is the most popular evangelical force of Hinduism within the West and is reasonably popular in India. Based on discussion and observation, it is reasonably obvious that many in India have been infiltrating ISKCON over the last few decades in an effort to encourage traditional Vedic thought in the West.

Śrīla Prabhupāda served as an example of who not to be, even in his own words. He was an uneducated man who came from a reasonably affluent portion of Indian society. Based on linguistic analysis of his works, he had an unhappy marriage and hated women. He did start a very positive movement in the West that also found its way into India, which celebrates sankīrtana. He also was the first to publish Kṛṣṇa's words from the Gītā (in Sanskrit) in the West, and his movement has been incredibly popular.

Despite that, his philosophy was heavily influenced by the Roman Catholic doctrine of absolution of sin. In fact, his organization teaches that accepting a guru eliminates sin, and that engaging in japa meditation also offsets karma. His general teachings are incredibly poisonous, and his organization preaches that one should crave death, rather than enjoying life and all of the amṛtam that saṃsāra has to offer.

The traditional yajña within the Hindu tradition is the Nāciketa sacrifice – that is the eternal chanting of the Lord's name within one's heart. Many traditions within Hinduism, in the English language, preach death and the longing for death in order to escape the suffering of life. In fact, the traditional Vedic point of view celebrates death – both in terms of our accomplishments in each lifetime and the beginning of the next. Those who provide missionary work in the West tend to demonize the concept of Kālī – equating her with kali, or vice, or more properly, conflict – when in fact She represents the Divine Feminine and the heart, as well as the concept of eternal life, which is experienced through birth in each lifetime.

Kīrtan is a form of devotional music that is popular in India and popularized in the West by Prabhupāda. It is in fact a representation of the Nāciketa sacrifice – we are to learn to sing simultaneously with our soulmate and the community – and eventually, if the lesson is learned, it occurs within the heart, as well. Kīrtan is one of the highest forms of prasādam, and the spiritual version, which is practiced between soulmates – is one of the highest of all.

ISKCON is the most popular evangelical force of Hinduism in the West. Unfortunately, through Prabhupāda, it has introduced a number of Roman Catholic ideas into the tradition. However, as it is very successful in providing both good food and kīrtan to Hindus and is very successful in attracting Westerners, it is an institution that can be leveraged to further the aims of those who believe in spreading the original Vedic point of view.

Prabhupāda's work was not only influenced by Roman Catholic doctrine, but his instruction in Sanskrit was in the English language and he was not fluent enough in English to determine some of the finer points of meaning (in terms of English definitions). He was also not provided traditional Vaiṣṇava or Hindu education – and both he and his guru, Bhaktisiddhānta Ṭhākura, were inept in Sanskrit grammar, and neither would have passed a serious course in Sanskrit without serious study and tutoring. Unfortunately, Prabhupāda's work has found its way into the academic community and affected current Sanskrit scholarship, which in turn has found its way into the Indian community, as well. Due to the prevalence of the English language in India, translations in English have an effect on Indian culture. This is part of a long-standing tradition starting potentially with European Sanskritists and has been further compounded by the fact that those seeking publication have traditionally been associated with the modern role of the sannyāsin, or one who "renounces" life and potentially seeks fame, money and or sex from their reputation and teaching. This has been further affected by Western yoga culture, which teaches a variety of harmful notions, such as the modern concept of meditation, that Hindu culture and religion are "mysterious" and that physical exercise is a path to enlightenment.

An important step in reclaiming Vedic culture is the availability of scripture which has an accurate translation and sufficient commentary based in traditional Hindu thought to help offset and undo some of the damage by those whose intentions were not pure or who had little to no education. Currently, accurate translations of the Brahma Saṃhitā and Śrīśopaniṣad exist, and with the release of this book, there is now an accurate translation of the Bhagavad Gītā. Most temples with translations from the Gītā posted are using Western translations – one important step will be to update these with translations based in Vedic tradition. Another important step will be to distribute the śāstras with proper translation to families and individuals, as well as potential new converts – the above works are provided free on Facebook to anyone in the world. And yet another step will be to encourage rational discourse within the Hindu community to help promote the Vedic viewpoint and to help encourage religious leaders to discard the previous notions that have been popularized in recent centuries and to seek a return to traditional Vedic culture. The traditions based in Rāmānuja's work from South India have a reasonably effective method of instruction – but it has not been popularized in the West, and the general interest to the community should be focused on universality and also evangelism in the West.

As ISKCON is such a popular evangelical force in the West and has numerous temples world-wide, this organization should be a primary focus for influence – this will not only help to undo the damage that Prabhupāda effected, but they also have a ready infrastructure and reputation in place, as well as an excellent kīrtan tradition, which can help to provide services for the existing Hindu community world-wide, as well as to spread our message to other members of world society in an effort to bring new converts to the religion. Some believe that one must be born a Hindu – in many respects this is true, but it is not based in nationality or ethnicity – it instead is based in personal perspective and capacity for understanding – and spreading Kṛṣṇa's words far and wide (and in an accurate manner based in tradition) will help to bring in those who are capable of hearing His message. ISKCON also has one Hindu in the US Congress as of the year 2018 (she is not necessarily associated with the organization but grew up with their teachings) and there is a strong Hindu community in the Washington, DC area – with further influence and unification of the community, we can seek greater influence in Washington in an effort to help combat Western culture, while achieving sufficient influence to help promote important concepts, such as world peace and legal reform.

There are a handful of actions that will benefit the Hindu community, and support from leaders will be appreciated by many:

- Promotion of accurate translations and commentaries on the śāstras – this includes updating, as appropriate, translations posted in temples and encouraging devotees to access the freely available resources provided for this purpose.
- Promotion of kīrtan – it is extremely powerful, highly enjoyable and provides fellowship for all devotees and attracts others to Kṛṣṇa's message.
- Rational discourse among religious leaders – this includes āchārya's, temple leaders and scholars.
- In particular, rational discourse with ISKCON devotees and ISKCON leadership – unfortunately, their governing body consists of sannyāsins – many of which make a good living selling books and participating in paid speaking engagements – and so they will be resistant to change, for fear of losing celebrity status.
- Education focused on children to help the next generation understand traditional family values adapted to the modern age, and to understand the history of their culture so they are not poisoned by the Western concepts of yoga, Christianity and celebration of those who renounce life.
- Promotion of Vedic values within government – through the voting process,

discussion with leaders on policy and in working to place Hindus in political positions.

In addition, there are changes that would be very healthy for ISKCON to adopt, specifically, due to their history and current policies:

- Removal of Prabhupāda as an authority within ISKCON – this is not direction to adopt my books, but rather to eliminate the notion that he and his students are intermediaries between God and man.
- In doing so, his statues and images should be removed from temples and his teachings disregarded, as they have no basis in actual Vaiṣṇava tradition.
- Caitanya Mahāprabhu can always be credited with starting this movement, however devotees should be taught that we are all avatars of Kṛṣṇa and no single human being is the sole incarnation of God – and if devotees are taught more about what he did in life and taught, many would not want his image in the temple, and some temples have already adopted two women as Gaura-Nitai, instead.
- With the elimination of the regulative principles and in the interest of spreading the love of Kṛṣṇa to all of humanity, then dance clubs featuring music, kīrtan and refreshments would help bring Kṛṣṇa into popular culture around the world, as well as in providing funding.

I have been working to try and eliminate child abuse (and other sexual predators) from ISKCON. It has a well-known history going back at least to New Vrindaban of supporting and fostering sexual abuse of minors – and the only formal complaint process in the organization concerns the behavior of their sannyāsins. I have found that ISKCON has historically been able to influence its members and also control testimony in court – which is a trend that contributes to an environment of abuse, where victims and reporters are shamed, ostracized and discredited through lies and community accusation and influence from leadership. This edition of the Gītā lays the traditional ideological foundation to erase the mistakes that Prabhupāda and his forebears made, in order to help heal the organization and bring their members into the coming years with an appreciation for the Divine, rather than craving death and providing permission for the rape of their children.

It is important to note, that while there are needed reform efforts within Hinduism to help eliminate a variety of influences that have been particularly pronounced within the last few centuries, that the Sanātana Dharma encompasses most of the world's religions, in particular in looking at their mystical traditions. For example, the Kabbalistic tradition of Judaism and the Sufi tradition within Islam all closely mirror the Hindu viewpoint. And many consider these traditions to encapsulate all of the core values and teachings of the orthodox faith, even if not all of those who subscribe to these traditions are aware of them. There is one notable exception within the major world religions – which is Christianity.

Christianity teaches the concept of original sin, as well as the forgiveness of sin. Sin, if properly classified as such, cannot be forgiven. Depending on the circumstances, one can try and improve one's situations and or seek redemption through action, but the notion of forgiveness by God has been incredibly harmful to humanity. This same concept found within the religion has also made its way into secular society, in the form of prisons and a reluctance to implement the death penalty, as well as a fear of efficient, effective and humane warfare (which is also supported by the establishment seeking to improve or sustain the economy through excessive risk to the loss of human life and the purchase of very expensive weapons).

An important step for humanity will be to combat Christianity, as well as the various concepts that have influenced society within the East and the West. This will be done through ideological warfare, in teaching others about God and ministering to Christians. We should all serve as examples within our own lives, work on appropriate legislation and policy reform – as well as trying to help Christians see the light of God. Once one eliminates the Christian concept of sin, there is actually nothing left to the religion, as Jesus provided little that was redeeming in terms of teachings and without the need to forgive sin, then the "sacrifice" of Jesus has absolutely no value or rational basis.

Many believe that Vedic culture died out when the Aśvamedha was no longer performed in India. There are many stories about its practice and what it represented – it is well-known as the horse sacrifice and may have included the sacrifice of a number of animals. It was a representation of the sun and its cycle – and the fact that life is also very short (but joyful, once we are able to eliminate the most problematic elements of society).

The original Vedic culture was rooted in a more tribal society closer to humanity's origins, when women were considered extraordinarily holy and may have had a significant role in the governance of society. For example – the ancient sacrament of soma referred to the beauty and wisdom of women.

Unfortunately, for all of human history, there has been a great deal of difficulty in identifying some of the more problematic elements of society, but eventually, especially in a small community, one can eventually narrow down the source.

In the Aśvamedha there were a number of sacrifices throughout the day, celebrating the beauty of the sun and all it provides. It was also related to the concept of the rāja and the rāṇī and was a celebration of the soma sacrament. Many believe that the chief sacrificial offering was the horse, based on the name – however, the horse was just one of the offerings made on that special occasion. As mentioned in the commentary of the Gītā, after the sun set the final offering was made – which was one or more "demons." Some believe that the demon was actually sacrificed while alive by having the heart removed – although no one knows for sure. Depending on the nature of the crime that the offering had committed, the Aśvamedha may have also brought about a sense of peace for the community, through resolution and justice. It also served as a reminder to all what the penalty is for violating dharma. The ceremony was also a celebration of war and the peace that it brings.

The Christian church is a source of a great deal of the evil in this world today, even in secular society. Institutions such as prisons and expensive and inefficient warfare are all concepts that seem to have a strong basis in Christian culture (for example, the reluctance to execute when warranted). Ironically, the church was founded on the Aśvamedha itself but has unfortunately been allowed to propagate within society for centuries. Jesus was seen as a problematic element of Jewish society – there are numerous signs that some of the problems he "solved" may have in fact been problems that he started himself and he also declared himself to be the fulfillment of prophecy and the only Son of God. While some of the explanations for his "miracles" could simply be written off as the work of fiction, there are strange things in this world and Jesus himself may have been a "demon" and a form of criminal that has never been tolerated in earlier cultures (such as Jewish and Vedic society). The Jews and Romans did in fact eventually solve the problem – as they dressed him up as a king, presented him with a crown, flogged him like a horse and then executed him as a criminal and a thief. He truly was a sacrifice and offering – it is just unfortunate that the story was not presented properly in literature.

Caitanya Mahāprabhu and Śrīla Prabhupāda had some similarities to Jesus, which may be one of the reasons why they were so fond of the connection they claimed to Christianity. Caitanya actually declared himself to be an avatar of Kṛṣṇa and asked to be worshipped as God. Prabhupāda taught that he and his disciples are capable of absolving original sin through their "baptism" (also known in ISKCON as initiation). Also, neither were particularly likeable individuals and nearly all stories about them portray them as being quite unfriendly and extraordinarily hostile to women.

In my own lifetime, I am working on writing books and articles and working on eventual social and legal reform – much of that is tied to trying to eliminate the traces of Christian thought from society over time. In my own lifetime I can only accomplish so much but at least hope to eventually gain widespread support for the legislation of the death penalty for rapists – and over the millennia, hopefully the Gītā can be used to wage a holy war against Christianity. They represent evil (hatred of women and the abuse of children) and they have provided those who adopt its beliefs a very low sense of self-esteem (they believe they are born into sin and that a variety of actions are sinful, when in fact, depending on the situation, those actions may not be in violation of dharma). They also teach the concept of penance, which does not actually exist – society should be governed by the concept of karma – and there are consequences for our actions.

Those in ISKCON who recognize the signs of Christianity within its teachings should be working to support the effort to eliminate the signs of Jesus from the institution – that does not mean that ISKCON would need to adopt the work of any particular author, but they should be distancing themselves from both Caitanya Mahāprabhu and Śrīla Prabhupāda and their teachings, elimination of mandatory japa, as well as the concept of dīkṣa. While dīkṣa has its roots in traditional Hindu religion, there are no other traditions in Hinduism that attribute any true importance to it, as it is merely a formality during a process of education within certain specific sampradayas. Also, ISKCON is likely to die out within a few decades, anyway, for refusal to let go of the past and its roots in the 1960's and 1970's – it can be preserved over the millennia and become a force for change, but in order to do so it will have to let go of its ties to Prabhupāda and his traditions or people will lose interest as the older disciples move on. Given the age of the leadership in ISKCON, now is a good time to start planning for moving past ISKCON's roots and into the future – and change within the institution will help to preserve its existence – and of course, that will be of benefit to those practicing this particular form of Hinduism when the day comes that there is a true holy war against the Christians.

Hindus have a very long tradition of celebrating the śruti tradition. Western philosophers and writers from Vico to James Joyce and then Marshall McCluhan have predicted the eventual return of human society from the current visual age back to the original aural age – which is focused on a tribal society embracing family values, the worship of women and the Divine Feminine – and embracing true prosperity, over the concept of money – the focus on music as an important element of human society – and the rejection of the male-centric elements found within current Western religion and society. It is clear, based on trends in popular society, that we are in fact (as of the year 2018) returning to the aural age, which has been ongoing since the mid-20th century.

There is a group of people within human society who have existed potentially since the dawn of man – who do have quite a bit to offer humanity, and some of whom have been working on trying to restore Vedic culture world-wide (updated of course, for the modern era). Those working towards improving humanity's situation are known generally as the Sisterhood (that is my term, but in Western occultism they are known as the Great White Brotherhood) – although there is not actually a true organization, they are spread throughout the world's religions.

Some, over time, have experimented with a variety of notions, such as trying to teach people concepts such as "magic." We of course all know that magic does not actually exist, and a variety of concepts related to magic (such as redemption or forgiveness of sin through consuming bread and wine) are incredibly harmful to humanity. Those who do fall for the trick of believing in "magic" end up doing incredibly evil or selfish things for personal gain, which could come at the expense of others. Not all may think of it as "magic", but the manipulation of others for personal gain could potentially be classified as being sinful.

There are a variety of initiatory organizations and traditions that have existed for centuries. Originally, they just offered a few lessons concerning morality and the nature of existence – such as the concept of eternal life. Within Western culture they eventually evolved into organizations that provide "rigorous" programs intended to teach the individual through the process of initiation – something learned over time, is that there is no such thing as an initiatory process, outside of the initiation that life provides on its own. Instead – one will either understand a lesson once one has the appropriate level of maturity to understand it, or one may never understand. But for some, they may benefit from the lesson if properly explained, in plain terms. For those who understand the message, they tend to process it immediately.

The translations and commentaries within this book include the essential truths found within all mystery traditions and religions that are present in the current age, which all stem from the fundamental truths of the Sanātana Dharma – with the exception of Christianity, but their teachings and values are also well-explained in the commentary, with appropriate references to their various harmful concepts and teachings.

It is apparent through an analysis of modern culture, that in particular within in the last few decades the artistic community has been working towards exposing humanity to a coming change that may occur someday. These changes within society will eventually bring about world peace, prosperity and an improved opportunity for personal happiness. It will also help to eliminate some of the more destructive elements from society.

Some of these signs include films such as Star Wars – graphic novels such as Promethea – a variety of musicians ranging from Apoptygma Berserk to A Perfect Circle – and the various movies and books concerning telepathy, extraterrestrials and the unity of humanity.

Those who will eventually partially be responsible for bringing about these changes have probably been within the human race since the dawn of man. There are numerous signs within the Vedas, as well as potentially the structure of the Sanskrit language, that indicate that they were present in Vedic India, including during the original Aryan migration of the Dravidian people. Due to the timing of consistencies in a variety of concepts and related-definitions between words, and the older history of the writing system, this may even be traced to Ancient China. There are also other trends within human history indicating a great prevalence of these individuals within Germanic, Celtic and Near Eastern cultures. Based on timing, this may have originated through trade from the Assyrians (or even before). This is supported by a variety of influences within the Celtic languages, a variety of musical traditions and the various legends that are found in these aforementioned cultures. There is also quite a bit of evidence that there is a very strong genetic presence of these people within Indian culture – and no spiritual tradition in the world best captures many of the fundamental values shared by these people than that of traditional Vedic Hinduism.

Eventually, over time, some may come to realize that the subset of humanity referenced above can provide a great benefit – which is a greater degree of closeness between friends, family and in particular –

within a marriage. However, it is fairly obvious that right now modern science has not advanced to the point, yet, where a new set of laws can necessarily be enforced (without the death penalty for certain violations) in order to protect the rights of the individual and society from this reasonably large subset of humanity. However, it is clearly genetic in nature and there are recorded samples of DNA available to third parties which could be referenced, eventually, if an organized body of individuals with interest in these characteristics ever comes forward – and of course, in addition to those samples (which includes that of one individual with this quality and another which has a complementary quality in terms of being able to clearly perceive the other) others could also come forward and help advance the state of modern science. One of the DNA samples includes the strain of Irish which founds its way to Iceland during the age of the Vikings and intermarried into their society. Iceland is well-known for not only being the land of faeries and elves, but the DNA of nearly the entire population, which is very unique in nature, is on record and can be correlated with these existing samples, if proper studies are not already ongoing. Unfortunately, the other complementary known DNA sample with the active ability belongs to an individual of low intelligence – but the sample still preserves the proper genetic markers.

Genetic research could result in medication to curb bad behavior if the death penalty is not a desired consequence adopted by society. Further, genetic research will firmly expose the existence of this subset of the human race and provide concrete rationale for the development of new laws.

Some would be concerned that humanity would fear this sort of quality in others that is hinted at above. That should be fairly obvious given humanity's tendency towards genocide. However, in the current age we are becoming less concerned about the right to privacy – and anyone who understands the benefit associated with this genetic trend would quickly become open to the notion – assuming that those who do inflict pain and misery on others have a means of being dealt with. One should be concerned about the governments of the world, as they would attempt to use this to their advantage, and obviously we do need more enlightened governments.

However, those in the majority would have no desire to cooperate with the government and are concerned about ethical and moral behavior. The governments should understand that society will run far more smoothly, including their own administration of law, if laws are established that provide penalties for unethical and immoral behavior.

No means of protection exists for those who are not part of this trend within the human race. We must rely on ethics and morality – as well as punishment. Once society is able to determine the source of a great deal of current misery among various individuals who are affected, then proper punishment and laws can be defined and implemented – and the solution for humanity is self-realization and liberation, both of which are outlined in this book.

A notion introduced by Christianity is a reluctance to support assassination or the death penalty. There are few crimes where this should be applicable, but there are some, such as rape, that do require this as a solution. One motivation for working over time on eliminating the Christian religion and its traces that are found within society will be to eliminate rape from the human race by dealing with the issue as soon as it appears.

One benefit to exploring some of the notions listed above through scientific research and improved education within human society will be an improved relationship between human beings involving closeness and intimacy. It is something that only a few may have experienced in their lives so far – and hopefully, over time, others will experience for themselves and discover a greater means of being closer to God.

It should be noted that there are positive benefits to humanity in eventual exposure to society at large, in plain terms. Some of these individuals hurt others and or pose as God to some and providing awareness to others and enforcement of law will allow greater unity and safety in human society. In addition to providing awareness, both through open dialogue and some basic instruction for those who are unaware of the existence of this ability, law enforcement and investigation (such as those who look for those in trouble and a hotline to call to seek assistance) will help to keep behavior in check and allow for greater intimacy among those who care for each other and are compatible. If dialogue does occur, many will realize that if they have been led into believing that these individuals are actually superior, more intelligent – or even from another place or species, then it will become evident that they are simply human beings and are as flawed and unintelligent as the rest of us.

This book outlines the spiritual basis for the next age of man – by reclaiming the original thought and beliefs found within early Vedic culture. It includes a description of the beauty of Kṛṣṇa – which is that of the night sky and the universe. It also outlines a variety of values for humanity derived from the Vedas in the form of both extremely accurate translation and commentary that will eventually lead to world peace and prosperity – and the concept of self-realization for all and liberation for those who have no hope of rehabilitation.

This version of the Bhagavad Gītā is my Finnegan's Wake – as written and translated by a business man, minimalist and a devotee of the Divine Feminine. It includes the wisdom of the East and the West, the story of all of human history, it starts and ends reasonably close to the beginning (and end), consistent with the concept of the cakra and the yuga – it tells the story of Eve and the fall of man – but it also tells the story of the evils of Jesus and his church, celebrates the divinity of women – and will eliminate the concept of shame and sin – as if humanity learns from the lessons of Viṣṇu, then they will tend the garden, prune the tree – and provide swift justice as soon as we perceive a cancerous growth on the banyan tree of the human race.

Summary

For centuries writers in the Sanskrit language have created summaries of and commentaries on the Vedas, including such historical figures as Śaṅkara and those in his line of succession.

Below is my summary of the Vedas in Sanskrit:

brahmeśvara dharma karma yajña

Which can be further summarized as:

īśvara

And the woman to whom this book is dedicated (as well as all of my work in life) did an even better job, and simply summarized the Vedas as:

kiṃ

Chapter One

At the battle of Kurukṣetra, Arjuna was assembled at the beginning of a war between the people of Bhārata and that of the Kauravas. The below śloka, text 40, provides a synopsis of the reason for warfare – which was to protect the soma of India from the unbelievers.

-

adharmābhibhavāt kṛṣṇa praduṣyanti kula-striyaḥ
strīṣu duṣṭāsu vārṣṇeya jāyate varṇa-saṅkaraḥ

-

Kṛṣṇa, without dharma one is defeated;
the community of women will become polluted,
and females dear to you will
have been defiled and produce unwanted children.

-

Commentary

This text relates to the only actual absolute law related to dharma – which is "thou shalt not rape."

Chapter Two

Much like Chapter One of what has always been known as the Bhagavad Gītā, Chapter Two is simply transition from the Mahabhārata into the actual text of the Gītā and does not have much substance to it. It does however set the stage for the opening of Chapter 3, as Arjuna is afraid of getting blood on his hands.

The Gītā is a very old text that originates from an oral tradition, a fact that is supported by the language of the śāstra, as well as the opinion of modern scholars. Most Hindus do realize that Kṛṣṇa (and the other avatars of Viṣṇu) never actually walked on the Earth and that these stories are mythology that serve as explanation of the universe and human society. Hindus are incredibly sophisticated and outside of a few, tend to understand the meaning of their religion, which is evident from review of all literature (for the most part) outside of that of the Gaudiya tradition. Unfortunately, their teachers were not very educated or intelligent.

The Gītā was authored by a woman and is essentially a bed-time story told to her husband to get ready for bed. Those who are familiar with women will pick up on that when reading this translation.

For future generations, if parents continue to chant the Gītā in study groups, I hope that their children, after reading this book pick up on the message of the text and understand that it is a love story about God and man, as told by a beautiful woman to her equally beautiful husband. And hopefully they read this book and understand that the Maha Mantra encapsulates all of the truth of the Gītā – the balance and unity of male and female, with an emphasis on the feminine – the beauty of both men and women – and the darkness of the night sky and the ferocity of the warrior spirit. The book also explains the meaning of the guru – who is our spouse.

I hope that someday the woman I wrote this book for appreciates this gift, which has no expectation attached to it – but maybe will contemplate the friendship I promised someday in the future. She is a grove in the forest and a twin – and this gift was written by a twin, as well, and a water-bearer – who is also a born Hindu and who has been covered in flame since birth and who is descended from both the Vikings and the Celts.

Chapter Three

Text 1

arjuna uvāca
jyāyasi cet karmaṇas te matā buddhir janārdana
tat kiṃ karmaṇi ghore māṃ niyojayasi keśava

-

Arjuna said:

Keśava, You will conquer
through the venerable duty
You have given me –
my mind enjoys Your obligation
and the duty You have given.

§

Text 2

vyāmiśreṇeva vākyena buddhiṃ mohayasīva me
tad ekaṃ vada niścitya yena śreyo 'ham āpnuyām

-

Like two outstretched arms,
I have two choices
and am confused.

Please advise me
so that I am assured
through You –
I want to be victorious.

§

Text 3

śrī-bhagavān uvāca
loke 'smin dvi-vidhā niṣṭhā purā proktā mayānagha
jñāna-yogena sāṅkhyānāṃ karma-yogena yogināṃ

-

Śrī-Bhagavān said:

In this place
there are two states of being,
given that the body and mind
have been anointed
with My presence –
compare yourself to Kṛṣṇa,
who is perfect.

With jñāna yoga
one deliberates through reason,
and with karma yoga
one seeks to be joined with Me.

§

Text 4

na karmaṇām anārambhān naiṣkarmyaṃ puruṣo
'śnute
na ca sannyasanād eva siddhiṃ samadhigacchati

-

The Puruṣa enjoys
those who do not
abandon their duties
nor renounce the world –
as He performs
them with you.

§

Text 5

na hi kaścit kṣaṇam api jātu tiṣṭhaty akarma-kṛt
kāryate hy avaśaḥ karma sarvaḥ prakṛti-jair guṇaiḥ

-

He is not with those
who perform non-action
or act without
a pure heart –
all of those born from Prakṛti
are accompanied by the guṇas.

§

Text 6

karmendriyāṇi saṃyamya ya āste manasā smaran
indriyārthān vimūḍhātmā mithyācāraḥ sa ucyate

-

Kṛṣṇa inhabits the intellect
and assists in being mindful

of karma and the power of the senses.

The senses are the companion of Indra –
it is foolish to have
improper conduct with respect
to their objects –
Kṛṣṇa is the ātman.

-

Commentary

Karmendriya is a technical term that historically relates to the five organs of action which pertain to the most part in positive interactions with people and the world, including that of speaking, touching, walking, worshiping and procreation. However, the term can also refer both to action or karma, as well as the sense organs, in general – which ultimately has the same meaning, although the term karmendriya has a very specific meaning if taken as a compound word.

Indra represents the intellect, in addition to being an early representation in the Vedas of Kṛṣṇa. Indriya refers to the senses, as well as the companion of Indra – which has the same meaning, as our senses are the means through which we interact with the world in cooperation with and on behalf of our intellect.

§

Text 7

yas tv indriyāṇi manasā niryamyārabhate 'rjuna
karmendriyaiḥ karma-yogam asaktaḥ sa viśiṣyate

-

Arjuna –
restrain your senses
with your intellect –
he who is free from the senses
and practices karma yoga
is distinguished from others.

§

Text 8

niyataṃ kuru karma tvaṃ karma jyāyo hy akarmaṇaḥ
śarīra-yātrāpi ca te ṇa prasiddhyed akarmaṇaḥ

-

You are answerable for your actions –
always act within dharma
and do not abandon one's duty.

The jīva comes from the mother
and is like Kṛṣṇa –
you do not want
to achieve the result
of inaction.

-

Commentary

Śarīra relates to the body and has two suspected sources etymologically: śri, which is related to Śrī, can refer to support, resting on or leaning on; as well as śṛ, which can refer in this context to that which can be destroyed. Both of these meanings relate to the physical body – we come from the mother and we will also experience death.

Yātrā can refer to the support of life but it can also refer to movement, traveling and seeking (which is a separate word (yātṛ) with the same declined form) – the latter word would appear in this text in the instrumental and has the further meaning of "charioteer."

Siddhyet refers to reaching a goal or result, but also has a relationship to archery – in the Sanātana Dharma, arrows are associated with many of the representations of God, including Śiva and Rāma. In the Hindu context, archery is associated with good things, such as accomplishment and aspiring towards God – in the Judeo-Christian traditions, the origin of the word that is typically translated as "sin" also relates to archery and refers to missing the mark or falling short. Many concepts found within the Judeo-Christian traditions, in particular Christianity, find themselves more or less inverted in our tradition – that which Christians find to be sinful, such as birth into each lifetime, is frequently considered very holy and sacred within Hinduism.

§

Text 9

yajñārthāt karmaṇo 'nyatra loko 'yaṃ karma-bandhanaḥ
tad-arthaṃ karma kaunteya mukta-saṅgaḥ samācara

-

Kaunteya –
your artha is a yajña –
in this world
one is bound to duty
but finds freedom
in devotion to it.

§

Text 10

saha-yajñāḥ prajāḥ sṛṣtvā purovāca prajāpatiḥ
anena prasaviṣyadhvam eṣa vo 'stv iṣṭa-kāma-dhuk

-

Prajāpati created
man for worship
and as My home –
He is my original creative aspect
and requests
that all perform service to Me
through procreation
and preservation –
you should seek this for yourself,
as a husband
provides love and affection.

-

Commentary

Prajāpati corresponds to Brahmā – while some associate Brahmā with the first created being (a deva sometimes confused with Mānu), He is actually the creative aspect of the Trimūrti, from the perspective of the creation of the universe, which happens continually. Brahmā is an alternate declined form of the nominative of Brahman – this form is used to distinguish the universe's creative force from the unknowable aspect of God. Those who have been raised within a traditional environment understand that Brahmā is rarely worshipped on His own – and that is because we better relate to the personal aspect of God, Īśvara. Those familiar with the Vedas will recognize this immediately, given that one of the principle commentaries on the Upaniṣads is the Brahma Sutra – Brahma is the other nominative form of Brahman, and is used when referring to Him in his unknowable form. Viṣṇu, or Kṛṣṇa, is the Preserver and represents life and procreation. The word Prajāpati consists of prajā, which refers to children, and pati, which corresponds to either a husband or wife. Brahman is very commonly referred to in the Vedas by the word tataḥ – which means father, and also diffuse or all-spreading. In this text prasa refers to extension, diffusion and procreation – and the accompanying word within the compound is viṣyadhvam, which is a command to act or perform sevā. Kṛṣṇa wants His very special creation – the universe, as well as the human race – to exist eternally, and procreation is an important aspect of this and part of the artha of many, if not most, human beings.

§

Text 11

devān bhāvayatānena te devā bhāvayantu vaḥ
parasparaṃ bhāvayantaḥ śreyaḥ param avāpsyatha

-

Others exist for worship –
love them
and together, with shared mantras
you will experience reciprocity
and together achieve the highest
through creation –
this is a gift from Śrī
and binds all of Us together.

-

Commentary

The word deva corresponds to any heavenly being, as well as those deities who were not always traditionally associated with being a direct aspect of God, and it also refers to human beings; this is a masculine noun, but in its feminine form, devī, it nearly always refers to the female half of God.

There are multiple means of parsing bhāvayatānena – the choice of words that makes most sense includes tānena, which is the instrumental case associated with a fiber, tone or monotonous tone – mantras of course do not need to be monotonous and are quite pleasing to Kṛṣṇa when sung with devotion. This word is also associated with the recitation of the Vedas, which were originally sung by Gāyatrī.

Avāpsyatha consists of ava, āp and syatha – these words together indicate the act of binding with the simultaneous sense of coming down from on high, as well as arrival. Further, the root of syatha (sā) is related at least phonetically to a word that means Lakṣmī, Rādhā and the sacred, as well as giving or bestowing. While Lakṣmī is associated among some as a goddess of fortune, throughout the Vedas She is associated with the concept of welfare, happiness and prosperity in the sense that is provided by the mother and wife, both in temporal terms, as well as in Her role as the Divine Mother.

§

Text 12

iṣṭān bhogān hi vo deva dāsyante yajña-bhāvitāḥ
tair dattān apradāyaibhyo yo bhuṅkte stena eva saḥ

-

My devotees
will give themselves
to each other
for the enjoyment of Viṣṇu
and help those
who do not know Me.

-

Commentary

Iṣṭān refers to those who are cherished or beloved and is related to the past participle for sacrifice, which also has the meaning of praise and worship – in addition to being a name in the Vedas for Viṣṇu, as well as Agni, who presides over the marriage ceremony.

Bhogān refers to the offering and relates to bhuj which refers to bowing and enjoyment through consumption, as well as the objects of consumption.

Dāsyante refers simultaneously to giving, including giving one's hand in marriage (with the verb root dā), as well as desire and exhaustion (through fire) – the root verb, das, refers to sight, light and exhaustion.

Dattān refers to that which has been given or honored – in this case, it is the devout Vaiṣṇava who hears Kṛṣṇa. This word appears in the accusative as the object of bhuṅkte, which refers to enjoyment and consumption, which Kṛṣṇa does with His offerings. Yaḥ is a name of Kṛṣṇa and means charioteer in this context. Pradāya has a relationship to prasādam and also refers to that which is given and is negated in the text – but it is also possibly an address to that which is not a gift or one who does not give. Through our offerings to Kṛṣṇa we can also assist Him in providing for those who have not yet received His blessing.

§

Text 13

yajña-śiṣṭāśinaḥ santo mucyante sarva-kilbiṣaiḥ
bhuñjate te tv aghaṃ pāpā ye pacanty ātma-kāraṇāt

-

You must punish
those who have
offended Me –
they have reached the end
of their lives –
they sought Me
and did not find Me.

They have consumed
and enjoyed evil –
I am the source of the ātman
but I also provide the basis for judgment
through my devotees.

-

Commentary

Many of the words within this text pertain to cooking and eating, however cooking in this particular context (due to āś, which is the source of āśinaḥ) also relates to coming to the end of one's life – while it may refer to doing so through old age, there is also a command within the Sanskrit that refers to punishment – and one of the multiple references to eating refers to eating and enjoying sin (the Hindu concept is not the same as that in other religions, as it is based in the law of karma, which is not necessarily absolute).

Mucyante refers to archery – aspiring towards Viṣṇu involves hitting the mark and has obvious associations to warfare within the historical context of the Gītā. It also refers to both liberation and slackening of the reins – as we are the chariot, and Kṛṣṇa is the charioteer, eventually within this lifetime we encounter a moment when we pass to the next one.

Kāraṇāt is in the ablative and can be paired with ātman – kāraṇam refers to the original source, as well as both the earthly and heavenly father, in addition to that upon which a judgment is founded (such as the law), as well as action.

§

Text 14

annād bhavanti bhūtāni parjanyād anna-sambhavaḥ
yajñād bhavati parjanyo yajñaḥ karma-samudbhavaḥ

-

They come from Me
and have always existed –
one who joins with Me
will also provide prasādam
for the Earth –
I am the yajña
and the source of both karma
and rebirth.

-

Commentary

Annam does refer to food, as well as prasādam – but it also refers to the Earth, water and Viṣṇu – we all originate from the eternal waters of creation, which proceed from and are a part of Kṛṣṇa, who has the likeness of the night sky.

Parjanyaḥ refers to rain, Indra and Prajāpati. Sambhavaḥ refers to union and the creation of existence – and samudbhavaḥ refers to rebirth, as well as Agni – the funeral pyre is a traditional practice and fire is of course relevant to yajña, in many ways. Through the union of devout Vaiṣṇavas and a loving upbringing, we provide the best opportunity for our children to contribute to humanity and provide for Kṛṣṇa's enjoyment – one's starting position in the next lifetime is determined through karma. Karma relates both to the actions of our free will as human beings, as well as the system that traditionally is considered to determine one's parents in the next lifetime. Not only is all of existence eternal, but it is also subject to His judgment, through us, and those who are devout and morally superior provide the best opportunity for those in the subsequent lifetimes.

§

Text 15

karma brahmodhbhavaṃ viddhi brahmākṣara-samudbhavam
tasmāt sarva-gataṃ brahma nityaṃ yajñe pratiṣṭhitam

-

Know that rebirth
comes from the imperishable Viṣṇu
through karma –
the universe flows
eternally from Brahman
like milk from the Mother.

§

Text 16

evaṃ pravartitaṃ cakraṃ nānuvartayatīha yaḥ
aghāyur indriyārāmo moghaṃ pārtha sa jīvati

-

One who is not accompanied
by Me
lives an impure life
without meaning.

§

Text 17

yas tv ātma-ratir eva syād ātma-tṛptaś ca mānavaḥ
ātmany eva ca santuṣṭas tasya kāryaṃ na vidyate

-

One wishes to rest
in the pleasure of the ātman –

I am satisfied with My creation,
but am most pleased
with one who performs his duty
with Me –
some do not understand –
some do not learn –
and some do not seek Me.

-

Commentary

The ātman refers to the self, as well as the Self – while paramātman does exist in Sanskrit and is the concept of the greater Self of which we all are part of, ātman can refer to both. It can also refer to the self in a more mundane sense – but in seeking the self, we find the Self – and vice versa.

Kāryam refers to action and duty, as well as punishment – it can also refer to a libation.

Santuṣṭaḥ can refer to sacred pleasure and delight – as well as pleasure and delight in the sacred. San comes from sat and refers to the good and the sacred – which comes from existence and the understanding and wisdom that comes from seeking the true nature of reality.

§

Text 18

naiva tasya kṛtenārtho nākṛteneha kaścana
na cāsya sarva-bhūteṣu kaścid artha-vyapāśrayaḥ

-

One performs his duty
and obligation;
another has no need of this world –
consider all actions
and rely on yourself –
some live with no meaning.

§

Text 19

tasmād asaktaḥ satataṃ kāryaṃ karma samācara
asakto hy ācaran karma param āpnoti pūruṣaḥ

-

One who has continually
acted without attachment
will have performed their duty
because of Him
and will achieve the Highest.

§

Text 20

karmaṇaiva hi saṃsiddhim āsthitā janakādayaḥ
loka-saṅgraham evāpi sampaśyan kartum arhasi

-

You will enjoy success

by remaining firm
in action –
you are entitled to conquer
if one sees Me
in everything, and in everything
you do.

-

Commentary

Interestingly, pārtha, which is referenced in Text 16 and typically translated as the vocative of pārthaḥ (Arjuna), also refers to the mantras chanted during an ancient ceremony used to consecrate a new rāja, which happens to include the soma pressing, a chariot race, archery and a dice game, the latter of which is associated with the rāja's creative and generative power.

Mānavaḥ, which appears in Text 17, can be used as a generic reference to a human being, but also relates to one's worth, as well as indicating the subject of a rāja.

§

Text 21

yad yad ācarati śreṣṭhas tat tad evetaro janaḥ
sa yat pramāṇaṃ kurute lokas tad anuvartate

-

A superior individual

knows both Kṛṣṇa and Śrī
and leads others
through action and example –
he is a rāja
who lives in harmony
with others and Me –
he is set apart
but especially from those
who have fallen and not found Me.

-

Commentary

Śreṣṭhaḥ refers to one who is most beautiful, or most excellent, and has additional meanings of rāja, Viṣṇu and Śrī.

Kṛṣṇa appears multiple times in this text, as many pronouns also relate to Him. Yad can also have the meaning of Puruṣa and yaḥ can refer to both a chariot, or a charioteer.

The word jānaḥ refers to a living person, but it also has the connotation of the common man. Pramāṇam not only refers to a scale or a standard, but more specifically the right standard for comparison – which relates to virtue – and also relates to unity.

Itaraḥ distinguishes between two individuals, but also has a further meaning of one who is vile and wretched.

§

Text 22

na me pārthāsti kartavyaṃ triṣu lokeṣu kiñcana
nānavāptam avāptavyaṃ varta eva ca karmaṇi

-

One who lives
in the three worlds
and does not live
for Me –
is lacking in jñānam.

One who is lacking –
one who refrains from action –
one who acts without Me –
will not be received by Me.

§

Text 23

yadi hy ahaṃ na varteyaṃ jātu karmaṇy atandritaḥ
mama vartmānuvartante manuṣyāḥ pārtha sarvaśaḥ

-

Arjuna:

I may not want
to carry out this obligation
with complete assurance.

Śrī-Bhagavān:

Know that I am always
with you, and all people,
and accompany you in all actions.

§

Text 24

utsīdeyur ime lokā na kuryāṃ karma ced aham
saṅkarasya ca kartā syām upahanyām imāḥ prajāḥ

-

They long for death and sacrifice –
I am the Creator – the Doer –
you belong to Me
and I act through you –
I want to slay them with you.

-

Commentary

Sad (sīdeyuḥ) refers to sitting but can specifically refer to sitting before the sacrificial fire – and is modified by ut, which refers to an upwards direction, or above.

Hanyām refers to execution (in terms of the death penalty), but also refers to beating the war drum and is modified by upa, which indicates with, or doing something side-by-side. Saṅkarasya also refers to doing something with assistance, as it can refer to the breadth of twenty-four thumbs – and can refer to the elephant's trunk, which removes obstacles and performs work – Gaṇeśa is the remover of obstacles and relates to the intellect, which is a part of the mind of which Kṛṣṇa is a part, as both the chariot and the charioteer.

§

Text 25

saktāḥ karmaṇy avidvāṃso yathā kurvanti bhārata
kuryād vidvāṃs tathāsaktaś cikīrṣur loka-saṅgraham

-

They have committed themselves
to action, without understanding Me –
your people – Bhārata –
are my agents.
One wants to have wisdom
and understanding –
do not be intent
on desiring this action –
instead focus on understanding
the sacred –
demons who attempt
to steal what is precious
to Me meet with destruction –
and the sacred cannot be obscured.

-

Commentary

Kurvanti refers to those who act, or act as agents. Bhārata can refer to a descendant of Bhārata, or it can refer to all of India. Of course, this is an old śāstra, but we can all find our spiritual home within the Sanātana Dharma, if we are capable of hearing and understanding Kṛṣṇa's message. Bhārata also refers to one who bears the oblation – which refers both to Agni, as well as the one who lights the homam fire, which in the Śrī Vaiṣṇava tradition are typically the female attendants at the yajña (which is a ritual dedicated to bhakti, rather than requests to the devas).

Saṅgraham refers to seizure, conquering, perceiving and understanding, specifically related to the sacred nature of existence – the base component word, graham, can also refer to one who eclipses the sun, and refers to the myth of the demon Rāhu who attempted to steal the elixir of immortality from Viṣṇu (amṛtam refers to both immortality and an elixir) and swallowed the sun multiple times in their chase through the heavens, but was never able to completely obscure it – and eventually was slain by Viṣṇu through decapitation. Incidentally, it also refers to the soma ladle.

§

Text 26

na buddhi-bhedaṃ janayed ajñānāṃ karma-saṅginām
joṣayet sarva-karmāṇi vidvān yuktaḥ samācaran

-

Those who lack

understanding and reason
cannot discriminate
and long for ignorance –
the wise have understanding
and desire to be united with Me
and act in My name.

§

Text 27

prakṛteḥ kriyamāṇāni guṇaiḥ karmāṇi sarvaśaḥ
ahaṅkāra-vimūḍhātmā kartāham iti manyate

-

One separates and spins
the fabric of Prakṛti
with the mind –
I am the Doer –
the world arises through the self.

-

Commentary

Karta refers to separation and distinction, as well as a spindle. It is related to both action and discrimination. The three guṇas, as traditionally described, represent various qualities of reality and our minds process everything we encounter – this affects perception, belief and decision-making.

Ahaṅkāra refers to the individuation of the world through both the mind and senses. It is related to indriya – the companion of Indra – which relates to the various organs of sense and discrimination. Indra relates to the intellect and mind, as well as Kṛṣṇa. This term has a historical philosophical meaning which came after the original writing of the Gītā – many assume that Buddhism evolved from Sāṅkhya philosophy and may be the original school of thought in India that rejected the sanctity of existence and led to the rejection of life and the world in favor of mokṣa – mokṣa refers both to self-awareness, as well as liberation from saṃsāra – Buddhism and related philosophies are fundamentally atheist in nature. Those who believe that life and the universe are impure and that life is equivalent to suffering desire to leave saṃsāra – those who love life understand that one must live life to its fullest and appreciate the sacred nature of birth and existence, and desire to drink the nectar of immortality. While there is a philosophical relationship to Sāṅkhya in this term, the school of thought developed later than the writing of the Gītā and the association with traditional terms related to the senses and the mind indicate that it existed at least several hundred years prior to the development of Sāṅkhya.

Māya refers to our perceived separation from God. Prakṛti is the world of which we are a part – we can touch and feel everything we perceive with our body, senses and mind. Once we achieve mokṣa and experience the jñānam associated with intuitive understanding of the divine, then we can pierce the veil of māya and see the universe as it truly is. Aldous Huxley, who was a student of the Gītā and helped to popularize the term Sanātana Dharma in the West is famous for quoting William Blake: "If the doors of perception were cleansed every thing would appear to man as it is, Infinite."

In the Sanātana Dharma the mind is considered to be a part of the soul, or ātman. While we are divine and a part of Rādha-Kṛṣṇa, we are not the entirety of existence and must remember to realize that we are not the totality of existence on our own and remain humble before Him/Her – and those who worship man as the highest form of god also adhere to a form of atheism, as well (in addition to those who believe the universe is impure and corrupt).

§

Text 28

tattva-vit tu mahā-bāho guṇa-karma-vibhāgayoḥ
guṇā guṇeṣu vartanta iti matvā na sajjate

-

Together with Me understand
the true nature of reality –
I am the entirety of the Universe –
do not hesitate
to unite with Me – continually –
in thought, belief and experience.

-

Commentary

Tattvam refers to the true nature of reality. While a single word, it can also relate to a phrase found in the

Vedas – older English language translations use the phrase "thou art that." The verb "to be" is optional in Sanskrit.

Vit can either refer to knowing, perceiving and understanding (with connotations of remembrance), as well as piercing – piercing the veil of māya is a common historical phrase associated with the Sanātana Dharma in the English language, and one of the many names of Viṣṇu is the sword. Bāhu refers to a measure, such as that of an arm, as well as the support of a door.

Na has common meanings of negation, not and neither – however, specifically within the Vedas, later śruti śāstras and some Classical period smṛti literature, it can be used to provide emphasis to other particles, in particular if found within a later clause in the śloka and can indicate a request to do something in a particular manner.

Sajjate in the passive voice refers to attachment, devotion and yoga.

§

Text 29

prakṛter guṇa-sammūḍhāḥ sajjante guṇa-karmasu
tān akṛtsna-vido mandān kṛtsna-vin na vicālayet

-

Those who are confused
about reality

are concerned with worldly action –
some of those who
have understanding
help them to change their course –
but all who have jñānam
should do so.

§

Text 30

mayi sarvāṇi karmāṇi sannyasyādhyātma-cetasā
nirāśīr nirmamo bhūtvā yudhyasva vigata-jvaraḥ

-

All actions which are surrendered
through the heart and mind
to Me are precious.

Pray for wisdom –
fight and abstain from
mental anguish.

-

Commentary

Āśīḥ refers to prayer and a blessing, as well as being a reference to healing – it can also refer to the fang of a serpent. In many cultures the serpent is associated with wisdom – which has even frequently been personified as a female aspect of the divine in some Near Eastern cultures that evolved prior to modern Christianity – and in some of the esoteric traditions associated with the Sanātana Dharma, the kuṇḍalinī serpent, which represents the combined breath and energy uniting the macro and microcosm, relates to Śakti, the active and feminine aspect of God. Wisdom comes through the combined grace of Kṛṣṇa and our intellects – and we obtain the grace of Kṛṣṇa in offering our hearts. Jñānam is associated with wisdom rather than purely intellectual seeking.

§

Text 31

ye me matam idaṃ nityam anutiṣṭhanti mānavāḥ
śraddhāvanto 'nasūyanto mucyante te 'pi karmabhiḥ

-

Those who are faithful to me
act continually
with devotion and certainty –
their karma is drawing near
and they should not be
allowed to procreate.

-

Commentary

Śraddhā refers to both faith and certainty – as well as having an association to an ancient practice of honoring the dead.

Anasūyantaḥ refers to not producing children – which refers both to those who do not procreate, as well as having the connotation that not producing children for Viṣṇu is not pleasing to Him.

Mucyante is in the passive voice and refers to liberation, slackening and allowing one to depart from life.

Nitya refers to one's own people – who are constant and loyal and belong to the community – as well as referring to continually performing sacred acts to Viṣṇu, such as yajña.

§

Text 32

ye tv etad abhyasūyanto nānutiṣṭhanti me matam
sarva-jñāna-vimūḍhāṃs tān viddhi naṣṭān acetasaḥ

-

They do not live
for Me –
they have gone completely astray –
are lacking in knowledge of Me –
and have lost the splendor
of both the mind and heart.

-

Commentary

Naṣṭa refers to loss and destruction, but also has meanings associated with losing sight of that which one cannot be seen, as well as passing judgment (and being on the losing side).

§

Text 33

sadṛśaṃ ceṣṭate svasyāḥ prakṛter jñānavān api
prakṛtiṃ yānti bhūtāni nigrahaḥ kiṃ kariṣyati

-

The wise live in the world
and know that I am present –
they act on behalf
of their own –
they join together in union
and provide offspring worthy of Me –
and will punish those
whose actions
violate My law.

-

Commentary

Jñānavat refers to one who has wisdom and knowledge of the various levels of understanding of Kṛṣṇa – this includes knowledge of the physical and spiritual, as well as science.

Yā refers to movement – it can refer to restraint – but also attainment and has associations with Lakṣmī. Bhūta refers to those who live and refers both to that which has happened before and to that which will happen in the future – it also refers to yoga, prosperity, devotees of God and children.

Nigrahaḥ refers to punishment, and also has associations with both Viṣṇu and Śiva.

Note that during mantra recitations in a homam setting some change the usual namaḥ to svāhāḥ – which is an address to all of those present, indicating that all those worshipping Kṛṣṇa are together and are of one people.

§

Text 34

indriyasyendriyasyārthe rāga-dveṣau vyavasthitau
tayor na vaśam āgacchet tau hy asya paripanthinau

-

Together we have a great purpose –
and are of course unhappy
that they are in our way
and have forced us to leave our home –
unite in yoga with Me
and live for Me.

-

Commentary

Indriyasya is the genitive of indriya and implies possession or interest in the companion of Indra (the mind or sense organs). Indriyasyārthe is a compound word indicating that which belongs to or has interest in the companion of Indra (or that which is suitable for Indra) and great purpose – or it can refer to the sense organs and the sense object. If one does not assume that this is a compound and rather a genitive with a standalone dual noun, then some existing translations do not make sense, as one wonders why the dual person is used in the text – one could assume that indriyasya is stated twice for emphasis, and arthe is dual with respect to that, however there are other indicators in the text that would suggest otherwise. Given sandhi rules, the final component word could be arthe – which refers to one's occupation or purpose – or ārthe, which refers to something that is significant. When used in the dual person this concept implies that both Kṛṣṇa and Arjuna are working together. When considering this as a compound, there are other means of constructing it, however a traditional construction would suggest the purpose of the companion of Indra, rather than the combined purpose of one who is suitable to Him – and either way, the repeated use of indriya in the genitive, if not considered as a compound, implies emphasis of the sanctity of the mind and senses to Kṛṣṇa and all comments on person and sandhi rules also still apply.

The word associated with hindering is paripanthinau, which according to Paṇini means hindrance in a Vedic context. The Gītā was written reasonably close to the beginning of the Classical period, and it is well known as being a summary of the Upaniṣads, and therefore having a Vedic influence – either stylistically, or as a carry-over from an earlier text or oral tradition –

makes sense, given both the time period and subject matter. While some could argue this applies to the sense organs and their use, the interpretation of arthe as being a sense object does not make a lot of sense given the dialogue between Kṛṣṇa and Arjuna, as well as for theological reasons and the date of the text. If one eliminates later philosophical interpretations of the nature of reality and our aim in life that existed well after the writing of the Gītā, then maintaining the highly spiritual dialogue of the Mahābhārata reveals a message consistent with historical Vedic thought and tradition, especially given Kṛṣṇa's relationship to Indra in the evolution of the Vedas away from the original Ṛg Veda. This word has a later meaning in Classical Sanskrit that refers to an enemy or robber – which is very interesting, given the currently popular translation and commentary on this particular text authored by Śrīla Prabhupāda and with respect to his claim that he was attempting to destroy Western civilization by teaching them about his own way of life.

Rāga can mean interest or affection, which could relate to attachment – however, it also refers to coloring, in particular with the color red. It also means passion from the perspective of love. Dveṣa refers to hatred or dislike.

Artha, in addition to referring to purpose also refers to wealth – and Kṛṣṇa's general message in terms of motivation for eliminating the threat from the opposing faction is in protecting his family or future family.

Vyavasthiti refers to being apart or away from stability and rest or being away from one's home.

Āgam in this context most likely refers to the desire to ascend or approach, and the generic "one" to whom it applies does not have the authority to do so (vaśam).

The combination of great purpose and the association of Kṛṣṇa to the self and uniting with Him in action, in particular given the preceding dialogue between Kṛṣṇa and Arjuna, and the togetherness implied in the grammar within this text, indicates that He continues to refer to karma yoga, the yoga of action, within the highly spiritual instructions to Arjuna to fight for his family, in God's name.

§

Text 35

śreyān sva-dharmo viguṇaḥ para-dharmāt sv-anuṣṭhitāt
sva-dharme nidhanaṃ śreyaḥ para-dharmo bhayāvahaḥ

-

Women – in particular those
who are dear –
are the highest dharma –
fear of their loss
is an ordeal –
and encourages one to sacrifice.

-

Commentary

Śreyaḥ is a comparative term referring to that which is better than or more beautiful and modifies the base word śrī, which refers to yoga, union, prosperity, Lakṣmī and women. Śrī represents the female half of God (Rādhā), as well as one's own wife or mother.

Nidhanam refers to having wealth, as well as death.

Either avahaḥ, which can refer to undergoing an ordeal through fire or āvahaḥ, which can refer to one of the tongues of Agni, can appear in this text.

§

Text 36

arjuna uvāca
atha kena prayukto 'yaṃ pāpaṃ carati pūruṣaḥ
anicchann api vārṣṇeya balād iva niyojitaḥ

-

Arjuna said:

One who moves in union
with You and is
not willing to commit sin
will develop inner strength
in being near Kṛṣṇa.

§

Text 37

śrī-bhagavān uvāca
kāma eṣa krodha eṣa rajo-guṇa-samudhbhavaḥ
mahāśano mahā-pāpmā viddhy enam iha vairiṇam

-

Śrī-Bhagavān said:

One has the choice between desire
and anger –
rebirth comes from heaven –
war is necessary
to eliminate sin
and to return home
and have children.

-

Commentary

Mahā relates to a cow, which is incredibly sacred – and is also related in a compound word or phrase to mahat, which is related to something that is great, the auspicious hour of the morning (mangala, which relates to Kālī and war), as well as prosperity.

Eṣa refers simultaneously to a choice or option, hastening or moving quickly, seeking and sending forth – this happens to relate to a verb in Classical Sanskrit, rather than Vedic.

Rajaḥ refers to the ethereal, the heavens and air, the pollen of flowers, cultivated land and the Vedic sphere of light – in addition to impurity. The very slight connotation of impurity, which may have been attributed to the word as India progressed beyond the original Vedic culture, comes from the fact that in some cultures (such as that of the Hebrews), many considered the time of the moon to be a moment of impurity in the cycle of a woman – however, as we bring Vedic culture into the modern age, we realize that this can actually be a quite pleasant time of the month, depending on the individual in question.

§

Text 38

dhūmenāvriyate vahnir yathādarśo malena ca
yatholbenāvṛto garbhas tathā tenedam āvṛtam

-

Truth cannot be obscured –
do not look too closely upon
the unbelievers –
the one
who provides nurture and love
will turn one's head towards home.

-

Commentary

Yathādarśaḥ can be broken down as yathā and ādarśaḥ or adarśaḥ. Adarśaḥ refers to not perceiving or viewing and ādarśaḥ refers to looking closely at something or up at the newly visible moon. Within this text both words have significance – however one must remember the duty that Arjuna is facing – with respect to both meanings.

Mala refers to dust, but it also refers to filth, as well as those who do not believe in Kṛṣṇa.

Śrīla Prabhupāda's translation of this text provides the definition of "by that lust" for tena. This is an instrumental pronoun – it also has a phonetic relationship to the perfect tense of the process of procreation (which refers to one having the likeness of the Divine Creator) in addition to the application of reason (related to spinning and weaving).

Dhūmaḥ can refer to either smoke or vapor – vahniḥ can refer to several aspects of God associated with the sky – and garbhaḥ refers to a place of nurture which is related to the name Bhagavatī, in addition to the process of evaporation leading to the clouds providing rain during the growing season.

§

Text 39

āvṛtam jñānam etena jñānino nitya-vairiṇā
kāma-rūpeṇa kaunteya duṣpūreṇānalena ca

-

Kaunteya –
one who has understanding

of the Divine
chooses to
satisfy his beloved.

-

Commentary

Kāma-rūpeṇa refers to one having the beautiful likeness of Kṛṣṇa or being covered in fire. Duṣpūreṇa refers to the difficulty of being satisfied; however, considering this definition with respect to the various individuals referred to in this text and the reference to the flames of Agni which are associated with our offerings to God, as well as marriage, gives a very obvious meaning.

Vairin refers to one who is hostile – which can be either an enemy, or a hero. Vīraḥ specifically refers to a hero, but vairin also encapsulates the combative nature as an adversary, rather than strictly virtue and his role as a husband and father.

§

Text 40

indriyāṇi mano buddhir asyādhiṣṭhānam ucyate
etair vimohayaty eṣa jñānam āvṛtya dehinam

-

Reflect on and understand Me
with the mind and senses –
consider what is at hand

and seek jñānam.

-

Commentary

Vimohayati consists of vimā (the instrumental of measuring or meting out) and ūhayati, which means "to consider."

§

Text 41

tasmāt tvam indriyāṇy ādau niyamya bharatarṣabha
pāpmānaṃ prajahi hy enaṃ jñāna-vijñāna-nāśanam

-

You come from Me
and have my likeness –
both within and through
the process of creation –
understand the wisdom
of destroying evil.

-

Commentary

Niyam refers to holding or sustaining something within, and also relates to inner extension – many words associated with Brahman relate to diffusion or extension, in addition to the father.

Praja is the vocative of husband and hi has a variety of possible meanings, but it is frequently used to indicate doing or considering something (quickly or with assurance) and it is emphasized through duplication.

Vijñānam when occurring in a compound indicates understanding the particular meaning of something and is combined with jñānam, or understanding of the divine. In other contexts, vijñānam can refer to scientific knowledge and worldly knowledge.

§

Text 42

indriyāṇi parāṇy āhur indriyebhyaḥ paraṃ manaḥ
manasas tu parā buddhir yo buddheḥ paratas tu saḥ

-

The mind and senses
are divine, as they belong to Me –
within the self,
the heart and mind are closest to Me –
Kṛṣṇa is the highest thought.

§

Text 43

evaṃ buddheḥ paraṃ buddhvā saṃstabhyātmānam ātmanā
jahi śatruṃ mahā-baho kāma-rūpaṃ durāsadam

-

Strengthen your mind and heart
because of Me –
execute your enemy –
I am the most beautiful
and unparalleled form
of desire.

Chapter Four

Text 1

śrī-bhagavān uvāca
imaṃ vivasvate yogaṃ proktavān aham avyayam
vivasvān manave prāha manur ikṣvākave 'bravīt

-

Śrī-Bhagavān said:

Saranyu taught yoga to Vivasvān –
and Manu in turn taught it to his son, Ikṣvāku.

-

Commentary

Vivasvān is another name for the ancient Vedic god of the sun – and his wife was Saranyu. They had several children, which included Manu, the first man, as well as the Aśvins – the twin horsemen. Saranyu was the goddess of the clouds, which are of course associated with fertility and the harvest. Vivasvat is a name of Surya that is associated with diffuse light and the early morning – which is also associated with Agni. Manu also has associations with Agni and one of Agni's roles in Vedic mythology is as Prometheus – but rather than being condemned for bringing light to man, his role is to bring our offerings to God.

Avyaya means imperishable, but also refers to the soma strainer. Soma was an early Vedic sacrament and has associations in Vedic history with the rāja and is another name for Candra – the moon. The moon of course has associations with Kṛṣṇa's other half. There is quite a bit of evidence in the Vedas that the original inspiration for, or even the author of, the Vedas were women.

Manu has associations with both Manu, as well as his wife – and there are associations with Rudra, one who roars or howls – Rudra is thought to be the representation of Śiva in the Ṛg Veda. The word manu is also related to mantras and prayers. The son of Manu is Ikṣvāku, which is also a name of an ancient vegetable associated with the bitter gourd. No one knows for sure which plant this refers to, but it could either be the bitter cucumber or the bitter melon – bitter melon, or karela, is a possible choice given that it has Ayurvedic associations with providing relief to women during a difficult time associated with the moon. Many believe that Rudra has His roots in South India and belongs to a pre-existing Dravidian religion that combined with the faith of those who migrated to India at a later period in time – there are many similarities between both Viṣṇu and Śiva and some consider them to be essentially duplicate concepts that were later integrated into the description of the life cycle of the universe, the path of the sun and our path in this and each subsequent lifetime.

§

Text 2

evaṃ paramparā-prāptam imaṃ rājarṣayo viduḥ
sa kāleneha mahatā yogo naṣṭaḥ parantapa

A philosopher-king
is wise and attentive
and will ensure succession
and progeny –
even to those who
have lost sight of Me,
he will appear to be
glorious and mighty.

Commentary

Parampara refers historically to a lineage or unbroken succession, as well as progeny. It historically relates to family and potentially the line of the rāja.

In Greek a philosopher is one who loves wisdom – and most scholars agree that Plato was educated in India. This is evident in his respect for wisdom, as well as a caste system that provides mobility based on personal merit and excellence.

The German philosopher Nietzsche, who was later given a bad reputation by irrational and evil propagandists in Germany, espoused the concept of the Übermensch – that is, a morally superior individual whose hands are overflowing with honey for the masses and who sees the eternal joy of existence – in the narrative of Also Sprach Zarathustra, his friends are the eagle and the snake:

The eagle represents majesty and nobility, as well as ascending to great heights and the snake historically represents wisdom (as well as the feminine and eternity).

In terms of spiritual succession from Kṛṣṇa, this is something we can all take part in – His words were recorded through the śruti tradition, and we can all listen to those same words with our own eyes, ears, minds and hearts in listening to what He/She had to say throughout the Vedas.

§

Text 3

sa evāyaṃ mayā te 'dya yogaḥ proktaḥ purātanaḥ
bhakto 'si me sakhā ceti rahasyaṃ hy etad uttamam

-

Listen to the wealth
of the sacred body and mind
of your companion
and her love and devotion –
carry a sword – for discernment and sacrifice –
and listen to the mystery
of Her sacred mantra.

-

Commentary

Ayam is either a demonstrative pronoun or it refers to the wealth of the Vedas. Pura refers to the body as the stronghold and home of Puruṣa, as well as the intellect – it is also the form within a compound that refers to placing one forward or in front of, as well as standing in one's presence. Ātanaḥ refers to having one's children near. Referring to "very old" as a translation of purātanaḥ, as occurs in Śrīla Prabhupāda's work, indicates the use of atanaḥ, instead, which means one who does not have children or wealth (Lakṣmī).

Bhakta refers to that which is a part of something, as well as division – and relates to the unity of yoga, as well as the process of discrimination required to integrate jñānam (which is obtained in part through bhakti) into one's life. It also refers to a devotee.

Asi is the verb "to be," but it also refers to a sword (which can represent Viṣṇu), as well as a knife used for slaughter.

Rahasyam refers to a mystery or esoteric teachings and is also another name for the Upaniṣads, which refers to sitting near one's feet.

Uttamam refers to the highest and can specifically refer to the highest tone in terms of sound.

The Vedas were thought to have originally been sung by Gāyatrī (who is also known as Sarasvatī).

§

Text 4

arjuna uvāca

aparaṃ bhavato janma paraṃ janma vivasvataḥ
katham etad vijñānīyām tvam ādau proktavān iti

-

Arjuna said:

If I do not know Her – the Lord –
how can I understand
the origin of existence –
and experience reciprocity?

-

Commentary

Bhavataḥ is a term of respect given to both a lord and lady – and has a correlation to the dual for becoming and being – something that two people do together. Janma refers to rebirth, existence and a people – as well as a family. The verb is not intended in the text, as it is in the third-person; however, there is a relationship of meaning between this concept and much of this text.

Vivasvataḥ is the genitive and ablative of Vivasvān – the sun and refers as well to Agni's light. This refers to that which belongs to or comes from the sun. Within the text this can refer to Vivasvān's birth, but it can also refer to his family.

Ādau is the dual of receiving but can also refer to the beginning. Two can receive together – whether that is from Kṛṣṇa or from each other (who are really one and the same).

No one knows the true origins of Kabbalah – at least mythologically it dates to just after the Exodus from Egypt, although was never written down until far later. It likely originated in India but was thought to have been taught to Moses by God. The highest attainment in the Kabbalistic tradition is Tifaret – which refers to the sun and also represents the beloved. Men were instructed in this tradition to help them understand the nature of God, as well as to help them understand to approach God through their respective wives – the Kabbalistic symbolism for the Divine is equivalent to qualified monism.

Both Hebrew and Sanskrit are thought to have divine origins – both have interesting traits as a sacred language. Hebrew has a few notable and interesting mathematical relationships between words; however, Sanskrit has an extremely intricate relationship throughout the language to interesting semiotic relationships that refer to both the mundane world and theological correspondences – which includes a variety of extremely interesting synonym and antonym relationships between meanings for a single word – and multiple meanings with different uses that can create a variety of layers of symbolism within the text.

§

Text 5

śrī-bhagavān uvāca
bahūni me vyatītāni janmāni tava cārjuna
tāny ahaṃ veda sarvāṇi na tvaṃ vettha parantapa

-

Śrī-Bhagavān said:

Arjuna –
We have both been born
many times –
I comprehended all of them,
but you did not.

§

Text 6

ajo 'pi sann avyayātmā bhūtānām īśvaro 'pi san
prakṛtiṃ svām adhiṣṭhāya sambhavāmy ātma-māyayā

-

I am Īśvara –
the immortal ātman –
the Truth
which exists in union with
the universe in its entirety.

§

Text 7

yadā yadā hi dharmasya glānir bhavati bhārata
abhyutthānam adharmasya tadātmānaṃ sṛjāmy
aham

-

I provide for all –
creation emanates
from Me –
I am dual and non-dual –
the source of existence –
and the highest principle.

-

Commentary

In this text Kṛṣṇa addresses Arjuna and his people, Bhārata, but also those who have either lost or have never found their way.

Abhyutthānaṁ refers to offering praise or rising from one's seat in honor, as well as the rising of the moon, joy and care for one's family.

The concept of the ātman historically encompasses the individual self, which includes the jīva, as well, in addition to the nature of reality, the sun (which provides warmth, light and sustenance), children, the soul and the unity of all souls together and of course the entirety of the knowable and unknowable universe.

The feminine aspect of God is included within this text through multiple references as part of His/Her creative force, which includes the process of emanation from Godhead into Prakṛti – Kṛṣṇa also creates māya, so that we can once again experience the joy of reunion within this lifetime.

§

Text 8

paritrāṇāya sādhūnāṃ vināśāya ca duṣkṛtām
dharma-saṃsthāpanārthāya sambhavāmi yuge yuge

-

Protection and shelter
are provided by the virtuous –
one who has great purpose
preserves dharma –
I exist in union
in all yugas –
in all generations –
and in marriage.

-

Commentary

Duṣkṛtam has a specific connotation associated with crime and relates to a statement that those who protect humanity must eliminate evil committed by other human beings in offering protection to all.

Sambhū refers to existence and birth, but specifically with the meaning of existing together or complete existence.

A yuga refers to an age, as well as a generation – in addition to a yoke. Yuge is the locative for yugam and can be emphasized through duplication, such as "in each age" – but it is also the dual nominative, which can mean that Kṛṣṇa becomes each age, as this would indicate the predicate of "to be or to become," or that he exists in the union we can know through the duality of our separation from Him, as well as in the union we experience in one of the gifts He provided to us – love of the divine through other human beings.

§

Text 9

janma karma ca me divyam evaṃ yo vetti tattvataḥ
tyaktvā dehaṃ punar janma naiti mām eti so' rjuna

-

Birth and karma
are divine –
understand
the truth –
that all of reality emanates from Me.

One returns home
again and again
through rebirth into each lifetime –
one may approach Me or not –
but always offer yourself to Me.

-

Commentary

Deham refers to the jīva and is derived from "mould or fashion" – as we are created in His image.

One word for approaching through prayer also relates to flowing or spreading – Brahman (the unknowable aspect of Kṛṣṇa) is diffuse and is the Father – and encompasses all of existence.

The traditional Hindu view of mokṣa refers to self-realization and understanding of the divine – the concept of release from saṃsāra did not start to become more accepted in India until around the same time as the evolution of Buddhism, which taught that life is suffering and that one should seek escape from the cycle of rebirth.

One's starting position in each lifetime is determined by karma; however, our circumstances within each lifetime are determined by the collective karmas of all individuals, which includes the free-will and actions of each individual, including ourselves. Not all are fortunate in each lifetime – however, the traditional perspective on mokṣa indicates that one can try and rise above one's situation in this lifetime and attempt to attain knowledge of Kṛṣṇa and His divine nature, regardless. The highest form of karma yoga is to do His work – that is, to make the world a better place for future generations.

§

Text 10

vīta-rāga-bhaya-krodhā man-mayā mām upāśritāḥ
bahavo jñāna-tapasā pūtā mad-bhāvam āgatāḥ

-

Those consumed with anger
will not find Me –
those afraid of love
will not find Me –
those who feel the warmth
of spring
will be purified and understand Me.

-

Commentary

Vīta-rāga-bhaya-krodhā has a double meaning – it means one who is enveloped by and colored with anger – it also means one who is afraid of love. Some of the component words within this compound have interesting meanings on their own. Rāga is related to music and refers to a harmony or melody in Western terms, in addition to romantic love and beauty. Krodhā refers to fear of something – but also has a relationship to a bīja mantra associated with the sun salutation and the svadhiṣṭhāna cakra, which is related to procreation, the moon, water (which is associated with creation in the Vedas) and Brahmā.

Tapas refers to heat and warmth and can either be associated with austerity and pain, or it can also refer to the month of Phalguna, which is related to the constellation known in the West as Aquarius, has Vedic correspondences to water and is also the month in which Holi traditionally falls, which is sacred to Kṛṣṇa.

§

Text 11

ye yathā māṃ prapadyante tāṃs tathaiva bhajāmy aham
mama vartmānuvartante manuṣyāḥ pārtha sarvaśaḥ

-

I worship and enjoy
those who lose their way –
those who find Me –
those who live –
and those who die.

I live with you and in you –
and in everything.

-

Commentary

Most of the language in this text refers to one's course in life and one's path to knowing Kṛṣṇa – with simultaneous meanings of falling down and moving forward (related to the foot) and living (and being reborn) with Kṛṣṇa. Bhaj refers to worship and enjoyment and refers to His eternal love affair with man and the universe.

§

Text 12

kāṅkṣantaḥ karmaṇām siddhiṃ yajanta iha devatāḥ

kṣipraṃ hi mānuṣe loke siddhir bhavati karma-jā

-

Man is divine
in both body and spirit –
he desires complete attainment –
each lifetime is short
but offers the opportunity to find Me –
and one will be reborn.

-

Commentary

Devatāḥ refers to the divine nature of Kṛṣṇa, as well as our physical and spiritual divinity.

Bhū refers simultaneously to existing in the present and to becoming.

Mānuṣaḥ refers to the human condition.

Kṣipram refers to something that is fast and also has relationships to archery, in keeping one's self ready to aspire towards Kṛṣṇa. Multiple words in the text refer to something that is quick (or short, in this context) – karma-jā refers to acting or growing through action and is related to a word for parents, children, growth, origination, enjoyment, birth, as well as both Śiva and Viṣṇu.

§

Text 13

cātur-varṇyaṃ mayā sṛṣṭaṃ guṇa-karma-vibhāgaśaḥ
tasya kartāram api māṃ viddhy akartāram avyayam

-

I created the four varṇas
in accordance with the law of karma –
know that those who act
with Me will remain near Me.

§

Text 14

na māṃ karmāṇi limpanti na me karma-phale spṛhā
iti māṃ yo 'bhijānāti karmabhir na sa badhyate

-

One who is consumed
by karma that is not performed with Me
is not of Me –
enjoy your actions –
one who understands their karma
and aspires towards Me
will not be punished.

-

Commentary

Phalam has many positive connotations in Sanskrit, as it relates to the mother, in addition to our offerings to Kṛṣṇa. The combination of phalam and lip also relates to the traditional red bindu.

Spṛhā relates to real enjoyment, in particular that of a romantic nature.

Abhijña relates to knowledge and understanding of the divine, as well as in this conjugated sense having a phonetic relationship to birth.

Bandh relates both to yoga, as well as punishment.

§

Text 15

evaṃ jñātvā kṛtaṃ karma pūrvair api mumukṣubhiḥ
kuru karmaiva tasmāt tvaṃ pūrvaiḥ pūrvataraṃ kṛtam

-

Those who desire release
from māya –
attain knowledge of Him –
and do everything with
and through the Puruṣa.

-

Commentary

Jñātvam is a compound consisting of a word related to knowledge of the divine – it relates specifically to the aspect of the soul which is capable of thought, as well as being equivalent to the Puruṣa, and has a relationship to auspiciousness and Kālī (who represents time and eternal life through rebirth) via a correspondence to warfare – as well as the word for "you" with a specific reference to being near, as well as looking upwards. Jñaḥ also relates to Brahmā.

The word for first or ancient in this text relates to a unique concept – most words in Sanskrit corresponding to time refer to its cyclical nature – there are many associations with the wheel throughout the language and the simultaneous concept of before and next. Pūrvaḥ instead refers to the primal and refers to the first in a series – the universe is continually reborn in every moment, but the abstract representation of the universe is Brahman, who is mythologically personified as Brahmā, and represents the original cause of the universe, despite its eternal and timeless nature. Interestingly, pūrvaḥ also does refer to the cyclical nature of time but has specific connotations of being first.

§

Text 16

kiṃ karma kim akarmeti kavayo 'py atra mohitāḥ
tat te karma pravakṣyāmi yaj jñātvā mokṣyase 'śubhāt

-

Some act – others do not;
those who possess wisdom
remain close to those who do not.

I will speak to those who do not understand –
but you will execute those
who commit evil actions.

§

Text 17

karmaṇo hy api boddhavyaṃ boddhavyaṃ ca vikarmaṇaḥ
akarmaṇaś ca boddhavyaṃ gahanā karmaṇo gatiḥ

-

Know that seeing Me
leads to attainment –
do not break My law –
understand and comprehend
Her eternal darkness.

-

Commentary

Interestingly, gahanā refers both to a 32-syllable mantra, as well as the nearly impenetrable darkness and abyss leading to the grove within a forest – the Divine Feminine is closely linked to the later concept of Dionysos in Greek mythology – the underlying darkness of the universe and the human mind, as well as the eternal mystery that is the feminine. And of course, She is eternally a portion of Her husband – the night sky of this beautiful and magical universe – Kṛṣṇa.

§

Text 18

karmaṇy akarma yaḥ paśyed akarmaṇi ca karma yaḥ
sa buddhimān manuṣyeṣu sa yuktaḥ kṛtsna-karma-kṛt

-

One may experience non-action in action –
and action in non-action –
it is wise and rational
to act with Kṛṣṇa –
one who has been yoked to Me
does everything with Me.

§

Text 19

yasya sarve samārambhāḥ kāma-saṅkalpa-varjitāḥ
jñānāgni-dagdha-karmāṇaṃ tam āhuḥ paṇḍitaṃ budhāḥ

-

My devotees are like Me –
those who do not offer their saṅkalpa
in desire and love
are unable to reach Me –
those who offer their hearts, minds and actions
to Me are consumed by Agni
and are able to see Me.

-

Commentary

There are many references in this text to the homam fire, including saṅkalpa, yasya (which has a shared meaning between "His" and striving and transformation – which has a relationship to ghee), as well as jñānāgni, which is related to the flames of Agni associated with bhakti. Overall the text in general refers to the process of offering our hearts to Kṛṣṇa in the yajña of the Nāciketa sacrifice, which is the eternal chanting of His/Her name within our heart. True jñānam comes from bhakti (which is stated throughout the Vedas, including in works from the Classical period).

§

Text 20

tyaktvā karma-phalāsaṅgaṃ nitya-tṛpto nirāśrayaḥ
karmaṇy abhipravṛtto 'pi naiva kiñcit karoti saḥ

-

Offer yourself to Me –
love one another
and produce fruit together –
one will find satisfaction
in providing one's gift to the world.

-

Commentary

Tyaktvā can refer to giving up – it refers simultaneously to the surrender that comes from love – but can also refer to giving up on life. It refers to the renunciation of one who has abandoned material responsibility and productivity – it also refers to death – but has another meaning referring to bhakti through the definitions of yajña and distribution, which makes more sense in the overall context of the text.

Karma-phalāsaṅgam refers to bearing and bringing fruit to maturity – specifically in the context of close contact, including physical touch. Phala is actually an imperative command in this context conjugated from phal, which refers to producing fruit, and has several fruit-related definitions, some of which also refer to bhakti (specifically the distribution aspect of bhakti) – even if taken in the context of a compound, the fruit association is firmly intact given that is a primary definition of the noun, but the context of interpreting this as a verb makes more overall sense in this context given the relationship of all words taken together, as well as comparing to Hindu tradition.

Abhipravṛttaḥ refers to perfection, attainment and setting something in motion (in the context of a wheel). We are all microcosmic reflections of the macrocosm – the universe is eternal, as are we – our lives, whether through the cycle of each day or our movement through the sacred process of saṃsāra reflects the eternal līlā of Rādha-Kṛṣṇa.

At the end of this text there is a statement indicating that one will derive satisfaction even in offering only something small – this can be interpreted in many ways and relates to a later fruit-related text of the Gītā.

Note that while there is a very strong association with marriage in this Sanskrit text – we can all provide our fruits to the world in love, regardless of what they are, and those who are unable to procreate themselves can also adopt children and provide happy families and help make the world a better place.

§

Text 21

nirāśīr yata-cittātmā tyakta-sarva-parigrahaḥ
śārīraṃ kevalaṃ karma kurvan nāpnoti kilbiṣam

-

One who reaches outward
in prayer to heal
the heart of another –
his eyes will be opened.

One who honors
the gift from the Mother
will be whole.

§

Text 22

yadṛcchā-lābha-santuṣṭo dvandvātīto vimatsaraḥ

samaḥ siddhāv asiddhau ca kṛtvāpi na nibadhyate

-

One who is unselfish
may spontaneously
attain and enjoy knowledge of the divine –
striving for attainment is not relevant –
instead, one should do
that which does not cause internal suffering
and continue to seek Me.

-

Commentary

Some of the language used in the Vedas is very geometric in nature – literally, in that some words are paired together to show relationships between concepts – which requires interpretation rather than word-for-word translation. Not all texts in the Vedas are intended as complete phrases on their own, but instead demonstrate theological concepts via the combination of vocabulary and grammar – and this is one reason why so many commentaries have existed. The combination of samaḥ siddhāv asiddhau is an expression demonstrating the parallel equivalency between methodically seeking attainment, and not seeking it – instead one must wait for His/Her grace, and a great way to do that is to have a pure heart, to act responsibly and grow as a human being – and potentially meet the person who is right for you, some day. The reference to dvandva is a reference to duality, in the sense of a pair – however, it is not associated with atitaḥ and is only combined in the text due to sandhi rules, as atitaḥ is intended in this text as fulfillment, rather than liberation (from). Later summaries of the Gītā are very explicit in mentioning that we seek Him together, and those who do so will achieve enlightenment together.

There are multiple words in the text related to seeking and attaining, and the process of both seeking and attainment within Sanskrit has associations, of course, with Lakṣmī, or Rādhā.

§

Text 23

gata-saṅgasya muktasya jñānāvasthita-cetasaḥ
yajñāyācarataḥ karma samagraṃ pravilīyate

-

One obtains enlightenment
through yoga with another devotee.

-

Commentary

It may go without saying, but the yoga referenced is not a reference to anything other than the union achieved between soulmates who both understand the Nāciketa sacrifice – and of course, one may benefit from the devotion of another. It does not preclude living out the divine interplay that exists in the union of Rādha-Kṛṣṇa, nor the role of Viṣṇu as the preserver, as this is natural and complimentary. This text refers to the spiritual; but, of course, all of Prakṛti, including the jīva, emanates from the spirit.

§

Text 24

brahmāpaṇaṃ brahma havir brahmāgnau brahmaṇā hutam
brahmaiva tena gantavyaṃ brahma-karma-samādhinā

-

Those who offer themselves in oblation to Kṛṣṇa will join with Him.

§

Text 25

daivam evāpare yajñaṃ yoginaḥ paryupāsate
brahmāgnāv apare yajñaṃ yajñenaivopajuhvati

-

One who offers
will attain the highest –
we offer ourselves as ghee
into His fire.

-

Commentary

Daivam means divine and also has connotations of royalty, as well as a form of Hindu marriage.

Apare refers to superior, which has no equal.

§

Text 26

śrotrādīnīndriyāṇy anye saṃyamāgniṣu juhvati
śabdādīn viṣayān anya indriyāgniṣu juhvati

-

All of the senses
are insatiable –
one desires to consume
and devour the Vedas –
which were sung by Her
in the beginning.

One offers the senses
and their objects
to Me –
I am Oṃ –
the breath which
creates every beginning –
offer yourself to Me.

-

Commentary

Some translators frequently translate the word anyaḥ as a pronoun – it can be used as such and is used as a relative pronoun in some texts, but it also refers to the inexhaustible supply of precious milk and nectar that exists in the eternal cycle of saṃsāra – one of its definitions refers to the next body that we are born into and is intimately linked with the concept of eternal rebirth.

Śrotrādi simultaneously refers to the fact that the Vedas were first received from Gāyatrī, as well as the act of listening and understanding voraciously.

Saṃyama merely refers to doing something attentively and with effort, as well as enjoying the act of closing one's eyes while listening. It also has a relationship to Śiva – which has a number of possible meanings but can also refer to the fact that our universe arises from the perception and understanding of the mind, and while it does not go away when we close our eyes, we do not perceive it in the same way and the act is reminiscent of sleep.

Śabdādīn refers to the sacred syllable Oṃ, which is a symbol of God and the universe (who are equivalent) and is found in various forms throughout the Vedas. Brahmā is a personification of Brahman and represents His original creative force, rather than that which exists in each lifetime – Brahmā's wife is Gāyatrī, or Sarasvatī, who originally sung the Vedas and also represents sound and music. Sacred sound is associated with both the male and female halves of God. However, it has a specific reference to each individual human being, and their respective lifetimes, as well as the eternal lifecycle of the universe.

There are also many references in the Vedas to the notion that spending one's life in meditation and rejecting the world and its sense objects is essentially what one would consider a sin in the West – which in the Sanātana Dharma is better translated as "offence." It is reasonably well-known among those who have been given the gift of knowledge that some do not understand that message and waste a precious gift – this particular lifetime – but that they can try again in the future. Singing and listening are one of the true paths to understanding the Divine and relate both to the sacred acts of breathing and listening.

§

Text 27

sarvāṇīndriya-karmāṇi prāṇa-karmāṇi cāpare
ātma-saṃyama-yogāgnau juhvati jñāna-dīpite

-

All perception –
that of the mind and the senses –
which are one with each other –
comes from My eternal breath.

Union with Our eternal music
is the highest yajña
and one is inflamed with the prayer
of bhakti and knowledge of Me –
seek Us in each other.

-

Commentary

Interestingly within this text is another word referring to the cyclical nature of time and existence (aparaḥ) – and while it can have highly positive connotations, being associated with sleep (the setting of the sun) – it also has multiple connotations that are highly negative and can also indicate finality – one reading of this word could indicate that the concept of not finding birth once again into this world is a negative thing. Consistent with previous notes regarding instruction provided to individuals based on the instructors' opinion of the student in question – one meaning of this word refers to the hind foot of an elephant; if one considers the relationship between the elephant and Gaṇeśa to the intellect, one can draw certain conclusions.

Dīpitaḥ can refer to the singular of one who has been consumed in the flames of bhakti, which leads to knowledge and understanding of the divine – however, it is also dual, which refers specifically to two people – one can of course experience bhakti alone with Rādha-Kṛṣṇa; however, later summaries of the Gītā, as well as various texts within the Gītā, specifically refer to the Highest form of attainment as seeking Him/Her together with one's spouse (Brahma Saṃhitā, Text 58):

Those who experience
the joy and consciousness
of the ātman
and aspire towards Bhagavān through bhakti
will ascend and experience enlightenment together.

§

Text 28

dravya-yajñās tapo-yajñā yoga-yajñās tathāpare
svādhyāya-jñāna-yajñāś ca yatayaḥ saṃśita-vratāḥ

-

I created the setting
of the sun
as a reminder to all –
master sacred knowledge –
one strives towards me in the sanctity
of marriage.

-

Commentary

Yajña is another name for Viṣṇu – and does not just refer to sacrifice, but also the process of offering, as well as praise and worship. Most from a traditional background who have been provided proper instruction understand that the sacrificial fire is not for asking for favors from the devas, but rather a representation of offering ourselves and our hearts to Kṛṣṇa.

Apare can refer to the negative aspect of not experiencing rebirth, but it can also refer to the fact that the setting of the sun can at times have no rival – of course in modern society, due to our flexible schedules, that is not always a defining moment of the day.

Yatayaḥ refers to a devotee, but specifically one who strives – and the process of striving for attainment (as well as movement) relates in Sanskrit to Lakṣmī (as does dravyaḥ). Those who are too materialistic tend to mistake the concept of wealth in the Vedas for money and possessions, when the traditional meaning actually refers to the Divine Feminine.

Saṃśitaḥ refers to preparation and relates indirectly to archery – which of course relates to trying to reach (and attaining) knowledge and understanding of Kṛṣṇa (jñānam).

Svādhyāyaḥ refers to the recitation of the Vedas (and internalizing their message) and relates to vrataḥ, which refers to one who is committed to understanding their message.

§

Text 29

apāne juhvati prāṇaṃ prāṇe 'pānaṃ tathāpare
prāṇāpāna-gati ruddhvā prāṇāyāma-parāyaṇaiḥ
apare niyatāhārāḥ prāṇān prāṇeṣu juhvati

-

Living life and breathing together
as Rādha-Kṛṣṇa in the setting of the sun
brings joy –
those who are fully devoted to one another
will not lose their shared wealth –
offer one's breath to that of the other.

-

Commentary

Apānaḥ refers specifically to the opposite of prāṇaḥ (which is the breath of life) – one who performs yajña even in times of unhappiness will achieve happiness together. Prāṇe which represents both fulfillment, as well as prāṇā, is in the dual person.

Niyatāhārāḥ has two possible meanings. Niyam refers to holding something in and keeping it close, in addition to giving to, or receiving from, another. Ahāraḥ refers to not losing one's wealth; āhāraḥ refers to receiving near one's self, as well as enjoyment and consumption (such as that of prasādam).

Parāyaṇaḥ refers to being completed devoted to and focused on one objective (Rādha-Kṛṣṇa).

§

Text 30

sarve 'py ete yajña-vido yajña-kṣapita-kalmaṣāḥ
yajña-śiṣṭāmṛta-bhujo yānti brahma sanātanam

-

All have free will –
one can know Me –
one can obey the law.

One wise enough to rule
must implement strict punishment
for those who stray too far –
the educated enjoy
all that immortality has to offer
in each lifetime,
as they are able to seek Me, eternally.

-

Commentary

The combination of sarve 'py ete has a number of possible meanings: "all near-term choices," "all choices in this lifetime," "many choices in this lifetime," "everyone has more than two choices," et cetera. There are many more ways of phrasing this – in the Sanātana Dharma, the concept of sin and the sinner (as frequently translated in English) refers either to doing something that is offensive (such as wasting one's life) or in breaking the law.

Vidaḥ refers to the knower, the seeker, one who finds what he seeks, as well as one who obtains or receives prasādam (related to either anna prasādam or the message of the Aśvamedha).

Śiṣṭa has a variety of meanings ranging from punishment, governance, teaching and a variety of other meanings indicating that certain actions are praise-worthy (such as just punishment) and that admitting to one's faults is also commendable. Śiṣṭā, which could also appear, refers to that which is remaining (and has an obvious connotation related to

Śeṣa, or eternity – and the serpent on which Viṣṇu reposes), law, wisdom, education and discipline.

Amṛtam refers to immortality and nectar, as well as being alive. It is not used in this text, but appearing on its own, amṛta also refers to one who dies.

Bhujaḥ refers to enjoyment, ruling, eating or partaking, bowing – and at the end of a compound it can refer to any significant portion of the body, such as the arm. There are many ways of translating yajña-śiṣṭāmṛta-bhujo – there are actually too many to count, but overall it implies that the followers of Viṣṇu will enjoy saṃsāra eternally in eliminating destructive elements from society – there is a reference to the "arm of the law" within this phrase – as well the enjoyment of wisdom and education, in addition to the need to apply strict punishment to crimes that are very offensive to Viṣṇu and humanity. There are multiple references to royalty within this text, as well.

Yā refers to movement – such as moving through one's life, the path of a chariot on the battlefield – as well as the process of seeking and attainment – both seeking and attainment are of course elated in the Vedas to Lakṣmī, and there is also a relationship, both in terms of pronunciation and in meaning, to a key word representing both humanity and Kṛṣṇa (yaḥ).

Kṛṣṇa is of course equivalent to Brahman, as Brahman is His unknowable aspect.

§

Text 32

evaṃ bahu-vidhā yajñā vitatā brahmaṇo mukhe
karma-jān viddhi tān sarvān evaṃ jñātvā vimokṣyase

-

All who are born
perceive themselves as being
separate from Me –
understand others,
as well as their actions.

Seek the wisdom and understanding
of Kṛṣṇa –
and liberate those who do not understand.

-

Commentary

There is a frequent pairing within the Vedas (and related commentaries and summaries) between vid and jñā. Vid relates to intellectual understanding, and has a relationship to the sword, as well as Viṣṇu. Jñā relates to wisdom and understanding of God. It takes both the intellect and intuition (as well as Kṛṣṇa's grace) to understand Him – and one cannot make use of jñānam if one does not also use the intellect to integrate it into one's life and overall understanding of the universe and humanity.

Mokṣyase has two related meanings which are incredibly interesting. The two verb roots in question are mokṣ and muc. Mokṣ relates to the desire for enlightenment and understanding, the act of liberation, the extraction of truth from reality, providing understanding and knowledge to others, as well as blood shed (liberation). Muc also relates to liberation but has many more connotations within its various definitions related to the death penalty for those who did not achieve understanding and committed crimes that are unforgiveable.

Those who have achieved sufficient knowledge of Kṛṣṇa's nature have a responsibility to share this with others – in various ways – and it is the role of an enlightened society to enforce His law with humanity. Unlike in some traditions there are really no specific codes defined by God, but rather He leaves this to humanity to determine; but clearly, based on all of His instruction, we are to safeguard the happiness and well-being of others, as well as ensuring that society produces quality and happy progeny for future generations.

While in the traditional Vedic point of view there is really no concept of leaving saṃsāra, and instead mokṣa relates to self-awareness; there is an obvious conclusion, which is that certain pieces of the divine and the associated remnants of past jīvas may not experience rebirth depending on the Earth's population level and who chooses to procreate and contribute in meaningful ways to future human society. That is a subtle (and not so subtle) message underlying much of the text in the original Sanskrit throughout the Gītā.

Much of the Vedas celebrates the gift of human reason, the ambiguous (and unambiguous) nature of crime and His/Her love of family – and the role of the enlightened to help others determine proper punishment (which is of course enforced by the government).

Previous commentaries within Chapter Four indicate the relationship between the traditional red bindu and these concepts, as well as the theory that the Vedas were originally authored or inspired by women.

§

Text 33

śreyān dravya-mayād yajñāj jñāna-yajñaḥ parantapa
sarvaṃ karmākhilaṃ pārtha jñāne parisamāpyate

-

Our women are the
most valuable wealth –
both mothers and young women –
life is short –
understand
the wisdom of sacrifice,
for they will lead one to fulfillment.

-

Commentary

Maya (as opposed to māya) refers to an ancient Vedic concept in terms of God which later became known as Rāma. Many of the later Sanskrit names for

God came after the original Vedas, but they are still referenced within the texts. Maya also refers to a horse, which is a reference to moving quickly and historically represents one's perception of each lifetime. It also refers to injuring one's enemies and relates at the same time to the concept of Rāma, the Aśvamedha and the duty that some have in engaging in warfare. Maya can also act as a suffix indicating that something is composed of something (such as ānandamaya, which means "made of joy and bliss").

In Chapter One of the Gītā there is a reference towards much of the future dialogue concerning Arjuna's motivation for entering into battle – which is that the enemy has lost dharma and if victorious, will plunder all of the wealth of Bhārata, including hurting their women and children.

Akhilam and ākhilam refer to related concepts – akhilam refers to cultivated land that has not gone to waste, and ākhilam refers to as yet untilled land that one must keep close to one's self (for protection). The concept of protection is not that which Prabhupāda referred to in Chapter One – he indicated that women cannot be trusted and must be protected for their own good so that they do not engage in immoral activity, but this is actually a reference to the fact that all people must fight together to protect society, and while women are capable of protecting themselves, historically men are the ones who went to war. In modern society this is not always true and today there are many weapons and forms of combat that assist in overcoming any physical differences. One also keeps one's children close to one's self as they are growing and maturing to provide love, affection and guidance in life.

§

Text 34

tad viddhi praṇipātena paripraśnena sevayā
upadekṣyanti te jñānaṃ jñāninas tattva-darśinaḥ

-

Understand what they have to teach –
fall at their feet in devotion
and realize they are filled with wisdom.

My law exists to protect humanity.

-

Commentary

There are multiple layers of meaning in the above text (approximately three).

Nearly all of the words in the text relate to the judicial process in determining the outcome of an alleged crime. However, praṇipātena, which refers to prostration, indicates the primary reading of the text is related to wisdom.

One can learn through observation – and one can learn from direct instruction. Darśi refers to investigation and inquiry, as well as observation and understanding, in addition to teaching someone directly.

Sevā refers to service, worship and devotion – and has numerous definitions that relate to engaging in frequent enjoyment.

Enforcing the law and protecting society is a sevā for humanity, as well as our families. Incidentally, the word seva (from sevam) actually refers to fruit, specifically an apple.

§

Text 35

yaj jñātvā na punar moham evaṃ yāsyasi pāṇḍava
yena bhūtāny aśeṣāṇi drakṣyasy ātmany atho mayi

-

Arjuna, do not be confused –
you will be reborn with Me
and see that we are together.

§

Text 36

api ced asi pāpebhyaḥ sarvebhyaḥ pāpa-kṛt-tamaḥ
sarvaṃ jñāna-plavenaiva vṛjinaṃ santariṣyasi

-

You are My knife –

all sin comes from
those who choose to commit evil –
let them pass over you
and realize the sanctity of life and existence.

§

Text 37

yathaidhāṃsi samiddho 'gnir bhasma-sāt kurute 'rjuna
jñānāgniḥ sarva-karmāṇi bhasma-sāt kurute tathā

-

Everyone – and all karma –
is consumed by Agni
if offered to Me –
and one finds jñānam
in the flames of bhakti.

-

Commentary

The Brahma Saṃhitā is a summary of the Gītā and encapsulates much of Rāmānuja's interpretation of the Vedas, which is fundamentally the traditional Vedic point of view prior to Sāṅkhya philosophy and Buddha. Within the Brahma Saṃhitā is contained this text, which is related to the above (Brahma Saṃhitā, Text 54):

Without the protection of Indra one will be chained
to the fruit of their karma –

those who practice bhakti will have their karma consumed
by the flames of Agni.
I worship Govinda, the Puruṣa who existed in the beginning.

§

Text 38

na hi jñānena sadṛśaṃ pavitram iha vidyate
tat svayaṃ yoga-saṃsiddhaḥ kālenātmani vindati

-

Remember this sacred knowledge:
one achieves the Highest
when one finds union
together with the Self –
discover each other as being One
over time.

-

Commentary

Some of the Vedic texts refer to attainment between the spiritual union of Kṛṣṇa and Rādhā in terms of the dual person (a grammatical feature) – this is a natural part of early languages that denotes two people or objects together. However, in this text, the same concept is expressed, but there is only a reference to one person – but expresses the ideas of union and togetherness.

Interestingly, some traditions in both Eastern and Western culture expect students to eventually leave the method of instruction on their own – while some recognize this immediately, take the lesson and integrate that into their lives, others continue to study and practice within the tradition and ultimately pay the price for that. It is an unfortunate means of instruction and does many a disservice, as those who get the message would have understood it after hearing it the first time, and it otherwise takes advantage of and punishes those who do not have the appropriate level of intellect or insight. Siddhaḥ has one definition in reference to this, which is the meaning of being scared off – and has further meanings which are far more prevalent referring to attainment. Note that the traditional final stage of varṇāśrāma actually refers to one who no longer thinks about worldly affairs – one may wonder how many aging men actually left their wives and went to the forest to meditate.

Pavitram has many interesting meanings which are familiar to those of a traditional background – in addition to being related to the process of purification, it also refers to various sacred items such as the sacred thread, ghee, honey, water, argha, kuśa (and in this context it refers to two kuśa but without using the dual person), as well as the tradition of Hindu hospitality.

Mysticism is a frequently misunderstood term, which simply refers to yoga. All of the world's true mystical traditions have a similar message, which is union with God – and have common elements of romantic love, family, music and dancing.

§

Text 39

śraddhāvāṃl labhate jñānaṃ tat-paraḥ
saṃyatendriyaḥ
jñānaṃ labdhvā parāṃ śāntim acireṇādhigacchati

-

You fill find faith and certainty
in marriage –
you will find peace and wisdom
in providing for your family
and comprehending her
and Me.

-

Commentary

Indriyaḥ does refer to the senses, but it also refers to people, as well (who are the companion of Indra).

Saṃyataḥ can refer to control, or even imprisonment – but also refers to being held together through strong bonds.

Śāntiḥ has a variety of meanings – it has the most well-known meaning of peace and tranquility, but also is one of the many words referring to welfare and prosperity, as well as bliss – it has a side definition referring to one who is indifferent or who has no passion and can also refer to destruction and extinguishing fire. Śāntiḥ can also refer to an interruption or cessation – while this could be an interruption from the stress of one's day, it could also refer to the many references within this text to meditation, attainment and contemplation, which historically within the sacred language of the Vedas, refers to the knowledge, understanding and union between Kṛṣṇa and Rādhā.

Adhi is a valid portion of this text and when paired with gam, it would refer to attainment (moving upwards). Ādhiḥ can also appear and relates to meditation, reflection, hope, longing and care – as well as a vessel, a foundation and it also refers to a good father who provides for his family. Movement in Sanskrit can also refer to the general movement through life and our various lifetimes.

§

Text 40

ajñaś cāśraddadhānaś ca saṃśayātmā vinaśyati
nāyaṃ loko 'sti na paro na sukhaṃ saṃśayātmanaḥ

-

One lacking in understanding and faith
is uncertain in himself
and is lost –
he lacks both material and spiritual wealth –
he is unhappy, lives a difficult life
and poses a danger to himself.

-

Commentary

In Sanskrit a common word related to happiness is sukham, which is a reference to the axle of a wheel which turns easily. Education and reflection are necessary to achieve the degree of understanding required to know oneself – and one also requires inspiration from Kṛṣṇa, as well. However, much of the Vedas do tell us that we should focus on experiencing His/Her presence in our lives and to focus on being a responsible member of society, while also achieving happiness without extreme austerity – and to see beyond the material world. A related concept appears in the Brahma Saṃhitā (Text 25) – this text also relates to the overall concept discussed in Chapter Four of the Gītā related to understanding the spiritual and focusing on one's loved ones, as if one is lost in unproductive spiritual practices then one misses out on one's true means of attainment – and the only real austerity we need is that of freeing ourselves from attachment to the material world:

Austerity practiced easily
will bring complete attainment.

§

Text 41

yoga-sannyasta-karmāṇaṃ jñāna-sañchinna-saṃśayam
ātmavantaṃ na karmāṇi nibadhnanti dhanañjaya

Arjuna, conqueror of wealth –
one who gives up his wedding vow
is cut off from knowing the divine
and leaves the world – as if asleep;
he is selfish
and is tormented by his actions.

-

Commentary

Sannyasta means one who has died on the inside, given up on life and abandoned his wedding vow.

Na can be used for negation but has an almost endless number of uses (just as with most particles) and can be used for emphasis, affirmation and certainty. One reading of karmāṇi nibadhnanti refers to inner turmoil because of one's actions – and the preceding na refers to the certainty and declaration of this fact, rather than providing negation.

§

Text 42

tasmād ajñāna-sambhūtaṃ hṛt-sthaṃ
jñānāsinātmanaḥ
chittvainaṃ saṃśayaṃ yogam ātiṣṭhottiṣṭha bhārata

-

Bhārata –
one who is ignorant of this fact

chokes on his heart
and is cut off from himself –
he is destroyed
and unable to experience the Highest yoga –
he is weak and prone to pride.

-

Commentary

While tiṣṭha is the second-person imperative for standing, existing or being – ud relates to something that is over or above, but contrasts with ātiṣṭha, which refers to something that is both near and above and is more commonly used as a term for being superior. Ud has implications of something that is "superior" in the sense of pride and seeking fame, and also implies weakness. Ātiṣṭha uttiṣṭha is ambiguous, as it can be a combination of modified imperatives or vocative nouns. If imperative, then this is a command that has a variety of possible meanings – if vocative then it addresses two concepts related to "superiority" and does not express equivalence, as occurs in some of the other texts. The above translation makes most sense given the rest of the text and those preceding – and possibly considering the number of times Kṛṣṇa has already instructed Arjuna to fight.

Chapter Five

Text 1

arjuna uvāca
sannyāsaṃ karmaṇāṃ kṛṣṇa punar yogam ca śaṃsasi
yac chreya etayor ekaṃ tan me brūhi su-niścitam

-

Arjuna said:

A sannyāsin is of low birth
and continues to leave the world
in everything he does –
sing to me at the sacrificial fire –
one who aspires to the Highest
in the movement and choices
of two living as one –
declare our offspring
to be Yours.

-

Commentary

Another interpretation of the term sannyāsin involves one who consists of ashes and dust, who has the qualities of the posterior of the body and who is of low birth. Those who realize the difference between the sannyāsin and the final stage of varṇāśrāma realize there is a difference from being freed from material cares, responsibilities and needs and the very traditional role of the holy man in India who begs for alms on the street. In the modern age many make a very good living dressing in saffron robes and performing in the public eye – however, the concept is quite similar, even if some are taken in by affected mannerisms and public speaking.

Etayoḥ refers either to two choices, or to two who are moving together through life and making choices together – ekam tan me indicates unity. While su-nisćitam could refer to a highly positive emphasis on the notion of decisiveness, su refers to the good – but has a specific meaning related to parents and children, in particular children. The use of brū in the second-person imperative can be interpreted as a declaration that Kṛṣṇa claims something for Himself.

§

Text 2

śrī-bhagavān uvāca
sannyāsaḥ karma-yogaś ca niḥśreyasa-karāv ubhau
tayos tu karma-sannyāsāt karma-yogo viśiṣyate

-

Śrī-Bhagavān said:

A sannyāsin is a fraud –
the highest bliss comes
from the knowledge experienced
by two living together, without renunciation,
and acting together –
a sannyāsin is rejected, seen with disdain
and should be chastised.

-

Commentary

Consistent with the concept that some spiritual or social practices are seen with some degree of humor and disdain by those who appreciate the value of living, the word yoga, while referring to union with God in this lifetime – also does refer to the equivalent of sleight of hand or a parlor trick – and can refer to deceit. That is probably more of a slang term, and one must remember the context anytime a word is used in any language to determine what is meant, and Sanskrit is particularly prone to this.

Viśiṣyate can refer to something that is held in high regard, but that is only a slight meaning to the word and refers to situations where one punishes an evil-doer, or one worthy of reproach – it is also praise-worthy to confess one's crimes to the authorities. Otherwise it refers to punishment, disdain and reproach.

§

Text 3

jñeyaḥ sa nitya-sannyāsī yo na dveṣṭi na kāṅkṣati
nirdvandvo hi mahā-bāho sukhaṃ bandhāt
pramucyate

-

One who has come to know
the ordinary and unchanging sannyāsin –
one neither shows hatred towards
nor hopes to become one –
as he is alone.
He seeks liberation
and finds none.

-

Commentary

Mahā-bāho sukham bandhāt pramucyate means "there are many measures of happiness that he escapes from."

§

Text 4

sāṅkhya-yogau pṛthag bālāḥ pravadanti na paṇḍitāḥ
ekam apy āsthitaḥ samyag ubhayor vindate phalam

-

There are two manners of speaking to people –
as one does to children, and the wise;
some live alone
and some live together –
understand their fruit.

-

Commentary

Sāṅkhya refers to enumeration – after the writing of the Gītā this referred to a school of philosophy that had a later adverse impact on culture in India. However, when looking at the language of the Gītā, one must remember the date that it was authored when interpreting the vocabulary in the texts. Note that Sāṅkhya and Advaita should not be confused with one another – Advaita was an early expression of Vedic philosophy but has no actual relationship to Sāṅkhya and was later clarified and brought into clear alignment with the Vedas by Rāmānuja. The various early schools of theological commentary up until the late Classical period were intended to assist others in interpreting the Vedas; however, the language of the Vedas is quite clear, which shows in that most saṃpradāyas have a similar message. The guru tradition was originally intended to teach young students.

§

Text 5

yat sāṅkhyaiḥ prāpyate sthānaṃ tad yogair api gamyate
ekaṃ sāṅkhyaṃ ca yogam ca yaḥ paśyati sa paśyati

-

One who has a family
and secure home has wealth
and lives with Me –
one who practices yoga by himself
can only look on
at others who possess that

which he does not have.

-

Commentary

Paś refers to seeing – but specifically refers both to seeing with ājñā and seeing people – and also refers to being a spectator. Paś also refers to worshipping with one's eyes and refers to the inspiration of the Vedas. Sthānam refers to security and standing firmly and has many associations with warfare, such as one who accurately shoots a bow, as well as the safety and prosperity of a kingdom, music, speech, the moon and an altar.

§

Text 6

sannyāsas tu mahā-bāho duḥkham āptum ayogataḥ
yoga-yukto munir brahma na cireṇādhigacchati

-

One who lives a life of renunciation
has great difficulty in reaching his goal –
his inner longing for Kṛṣṇa
does not last long.

One who cares for his or her family
is inspired to find Me.

-

Commentary

Interestingly, there are previous translations of this text that associate ayogataḥ with "devotional service" – this is actually a reasonably good definition, as it refers to being connected with prosperity and has associations with fathers, gold and the Vedas, as well. In this context it refers to that which one has difficulty in obtaining due to a life of renunciation. Na cireṇa can mean "without delay" – however, the meaning of "delay" comes from the undesirable qualities associated with waiting an unnecessary amount of time; the association of "delay" with a word referring to an extended period of time is an association within the language to one's perception of time. Interestingly, both adhigacchati and ādhi gacchati are valid in the text and Prabhupāda chose adhigacchati, which simply refers to aspiring towards God, whereas ādhi gacchati means the same thing but refers more specifically to devotional service, in particular that towards one's family, and refers more to the action of doing so, rather than the concept.

§

Text 7

yoga-yukto viśuddhātma vijitātma jitendriyaḥ
sarva-bhūtātma-bhūtātmā kurvann api na lipyate

-

Through successful yoga
one achieves self-knowledge

of the mind, body and senses
and is anointed by the Self.

-

Commentary

Yuktaḥ refers to one who has been yoked – if we are successful in uniting ourselves with Kṛṣṇa, then one of our responsibilities is to act on His behalf and perform His work. This is part of karma yoga and varies from individual to individual; however, Kṛṣṇa wants us to make the world a better place for ourselves and others through meaningful contributions to society – both in the community and our respective families.

§

Texts 8 and 9

naiva kiñcit karomīti yukto manyeta tattva-vit
paśyañ śṛṇvan spṛśañ jighrann aśnan gacchan svapan śvasan

pralapan visṛjan gṛhṇann unmiṣan nimiṣann api
indriyāṇīndriyārtheṣu vartanta iti dhārayan

-

Do not do just a little bit –
one should desire
to know and understand Truth –
do this through seeing, hearing, touching,
smelling, eating, enjoying,

doing, seeking, sleeping, dreaming,
breathing, talking, procreating,
producing and discovering –
the mind, body and senses are holy
and are intended to do My work.

§

Text 10

brahmaṇy ādhāya karmāṇi saṅgaṃ tyaktvā karoti yaḥ
lipyate na sa pāpena padma-patram ivāmbhasā

-

One who has offered
his actions to Kṛṣṇa
is anointed –
an offering cannot be
made in penance –
it is the lotus leaf
floating in the celestial waters.

-

Commentary

Offerings are made from our heart and are done so out of the purity and love of devotion. There is no such thing as penance – only doing good things. If we do something that would be considered evil, then all we can do is move on and do good things in the future. No action can be undone – and no offering to Kṛṣṇa will undo any of the results of our actions. There are no contemplative or devotional activities that undo what we have done – we and others have to live with the consequences of what we do. Spiritual activity does make us feel better, and God appreciates it and enjoys it along with us, if done with love, affection and purity of the heart – but what both God and society appreciate even more, is the offering of our actions which benefit both ourselves and others.

§

Text 11

kāyena manasā buddhyā kevalair indriyair api
yoginaḥ karma kurvanti saṅgaṃ tyaktvātma-
śuddhaye

-

Two give themselves to each other completely –
in body, mind and soul –
all actions are performed in yoga
and faithfulness to each other.

-

Commentary

This text is entirely about marriage. All meanings of kāya are related to marriage – this word has multiple references to the prājāpati marriage, music – it is also a synonym for sarvam – as well as relating to wealth, the home and the object of attainment.

Kevala is also a synonym for sarvam.

Interestingly, the verb tyaj appears multiple times in the Gītā and refers simultaneously to bhakti (through multiple shared meanings between the two words), offering one's breath to another, as well as the concept of shunning and the act of giving up on life and longing for death.

Śuddhiḥ refers to holiness and purity, the judicial process in terms of determining innocence, the absence of a dowry or reverse dowry (a characteristic of a prājāpati marriage) and also has a reference to making an offering to Yama (also a component of the prājāpati marriage).

§

Text 12

yuktaḥ karma-phalaṃ tyaktvā śāntim āpnoti naiṣṭhikīm
ayuktaḥ kāma-kāreṇa phale sakto nibadhyate

-

One who lives with Me
continually offers the fruit of their action
and easily arrives at the Highest –
one who continually
practices austerity
and rejects the marriage vow
is unable to achieve union
and has great difficulty
in feeling affection for My fruit –
and is bound

by the fetters of existence and sin.

-

Commentary

A naiṣṭhikaḥ is one who continually listens to others (such as a guru) and never leaves their guidance, and also refers to one who has taken the vow of celibacy. It can also refer to perfection, as well as one who has realized they received their final lesson (and graduated).

Kāraḥ refers to action, but it also refers to exertion. Saktaḥ can refer to attachment, but it also refers to one who is hindered or impeded.

§

Text 13

sarva-karmāṇi manasā sannyasyāste sukhaṃ vaśī
nava-dvāre pure dehī naiva kurvan na kārayan

-

All actions of the sannyāsin
are performed in his mind –
he enjoys sitting,
and may appear as a vine
growing on a healthy plant, constricting its growth –
he is surrounded by
by young students, who he sees as opportunity –
he does nothing
and does not cause them to do anything, either.

-

Commentary

Nava-dvāre pure can be interpreted in multiple ways. The city of nine gates can refer to the body – puraḥ alone refers specifically to the body unless it is used within the context of protecting a city. Navaḥ also refers to a young student, especially a potential novice monk – and also refers to the next generation. Interestingly, navaḥ can also refer to the act of sneezing, which could be a natural action in coming into contact with one who is covered in the dust from sitting too long. This phrase is a metaphor and has a variety of references related to protecting a city, and includes the seat of Kṛṣṇa, references to the body and mind, youth, leading and being surrounded. While number is not always fully respected in Sanskrit outside of situations where specificity is required, this typically only occurs with a few words, for the most part. In this text dvāre is not plural and is instead singular. A better translation would interpret dvāḥ as "opportunity," and this is more consistent with the text. "City of nine gates" would be redundant, considering this is also a meaning of puraḥ.

Vaśī has a variety of meanings traditionally associated with the sannyāsin, including being a reference to a parasitic plant.

§

Text 14

na kartrtvaṃ na karmāṇi lokasya sṛjati prabhuḥ
na karma-phala-saṃyogaṃ svabhāvas tu pravartate

-

His actions in this world
create nothing –
he does not reach Me
through the fruit of yoga,
in simply being
or in his movement through life.

§

Text 15

nādatte kasyacit pāpaṃ na caiva sukṛtaṃ vibhuḥ
ajñānenāvṛtaṃ jñānaṃ tena muhyanti jantavaḥ

-

One does not listen to the
understanding of the unfortunate –
morality and heaven do not
come through ignorance –
the wisdom sought
through a sannyāsin
is that of a miscarriage
and that of a worm.

§

Text 16

jñānena tu tad ajñānaṃ yeṣāṃ nāśitam ātmanaḥ
teṣām āditya-vaj jñānaṃ prakāśayati tat param

-

Through the jñānam
of the ignorant
one will destroy oneself –
those who resemble death
cause wisdom
to appear distant and remote –
those who shine like the sun
show others the light of Kṛṣṇa.

-

Commentary

Āditya has several meanings and can refer to the sun, or that which belongs to death (aditi). The reference to death with respect to aditi likely comes from the myth of Rāhu – interestingly, it has alternate meanings that are also associated with some early Classical to later interpretations of the goals of a sannyāsin from the perspective of desiring release from saṃsāra – it also refers to poverty, which is both associated (only historically, at least from a financial perspective) with a sannyāsin, but also refers to one who has eaten himself into poverty. It also has positive connotations, as well, which refer to the concept of cooking and eating – preparation, offering and consuming are all associated with bhakti. There is another possible reading of this text indicating that those who show others the light of Rādha-Kṛṣṇa can dispel the ignorance of others –

while this is potentially true, unless one reads a more conditional meaning into nāśitam than exists in the text, then that translation ignores the notion that others still have to choose to see His/Her light for themselves.

§

Text 17

tad-buddhayas tad-ātmānas tan-niṣṭhās tat-parāyanāḥ
gacchanty apunar-āvṛttiṃ jñāna-nirdhūta-kalmaṣāḥ

-

One whose thoughts
and actions deviate from Me –
those who are unclean
and approach in torment
do not find Me.

-

Commentary

Parāvanāḥ refers to those whose path in life moves away from Kṛṣṇa. The concept of movement away from Brahman (or Kṛṣṇa) combined with the idea of being focused in thought and existence on Him, implies a form of negation of the former concepts. It is interesting that Prabhupāda associated apunar-āvṛttiṃ with "liberation," when the phrase actually refers to one who does not live again – when the Vedic interpretation of liberation is associated with knowledge of Kṛṣṇa in this lifetime. It is also interesting that he translated nirdhūta as "cleansed" when it can either refer to being deprived of something or being tormented. There is one reading of jñāna-nirdhūta-kalmaṣāḥ that would mean "the wisdom of one deprived of destruction," however that is only one possible meaning and one would wonder why one would be afraid of death, when the traditional Vedic point of view equates death with birth.

§

Text 18

vidyā-vinaya-sampanne brāhmaṇe gavi hastini
śuni caiva śva-pāke ca paṇḍitāḥ sama-darśinaḥ

-

The education of the intelligent Brāhmaṇa
is based in morality – for the good of the people;
the dog is ignorant –
but the wise understand
and treat him fairly.

-

Commentary

The use of cases is generally fairly loose in the Vedas, however vidyā is in the nominative and is not instrumental. One could interpret vidyā in its compound form, but Prabhupāda's combination of knowledge and gentleness does not really form a concept but is instead a handful of words strung together. Instead vidyā likely refers to the education of the Brāhmaṇa – vinaya-sampanne means "endowed with training in morality," the Brāhmaṇa acts on behalf of the people (the children of Govinda) and is intelligent (he is the best of his kind and has the intelligence of Gaṇeśa and the elephant). Śuni caiva śva-pāke is a locative object of sama-darśinaḥ – which means to observe and or treat fairly. Śuni caiva śva-pāke means "the dog is certainly possessed of his own ignorance" and has a variety of connotations such as being a plague to society.

The above translation is most consistent with Vedic culture, as well as previous texts leading up to this one in the Gītā. In an enlightened society, leaders well-versed in morality are needed to help the people make the proper decisions, which includes education, the structure and laws of society, as well as treatment of those who have lost their way and ultimately make the wrong decisions. Moral education does include fairness, but it does not necessarily include gentleness, as demonstrated by Kṛṣṇa throughout the Gītā.

Prabupāda's translation is biased towards the teaching of the Gaudiya paramparā, which traces its teachings to Caitanya Mahāprabhu who insisted that he was an avatar of Viṣṇu – and possibly identified himself as Jesus. The proper source of education is in Kṛṣṇa's words, instead – one has to choose whether to accept that which was written down in the original śāstra, or in the interpretation of those who came later (using languages other than Sanskrit). While this particular teaching within his translation is consistent with some of the teachings of the Gaudiya lineage (such as supposed equality and supposed elimination of the caste system) – he also taught in his own writings that he wanted to preserve varṇāśrama – but the only way to become a brāhmaṇa and find salvation is to accept a human spiritual master through his own process – and yet, if one eats candy that has been offered to Kṛṣṇa, then one achieves the same effect – and yet, one cannot offer any food to Kṛṣṇa unless it has been prepared properly, which is not possible with store bought candy. He also taught that one cannot use intoxicants, and yet promoted the consumption of sugar. Overall, his works are highly irrational, inconsistent and his translation of this text is not consistent with Vedic culture (or the time period in which this text was written).

§

Text 19

ihaiva tair jitaḥ sargo yeṣāṃ sāmye sthitaṃ manaḥ
nirdoṣaṃ hi samaṃ brahma tasmād brahmaṇi te sthitāḥ

-

In this world there are those
who conquer and create –
they are just, stand firm
and are perfect in thought –
they come from Me, live with Me
and are like Me.

§

Text 20

na prahṛṣyet priyaṃ prāpya nodvijet prāpya cāpriyam
sthira-buddhir asammūḍho brahma-vid brahmaṇi
sthitaḥ

-

One should not be impatient
while waiting for one's spouse –
one should not choose one
too quickly –
remaining faithful and understanding
each other will bring satisfaction –
do not be foolish together –
know Me and live together in devotion.

§

Text 21

bāhya-sparśeṣv asaktātmā vindaty ātmani yat sukham
sa brahma-yoga-yuktātmā sukham akṣayam aśnute

-

With the knowledge of uninterrupted touch
one lives easily –
I provide happiness and enjoyment to those
who live together with Me.

§

Text 22

ye hi saṃsparśa-jā bhogā duḥkha-yonaya eva te
ādy-antavantaḥ kaunteya na teṣu ramate budhaḥ

-

Those who are born from love
are an offering –
while birth is difficult for the woman,
children are the aim of desire and love –
the enlightened never stop
enjoying each other and their children.

-

Commentary

Interestingly, the verb ram means to both delight in pleasure and affection, as well as becoming calm.

While yonayaḥ is a correct possible interpretation of yonaya appearing before eva, it is grammatically incorrect based on Prabhupāda's translation. Yonayaḥ is in the plural nominative and his translation indicates a perceived distress from thinking about or experiencing yonis. Instead, the correct grammatical interpretation is yonaye, which is dative and indicates discomfort for, rather than from – when appearing before eva, yonaye can also appear as yonaya.

§

Text 23

śaknotīhaiva yaḥ soḍhuṃ prāk śarīra-vimokṣaṇāt
kāma-krodhodbhavam vegaṃ sa yuktaḥ sa sukhī
naraḥ

One who is victorious
in liberating himself
from the lust of anger and wrath
will do so through yoga –
I provide happiness, pleasure and comfort.

§

Text 24

yo 'ntaḥ-sukho 'ntar-ārāmas tathāntar-jyotir eva yaḥ
sa yogi brahma-nirvāṇaṃ brahma-bhūto 'dhigacchati

I am beauty, comfort and delight –
I am the grove in the forest,
in which is found knowledge –
I am the fire
and the lightning which causes
it to burn –
one who immerses himself
in Me
achieves the Highest.

§

Text 25

labhante brahma-nirvāṇam ṛṣayaḥ kṣīṇa-kalmaṣāḥ
chinna-dvaidhā yatātmānaḥ sarva-bhūta-hite ratāḥ

-

In aspiring towards Me,
one seeks the moon –
the dispeller of evil
who eliminates all duality.

One finds happiness
with one's beloved.

§

Text 26

kāma-krodha-vimuktānāṃ yatīnāṃ yata-cetasām
abhito brahma-nirvāṇaṃ vartate viditātmanām

-

Sannyāsins attempt
to stop the music of lovers
through restraint of the heart and mind –
they seek death and annihilation
themselves, and wish others to do the same.

§

Texts 27 and 28

sparśān kṛtvā bahir bāhyāṃś cakṣuś caivāntare bhruvoḥ
prāṇāpānau samau kṛtvā nāsābhyantara-cāriṇau

yatendriya-mano-buddhir munir mokṣa-parāyaṇaḥ
vigatecchā-bhaya-krodho yaḥ sadā mukta eva saḥ

Two soulmates move together, in sacrifice to one another and Me,
experiencing each other's outward feelings, emotions and touch –
their inner feelings are felt together in the heart,
and they breath together, as one.

Do not seek an exit from this world, as you live together.

One guides the intellect and mind –
and senses and body –
by the inward desire towards liberation;
two birds desire anger to take flight –
sit before the fire with Me
and find release.

Commentary

This text relates very closely to Text 8 in the Brahma Saṃhitā:

Destiny – the beautiful goddess –
beloved friend; who desires
the eternal, radiant form of
Bhagavān, Śiva, Śakti and Lakṣmī

to move together in the union of liṅgam and yoni, and wishes for the preservation of eternal life.

§

Text 29

bhoktāraṃ yajña-tapasāṃ sarva-loka-maheśvaram
suhṛdaṃ sarva-bhūtānāṃ jñātvā māṃ śāntim ṛcchati

-

One who has enjoyed
union in the sacrifice
of the warmth of spring time
is like Me – Śiva and Viṣṇu –
all are reborn through Me
but knowledge brings peace
when one seeks and finds Me.

-

Commentary

This text relates very closely to Text 9 in the Brahma Saṃhitā:

All are reborn from Śiva
through the union of male and female.

Chapter Six

Text 1

śrī-bhagavān uvāca
anāśritaḥ karma-phalaṃ kāryaṃ karma karoti yaḥ
sa sannyāsī ca yogī ca na niragnir na cākriyaḥ

-

Śrī-Bhagavān said:

A sannyāsin will have
offered the fruit of his karma
with a sharp exhalation of breath –
and it is neither offered to
nor accepted by Agni.

-

Commentary

Prabhupāda's translation of anāśritaḥ as "without taking shelter" is reasonably accurate but appears to refer to the meaning of aśritaḥ in relationship to the home, where it refers to the corners of a room. However, this is actually a suffix only and pairing this with ana to indicate "without" is not a proper grammatical construction. Instead, anaḥ refers to the mundane breath, not that of the breath of life – and affixing aśritaḥ indicates a sharp exhalation of actual breath, rather than that of the spiritual.

Prabhupāda translates akriyaḥ as "without duty." Kriyaḥ appears similarly to some passive conjugations of kṛ, however it is not a valid conjugation and also does not relate to any noun stems formed from the verb. Instead, this relates to the verb krī, which means "to buy." In this text it is used to indicate acceptance (or lack of acceptance) by Agni, who mythologically carries our offerings to Kṛṣṇa.

Nir in a compound means "out" or "forth" and indicates pouring forth one's offering. In this text one who does not live with Kṛṣṇa in his heart is only able to perceive the mundane nature of existence and is unable to make a proper offering to Kṛṣṇa. He accepts our offerings made in love and devotion, but one that is empty of meaning is not accepted by Him. The meaning of this text relates to previous commentaries on the sannyāsins as they do not understand or know Rādha-Kṛṣṇa. Note that a sannyāsin is an old concept, but refers to one who renounces life, rather than being a reference to the āśrama of saṃnyāsin, which refers either to retirement or one who has transcended the material world.

§

Text 2

yaṃ sannyāsam iti prāhur yogaṃ taṃ viddhi pāṇḍava
na hy asannyasta-saṅkalpo yogī bhavati kaścana

-

They will have said
that about one who renounces life
and practices austerity –

observe that form of yoga, Pāṇḍava –
for one who does not give up on life
will become a yogi in his saṅkalpa.

§

Text 3

āruruksor muner yogaṃ karma kāraṇam ucyate
yogārūḍhasya tasyaiva śamaḥ kāraṇam ucyate

-

Pouring oneself
into each other creates the inner desire
for karma yoga –
one creates milk with yoga
and it brings peace and rest.

-

Commentary

This text relates to the traditional Vedic message that those who have been successful in kindling the Nāciketa fire provide prasādam to humanity – this relates both to our work created in devotion, as well as our work together in raising a family.

The eight-fold system of yoga was first recorded (at least in written language) approximately 600 to 1200 years after the writing of the Gītā. The traditional language within the Vedas refers to the love between God and man, as well as His/Her love affair with the universe. One finds God in other human beings, as well as in marveling at the beauty of the universe and the Self.

Āruruksoḥ uses the dual person due to the duplicate usage of ṛ, which is the compound form relating to raising up or seeking (and finding) attainment. While this is provided for stress, it also is consistent with an overall Vedic message that this is something we do together, specifically between two people. Hindus consider marriage to be incredibly sacred, which includes honoring the marriage vow. The use of ā indicates that this is something we do together, and we both aspire upwards towards God, as well as keeping each other near.

Śamaḥ is one of many words in Sanskrit that has many meanings – and captures both the meaning intended by, as well as what others who know better think about those who reject life. In addition to having a meaning that many would (in the modern era) consider to be a traditional concept in yoga, it also refers to peace and tranquility.

Most concepts found within aṣṭhāṅga yoga have very valuable and useful meanings – for example, we should keep ourselves healthy, we should look past the material world, we should practice a reasonable level of responsibility in life, and we should pursue union with the Divine – however, all of the traditional terms found within what those in the West consider to be yoga have other more traditional meanings – such as looking inward, experiencing love within our hearts, breathing together and also loving life and others (worship of the breath). Many of these terms have inverse meanings, as well, such as killing or stopping the breath. One can either enjoy life, or long for death – at the end of one's lifetime, one can look back and possibly determine whether this lifetime was wasted or not – and in anticipating this, one can also live one's life accordingly.

§

Text 4

yadā hi nendriyārtheṣu na karmasv anuṣajjate
sarva-saṅkalpa-sannyāsī yogārūḍhas tadocyate

-

It is said that the saṅkalpa
of a sannyāsin
is neither occupied in the senses,
their special purpose –
nor in action –
and that he does not aspire
to know the heaven of the clouds
nor their fertility –
and does not care for the taste of milk.

-

Commentary

This translation uses a play on words with respect to ūḍhaḥ compared to ūdhaḥ. An interesting note for posterity is that I had a typo when working on this particular text – however, ūḍhaḥ refers to one who is swept away or who gets married. In Prabhupāda's text he assumes ārūḍhaḥ based on his interpretation of sandhi – however, this means one who is either swept away in aspiration towards God, or it refers to one who is lost in the romance and excitement of marriage. The choice of words that makes more sense is instead arūḍhaḥ, which refers to one who is not and fits better with the context. Phonetically, outside of some possible slight differences, arūdhaḥ refers to one who does not aspire to the clouds (which are a symbol of the feminine and fertility in the Vedas) or to the breast (ūdhaḥ means "udder"). Milk of course has many meanings within the Vedas, and one meaning from the original Upaniṣads references the product of a devotee who has kindled the Nāciketa fire within his or her heart. While the spelling is different with these two words, the overall meaning is the same, and regardless of one's pronunciation, they sound more or less the same, as well.

§

Text 5

uddhared ātmanātmānaṃ nātmānam avasādayet
ātmaiva hy ātmano bandhur ātmaiva ripur ātmanaḥ

-

One should crave life
and not be led away from its enjoyment,
as you are part of Me –
any other understanding is self-deceit.

§

Text 6

bandhur ātmātmanas tasya yenātmaivātmanā jitaḥ
anātmanas tu śatrutve vartetātmaiva śatru-vat

-

All are connected to and are part of Kṛṣṇa
and exist because of Me;
one who does not understand the ātman
wants to find Me,
but is his own enemy.

§

Text 7

jitātmanaḥ praśāntasya paramātmā samāhitaḥ
śītoṣṇa-sukha-duḥkheṣu tathā mānāpamānayoḥ

-

One will have conquered oneself
in finding peace with Me –
live together through good times
and bad times,
and neither will consider themselves
greater than that of the two.

§

Text 8

jñāna-vijñāna-tṛptātmā kūṭa-stho vijitendriyaḥ

yukta ity ucyate yogī sama-loṣṭrāśma-kāñcanaḥ

-

Two live together – and understand
the mystery of the other;
through earthly and spiritual knowledge
of the Self
one will gain union
of the heart, mind and senses –
material gold is equivalent to dirt and stone –
but the marriage vow
is true wealth.

-

Commentary

Kāñcanaḥ refers to money and wealth, as well as the marriage vow – and the color yellow.

§

Text 9

suhṛn-mitrāry-udāsīna-madhyastha-dveṣya-bandhuṣu
sādhuṣv api ca pāpeṣu sama-buddhir viśiṣyate

-

One who attempts to come between
the virtuous who seek the sun together
in mutual friendship – in particular the union
between lovers who are of a similar mind –
is evil and will be punished.

§

Text 10

yogī yuñjīta satatam ātmānaṃ rahasi sthitaḥ
ekākī yata-cittātmā nirāśīr aparigrahaḥ

-

A yogi desires union
with the eternal ātman –
and to rest in its sacred
mysteries and truth.

One who is alone
restrains himself and seeks
relief from his troubles
and finds none.

-

Commentary

Rahaḥ refers to solitude and loneliness – as well as mystical truth, and the expressions of emotional, spiritual and physical love between soulmates. Many words are a sign that different students are either taught different lessons based on their character, that not all students understand the lesson or that some students who do not understand the lessons (or receive poor instruction) become teachers.

Nirāśīḥ has a number of meanings related to prayer – as well as seeking a medication to heal one's wounds.

It also refers to the fangs of a serpent – which can provide a cure – as well as representing a source of wisdom. Nir in a compound tends to have the meaning of pouring forth or even without, rather than indicating a lack of something.

One could potentially argue that everyone has a different means to happiness – however, in this particular text there is really only one reading. Nirāśīḥ specifically refers to pouring forth one's prayers outward and aparigrahaḥ refers to either not comprehending, not experiencing the warmth of embrace, not getting married and one who does not experience or bestow hospitality. There is one possible reading of the latter word indicating one who escapes a curse or punishment – interpreting this word with the latter meaning in this context is a psychological slip of the tongue. The optative mood only appears once in this text in relation to one's desire for yoga. All other statements in the text are declarative in nature.

§

Texts 11 and 12

śucau deśe pratiṣṭhāpya sthiram āsanam ātmanaḥ
nāty-ucchritaṃ nāti-nīcaṃ cailājina-kuśottaram

tatraikāgraṃ manaḥ kṛtvā yata-cittendriya-kriyaḥ
upaviśyāsane yuñjyād yogam ātma-viśuddhaye

-

Two radiant beings

exist and endure together
with the Self.

Son of Pṛthu,
take pleasure in the kuśa grass,
the yoke and aspiration towards the Highest.

One should desire union
and fixed attention
in thought and action –
in observation and the senses –
sit at her feet and enter into
shared existence with the Self –
experience perfect knowledge
and provide nourishment for one's children,
together.

-

Commentary

Cailājina can refer to "cloth and antelope skin" as a compound or it is linkage between two phrases and an address to Arjuna (ca can imply "therefore" in some contexts) which also equates pleasure with the concept of yoga (in the traditional context of the Hindu homam fire, which is a symbol of the Nāciketa sacrifice, and the phrase equates kuśa with pleasure and līla). Kuśa grass is also a traditional material for creating a yoke for cows who plough the fields.

Kriyaḥ refers to acceptance, rather than activity, as it is derived from krī (to buy) rather than kṛ (to do).

Viśuddha refers to perfect knowledge and two who are of the same nature (it is a synonym for sama) and is derived from the concept of entering into the state of providing milk.

§

Text 13

samaṃ kāya-śiro-grīvaṃ dhārayann acalaṃ sthiraḥ
samprekṣya nāsikāgraṃ svaṃ diśaś cānavalokayan

-

In drinking from the nectar
of marriage
one will be moved –
and play together
in faith, trust
and lasting eye contact.

Those who do not fight with each other
are seen as praiseworthy
by one's own people and family.

-

Commentary

Kāyaḥ refers to marriage. Grīvaḥ refers to the neck, but originally referred to the neck of a bottle – it also refers to the nape of the neck.

Nāsika can refer to the nasal, but nāsikya is more commonly used to refer to the nose – when nāsika is used with respect to the nose, it tends to either have a meaning that is not sacred and incredibly mundane or is a reference to sound. Nāsika is more commonly used to refer to the town in India.

Instead, nāsika makes most sense interpreted as na āsika. This refers to refraining from dueling with one another and is derived from asi, which means "you are" and is an old warrior term for the sword.

Ānavalokayan is the most sensible interpretation of sandhi within cānavalokayan and refers to being seen as praiseworthy and a cause for celebration.

Samprekṣya refers to that which is worth seeing.

Acalam can refer to "unmoving," but can also refer to "unagitated" and "not shaking one another free" – and also has a phonetic relationship referring to one declaring himself to having been moved and also refers to intoxication.

§

Text 14

praśāntātmā vigata-bhīr brahmacāri-vrate sthitaḥ
manaḥ saṃyamya mac-citto yukta āsīta mat-paraḥ

-

A studious and successful brahmācari
seeks the light
in his vow to learn the Vedas;
he perseveres in his intent

to give himself up to Me – together –
and seeks to find his home
in the Highest yoga.

-

Commentary

The purpose of the original brahmācarya āśrama was to teach young students the Vedas while they matured – and it was also to teach the basic fundamentals of worship – all as part of basic spiritual education, as well as in preparation for marriage. The student saved himself for his future wife and at the same time learned Vedic concepts and practices (such as offering ghee in the homam fire, use of the dual kuśa, bowing and enjoying singing and listening to mantras). He was also taught the concept of yoga, as well, in preparation for his gṛhastha years. While this tradition has been preserved in the original language of the Vedas and in many traditions within India, over the centuries this message has been lost in a variety of traditions, world-wide.

§

Text 15

yuñjann evaṃ sadātmānaṃ yogī niyata-mānasaḥ
śāntiṃ nirvāṇa-paramāṃ mat-saṃsthām
adhigacchati

-

One experiences yoga with Me
in yajña –
the yogi is connected in thought
and prayer and finds peace
in the ultimate bliss
that comes from living together
and aspiring to the Highest.

-

Commentary

The term nirvāṇa existed before Buddhism – and can either refer to the bliss of full immersion in the Divine – or it can refer to permanent death. The latter is a concept that came from both Sāṅkhya philosophy and Buddhism. Prabhupāda uses the later definition in his translation – and while the "cessation of material existence" can refer to the traditional interpretation of mokṣa, throughout his writings Prabhupāda continually encouraged devotees to seek an end to the cycle of saṃsāra, rather than piercing the veil of māya and experiencing the joy of existence in the spiritual world. The key difference between the Gaudiya interpretation of mokṣa and the Buddhist interpretation is that the former teaches that one will essentially go to heaven, rather than dissolving into nothingness – however, one can also experience heaven on Earth, which is a certainty and is the traditional goal within the Sanātana Dharma (and the aim of every lifetime).

§

Text 16

nāty-aśnatas tu yogo 'sti na caikāntam anaśnataḥ
na cāti-svapna-śīlasya jāgrato naiva cārjuna

-

Arjuna –
one who seeks enjoyment of life
can certainly find union –
but one who does not
will never wake from their sleep.

§

Text 17

yuktāhāra-vihārasya yukta-ceṣṭasya karmasu
yukta-svapnāvabodhasya yogo bhavati duḥkha-hā

-

One who experiences yoga
finds enjoyment
in every action and in movement
through life –
including in his or her dreams.

Understanding the lotus flower
of yoga and its blossom
provides comfort.

§

Text 18

yadā viniyataṃ cittam ātmany evāvatiṣṭhate
nispṛhaḥ sarva-kāmebhyo yukta ity ucyate tadā

-

One who does not have
inner support or direction
loses his footing –
he longs for and reaches out to grasp
everything.

-

Commentary

While we must enjoy life we should also strive to transcend the material world, and embrace the spiritual. Enjoying life and all it has to offer is very different from craving things which are irrelevant, such as unnecessary possessions or desiring sex outside of our marriage. Unfortunately, even within a "spiritual" community there are those who have affairs (gurus seem to be candidates, in particular) and many have unnecessarily nice cars and very large houses. While one can possess a material object and not be possessed by it, all too often this is not the case. Going one step further, many are even possessed by their spiritual practice and value adherence to rules or status in their community (such as titles, fame, reputation or their adherence to a routine) over the spiritual aspects of life and even use some of these so-called spiritual activities and status to claim their superiority over others. One should always beware of any spiritual leaders who have affairs with their disciples, or the spouses of their disciples – and one should always beware of spiritual leaders who claim they are superior as human beings and are deserving of worship – in particular those who claim they are an intermediary between the devotee and God. It is a fact that while we are all part of Kṛṣṇa's divinity that not all human beings are created equal – however, the superior are here to serve, in their own way, and no human being can stand between another and God.

Concerning the language in the text – some are confused by the term niyam and niyatam. Niyam refers to inner support or holding something within (such as that which is dear); it is frequently a misunderstood term in the West. Niyatam can serve as an indeclinable adverb referring to that which is constant or inevitable, but in this context would not be paired with a prefix, such as vi. Prabhupāda confused this term with his concept of "regulation," based on the common Western interpretation of this as being restraint. Inner strength is not the same thing as controlling one's life according to someone else's rules. Whether as an indeclinable or as a participle, it does not have the meaning of "regulation." When treated as a participle and combined with vi, it refers to one who has lost his or her inner strength. While words that have modifiers that encounter frequent use can take on meanings that seemingly go beyond the combination of prefix and modified word, the various meanings are generally consistent with the underlying components. In this case, Prabhupāda did use niyatam as a participle – the above is mentioned simply as a note to some of his translations of other texts (within the Gītā and other works) – but he appears to be applying the concept of distinction to his term of regulation. A good example of distinction applied to vi is vijñānam compared to jñānam – one refers to scientific and material knowledge, which is distinct from the knowledge of God.

Prabhupāda was frequently confused concerning the prefix nis or nir. This can mean "without" but in the context of outside of oneself. It refers to something that is directed "forth" or "without." It does not indicate a lack of something or negation. He seems to have been confused with nispṛhaḥ, which is the combination of ni and spṛhaḥ. Glancing very quickly at the word, one could potentially read nis into the word, but one will realize that is not actually there – the prefix is ni, which refers to something that is inside (inner). This term refers to inner desire, but specifically within the context of craving and potentially envy. If nis were the actual prefix, then he would have attributed the incorrect meaning of "without," as seems to be consistent with all of his translations; he also overlooked the fact that the "s" is part of spṛhaḥ. Nispṛhaḥ refers to the inner lust that comes with living in the material world – and not the desire or longing that comes from spiritual kāma, which is best felt between ourselves and Rādha-Kṛṣṇa, which includes ourselves and spouse.

§

Text 19

yathā dīpo nivāta-stho neṅgate sopamā smṛtā
yogino yata-cittasya yuñjato yogam ātmanaḥ

-

A light shining downhill
does not provide illumination –
one who remembers
that the yogi looks inside
and longs with the heart and mind
to experience union with the Self
is foremost.

§

Texts 20 - 23

yatroparamate cittaṃ niruddhaṃ yoga-sevayā
yatra caivātmanātmānaṃ paśyann ātmani tuṣyati

sukham ātyantikaṃ yat tad buddhi-grāhyam atīndriyam
vetti yatra na caivāyaṃ sthitaś calati tattvataḥ

yaṃ labdhvā cāparaṃ lābhaṃ manyate nādhikaṃ tataḥ
yasmin sthito na duḥkhena guruṇāpi vicālyate

taṃ vidyād duḥkha-saṃyoga-viyogaṃ yoga-saṃjñitam
sa niścayena yoktavyo yoga 'nirviṇṇa-cetasā

-

Performing sevā together with
one who was long awaited
provides rest and delight
and is like the flash of Agni's laughter –

one finds satisfaction seeing the Self
in the other.

One is happy in the divine presence
of the beloved and in joining
oneself together in the marriage vow;
the senses and mind are overwhelmed
in comprehension of the other –
one discovers Truth in the soulmate.

Attaining the Highest within oneself –
in thought and conception –
brings one nearer to Me;
there is no sorrow being close
to one deserving of worship –
one cherishes the differences in the other
and is moved in the ecstasy of līla.

One who desires knowledge of the Divine
must live in both union and separation –
despite any trouble that may arise in life –
and one will attain knowledge and splendor together.

-

Commentary

Uparamate refers to enjoyment at the side of one's soulmate, or at his or her feet – in particular, the connotation refers specifically to yoga. Any meaning pertaining to rest or calm refers to afterglow.

Niruddham specifically refers to the flash of the lightning bolt, which in the language of the Vedas is likened to laughter. Agni, who presides over the homam fire and marriage ceremony, is also known as lightning, in addition to fire.

Paśyan refers to beholding with the eye.

Tuṣ refers to satisfaction, but with the connotation of being satisfied with someone else, in particular in relation to the calm and tranquility that is accompanied by yoga.

Ātyanitikam refers to being in the presence of the Highest.

Grāhyaḥ refers to taking one by the hand and not letting go, as well as marriage and Hindu hospitality. It also refers to understanding or knowing "in a certain sense." Overall the word has many associations with understanding and knowledge (but with the meaning of specific understanding), reception, taking the marriage vow, perception and comprehension.

The Hindu marriage vow does not resemble the ones typically used in the West. It simply refers to the implicit promise of eternal friendship and happiness together in sacred love of the Divine.

Lābhaḥ has a very similar meaning to grāhyaḥ – grāhyaḥ refers to taking a vow and looking upon an object of desire and affection and lābhaḥ has the similar meaning of keeping something close, but instead also refers to conception.

Cal in the causative refers to cherishing someone and the word overall refers to ecstasy and play.

Text 23 encapsulates one of the core Gaudiya messages, which is worship of Rādha-Kṛṣṇa in separation. We are two separate people, and yet we can achieve increasing degrees of closeness and unity – while still perceiving the differences, and that we are separate. Without some form of separation, there would be no way of knowing and loving each other and appreciating being close.

The above texts all accompany each other conceptually and have linkages between each śloka in meaning – these texts together tell the story of meeting one's partner, discovering God in the other's eyes, discovering the joys of union, procreation and the discovery of each other and Kṛṣṇa throughout one's lifetime.

§

Text 24

saṅkalpa-prabhavān kāmāṃs tyaktvā sarvān aśeṣataḥ
manasaivendriya-grāmaṃ viniyamya samantataḥ

-

The saṅkalpa of the mother and father
is to continually offer their breath
to one another completely –
in desire and passion –
with limited separation between
heart and mind, senses and body
and ascending together
with shared mantras.

-

Commentary

In this context, viniyamya refers to aspiring with inner determination. The term is used within the context of those living together and being united in shared thought, love, passion and spiritual goals. Grāmaḥ is a common term for a village, but also refers to a collection and can refer to a range of tones in music. One translation of manasaivendriya-grāmam viniyamya samantataḥ refers to the shared mantras between the mother and father through kīrtan – and also has a relationship to that of the shared kīrtan offered by the community, which children benefit from, as well. This refers not only to the prasādam of actual music, but the purely spiritual form, as well.

The language in this text is plural – in this case, there are some possible references to the community, but it addresses mothers and fathers generally, instead, rather than specifically referring to a pair in the dual. Prabhavaḥ refers to the source of existence and includes both Rādha-Kṛṣṇa and the human mother and father.

§

Text 25

śanaiḥ śanair uparamed buddhyā dhṛti-gṛhītayā
ātma-saṃsthaṃ manaḥ kṛtvā na kiñcid api cintayet

-

One should desire quiet and gentle enjoyment
at each other's feet,
in līla and the pleasure of rest –
with supportive and shared ideas,
existing together in the Self
with the mind always directed
on caring for one another.

§

Text 26

yato yato niścalati manaś cañcalam asthiram
tatas tato niyamyaitad ātmany eva vaśaṃ nayet

-

In movement and aspiration
one is ecstatic –
if one's thoughts are not focused
on Me, then one will not be faithful;
one should desire to lead one another home.

-

Commentary

While this translation uses the pronoun "Me" above, the text has numerous references to both Lakṣmī and Viṣṇu. Tataḥ is a reference to both Brahman and the father. Most terms associated with movement, attainment, seeking and "meditation" relate directly to Lakṣmī, including those in this text. Cañcalam can refer to something which either flickers or moves about – and relates to the wind, which is an ancient term for Viṣṇu, or Kṛṣṇa, and also relates to Lakṣmī, or Rādhā. The verb nī in this text is singular, however it refers both to leading someone home, as well as marriage (in addition to other more mundane meanings), but this clause within the text refers to the desire to hasten towards God – given the preceding texts and the various references to the process of seeking, meditation and both the father and mother, it makes most sense to interpret this as a direction to lead each other and create a happy home, where the family will live together with Kṛṣṇa.

§

Text 27

praśānta-manasaṃ hy enaṃ yoginaṃ sukham uttamam
upaiti śānta-rajasaṃ brahma-bhūtam akalmaṣam

-

One who approaches her feet in prayer
finds peace and calm – of mind and thought –
and the Highest yoga
in comfort and happiness;
one who has found true peace
in the pollen of spring
will have found Me.

-

Commentary

Akalmaṣam has been previously translated as being freed from sin. There is no concept within the Sanātana Dharma related to what those in the West consider sin. The Vedic concept of sin is the violation of the laws associated with dharma – there is actually no way (in most cases) of undoing one's actions. Instead, this refers to not being consumed with that which is bad. The bad could be considered evil – or it could also relate to misfortune and unhappiness, which is a concept frequently associated with words in Sanskrit that Westerners tend to translate as "sin." Unhappiness and the actions of bad people are what are typically associated with the various terms related to this concept. Of course, within the context of the traditional definition of karma, if one does something evil, the only recourse is to try and do good things, instead.

Rajaḥ is frequently misunderstood. Historically, it relates to the sky and clouds – Viṣṇu and Lakṣmī. It is associated with the sphere of light and heaven. Rajaḥ is also associated with tejaḥ – the fire of Agni and passion – which also of course relates to tapaḥ, which is related to the spring time and Holi (the month of Tapas). Rajaḥ relates to pollen and dust, as well as phalam. Some associate rajaḥ with impurity – whether or not that was an actual association in Vedic culture is possibly unknown – it certainly has picked up a meaning over the centuries that means "impure," but historically speaking, if one looks at the tradition of applying the red bindu, then one may assume that there was not an original perception of impurity associated with this word.

§

Text 28

yuñjann evaṃ sadātmānaṃ yogī vigata-kalmaṣaḥ
sukhena brahma-saṃsparśam atyantaṃ sukham
aśnute

-

One who seeks yoga in this manner
continually enjoys the fruit of the Self –
sorrow will take flight with ease;
and he will attain Me
in the perfection and comfort of mutual touch.

§

Text 29

sarva-bhūta-stham ātmānaṃ sarva-bhūtāni cātmani
īkṣate yoga-yuktātmā sarvatra sama-darśanaḥ

-

All should worship the ātman
and all people –
one who is yoked to Me
has offered himself
and always sees Me
and teaches others.

-

Commentary

Darśanaḥ refers to observation, sight, knowledge, yajña and experience – and it also refers to teaching and showing others, which is a direct result of having known Him/Her.

Īkṣ has most of the same meanings related to darśanaḥ but focuses primarily on the aspects related to sight (whether with the eyes or the mind). It also has a relationship (indirectly) to an alternate form of the perfect tense of bhaj, which is related to the yajña and teaching aspects of darśanaḥ, which are part of the offering and distribution aspects of bhakti.

§

Text 30

yo mām paśyati sarvatra sarvaṃ ca mayi paśyati
tasyāhaṃ na praṇaśyāmi sa ca me na praṇaśyati

-

One who sees and experiences Me
in everything –
I belong to him
and he belongs to Me –
and we live together.

§

Text 31

sarva-bhūta-sthitaṃ yo māṃ bhajaty ekatvam asthitaḥ
sarvathā vartamāno 'pi sa yogī mayi vartate

-

I am everything that exists, and all who are born –
one who offers himself completely to Me
lives with Me.

§

Text 32

ātmaupamyena sarvatra samaṃ paśyati yo 'rjuna
sukhaṃ vā yadi vā duḥkhaṃ sa yogī paramo mataḥ

-

Arjuna –
one who sees that I am everywhere
and eternal –
whether he is currently happy or not,
he will have understood the Highest knowledge.

-

Commentary

While particles in Sanskrit have very little specific meaning, the combination of vā yadi vā tends to refer to a set of conditional terms indicating "whether or not," or "even whether or…". The interpretation of particles in this text helps to provide the meaning for mataḥ. Mataḥ can refer to that which ones thinks or understands, or what others think or understand. The rest of the language in this text refers more to Kṛṣṇa as the ātman, rather than the jīvātman.

§

Text 33

arjuna uvāca
yo 'yaṃ yogas tvayā proktaḥ sāmyena madhusūdana
etasyāhaṃ na paśyāmi cañcalatvāt sthitiṃ sthirām

-

Arjuna said:

One who finds union with Kṛṣṇa
is said to be like You –
I do not understand
how one can remain resistant to change
if one is consumed with Your ecstasy.

§

Text 34

cañcalaṃ hi manaḥ kṛṣṇa pramāthi balavad dṛḍham
tasyāhaṃ nigrahaṃ manye vāyor iva su-duṣkaram

-

Kṛṣṇa –
one who is moved in ecstatic thought
gains power and strength –
I am able to overcome my inner demons
because of You – and our breath;
like You, I am extraordinary.

§

Text 35

śrī-bhagavān uvāca
asaṃśayaṃ mahā-bāho mano durnigrahaṃ calam
abhyāsena tu kaunteya vairāgyeṇa ca gṛhyate

-

Śrī-Bhagavān said:

Kaunteya –
we do not abuse each other –
the mind is great and comes from Me –
one may be confused
through repetition –
and one who clings to routine is distasteful,
and like Rāhu, consumes the sun.

§

Text 36

asaṃyatātmanā yogo duṣprāpa iti me matiḥ
vaśyātmanā tu yatatā śakyo 'vāptum upāyataḥ

-

One who has no self-control
cannot attain Me –
bhakti provides one with the ability
to endure suffering,
if one looks for Me inside oneself.

§

Text 37

arjuna uvāca
ayatiḥ śraddhayopeto yogāc calita-mānasaḥ
aprāpya yoga-saṃsiddhiṃ kāṃ gatiṃ kṛṣṇa gacchati

-

Arjuna said:

Kṛṣṇa –
one who seeks attainment
approaches the one who
provides understanding of the Highest –
approaching with faith and certainty
causes one to be moved in the mind and heart.

-

Commentary

This text is not a question – some find a variety of aspects of Sanskrit grammar confusing; in this case, the śloka makes no sense phrased as a question due to the vocabulary within the text.

Ayatiḥ has numerous meanings depending on the context of the śloka. In this case, ayatiḥ refers to one who is married – being associated with one who has not lost her husband.

Calita does not really refer to "deviation." It can refer to being moved from one's path, or from one's current state of mind – however, the source of this word generally refers to being moved by ecstasy and the spiritual, rather than changing one's actual course (unless one does so through inspiration).

Aprāpya does not mean "failing to attain." Instead it is a reference to the "unobtainable" – which is a superlative term in Sanskrit, indicating that which is "out of reach."

Kām is best translated as "to whom." This is actually an older usage of language – while kim does appear in the Gītā, use of kām in this context is actually an indication of an older style, which is closer to the original Vedas. The clarity of this text is also a possible sign of its original age, and the text is best read in reverse.

It is interesting that Prabhupāda refers frequently to the word "mysticism" within his notes for this text. Mysticism is frequently misunderstood but refers specifically to finding union with God and is associated in nearly all traditions with the concept of romantic love and marriage. This text is also a general direction to the devotee that Kṛṣṇa values everyone in the relationship, and that we are all an object worthy of attainment.

§

Text 38

kaccin nobhaya-vibhraṣṭaś chinnābhram iva naśyati
apratiṣṭho mahā-bāho vimūḍho brahmaṇaḥ pathi

-

One does not want to be torn apart
and cut off from the showers of spring –
or their flash of lightning which strikes the Earth;
one who loses their support
is driven from the path to Kṛṣṇa.

-

Commentary

The thunder cloud is symbolic of a variety of concepts related to the Vedas – clouds providing rain are associated with Lakṣmī, lightning is associated with Agni and both the thunderbolt and wind are associated with Viṣṇu (Indra).

Prabhupāda frequently translates mahā-bāho as "mighty armed" – when in fact it is a reference to a measure of greatness and is frequently associated in the Gītā to the mind.

The phrase ubhaya-vibhraṣṭaś chinnābhram essentially means "two who are torn apart, divided and driven from the sky."

§

Text 39

etan me saṃśayaṃ kṛṣṇa chettum arhasy aśeṣataḥ
tvad-anyaḥ saṃśayasyāsya chettā na hy upapadyate

-

Kṛṣṇa –
two find complete union
in You, through the other;
Kṛṣṇa is the remover of doubt –
one who tries to separate those who
desire the yoganidrā
does not find Your feet.

§

Text 40

śrī-bhagavān uvāca
pārtha naiveha nāmutra vināśas tasya vidyate
na hi kalyāṇa-kṛt kaścid durgatim tata gacchati

-

Śrī-Bhagavān said:

Arjuna –
do not listen too closely
to this discussion on separation –
one who seeks Me
will not experience the path
to loss and poverty.

-

Commentary

While amutra can refer to both this lifetime, as well as the next – it is also a grammatical feature that refers back to what has been previously said. This is related in usage to etad which is found in Text 39 – a key difference is that etad refers more to the concepts within a single set of connected clauses or ideas within a text and in Text 39 it is used to indicate that the discussion is making Arjuna desire to lay down and rest (alternately, etad in that context can just be translated as "this").

§

Text 41

prāpya puṇya-kṛtāṃ lokān uṣitvā śāśvatīḥ samāḥ
śucīnāṃ śrītmatāṃ gehe yoga-bhraṣṭo 'bhijāyate

-

Those who do what is desirable
and right, who are virtuous and pure –
live together continually in
their radiance and beauty,
of home and body –
and having experienced separation
they join together in victory, praise
and creation.

-

Commentary

All who read the Vedas and their message bring their own perspective on life to understanding the scripture. Śrīmat refers to beauty, prosperity and wealth. Śuci refers to radiance and purity, as well as the sun, moon, wind, fire, the oblation and the yajña offered at the first feeding of an infant.

Yoga-bhraṣṭaḥ refers to one who has experienced separation from union.

Gehe can refer strictly to the home, or appearing in the dual, as occurs in this text, it refers to the home of the family, as well as the physical body.

Jāyate simultaneously refers to victory and praise, as well as procreation. This is the middle voice of jan; however, there are numerous associations between jan and ji, despite any subtle differences in their phonetic representations. The last clause in the above text is singular, rather than plural; however, the middle voice is reflexive, and this concept encapsulates the concept of reunification. In some texts this shows up in the dual person, and in others it is singular. And while this could refer also to "being born," ultimately the meaning is the same.

§

Text 42

atha vā yogināṃ eva kule bhavati dhīmatām
etad dhi durlabhataraṃ loke janma yad īdṛśam

-

I see and enjoy the birth
of those who are reborn through wisdom –
whose parents are focused on that
which is considered by some

to be out of their reach.

§

Text 43

tatra taṃ buddhi-saṃyogaṃ labhate paurva-dehikam
yatate ca tato bhūyaḥ saṃsiddhau kuru-nandana

-

One joins together in yoga
with one of a similar mind –
a new body is formed
and another is reborn, as the rising sun;
rejoice in achieving the Highest together.

-

Commentary

In this particular case, kuru-nandana most likely refers to "son of Kuru." I left this out of the translation, simply for stylistic reasons. Tato bhūyaḥ saṃsiddhau kuru also means "become greater together in successful attainment". Nandana refers to being happy and rejoicing, in addition to meaning "son." The references to yoga in this text are consistent with the preceding dialogue – saṃyoga refers specifically to yoga performed together – of course that is implicit in all definitions of yoga, but saṃyoga provides additional emphasis.

§

Text 44

pūrvābyāsena tenaiva hriyate hy avaśo 'pi saḥ
jijñāsur api yogasya śabda-brahmātivartate

-

One is carried into this lifetime
through the parents –
but it is not simply because
of the desire for union
that one seeks to hear and understand
the eternal music of saṃsāra.

-

Commentary

Most terms related to time and direction refer to the cyclic nature of existence. Pūrva is associated with the rising sun, and is associated with birth, just as the setting sun is also associated with death.

Śabda-brahmātivartate refers to the music of the universe which can be heard in the eternal cycle of saṃsāra, and which represents the universe and man – it represents the creative aspect of the universe, both as the male and female aspects of God, our journey through each lifetime and each subsequent one – and even our journey through each day within each lifetime. Śabdaḥ is a word associated with the Vedas, language, music and Oṃ. Ativṛt refers to moving continually beyond – in each revolution of the Earth about the Sun, and in each death and birth.

§

Text 45

prayatnād yatamānas tu yogī saṃśuddha-kilbiṣaḥ
aneka-janma-saṃsiddhas tato yāti parāṃ gatim

-

Through perseverance and effort
in seeking and attaining that which is good,
the yogi is purified –
in seeking and finding Me,
he will have reached the Highest.

§

Text 46

tapasvibhyo 'dhiko yogī jñānibhyo 'pi mato 'dhikaḥ
karmibhyaś cādhiko yogī tasmād yogī bhavārjuna

-

Arjuna –
in his desire for life,
the yogi seeks wisdom –
in thinking about future lifetimes
he engages in activity;
he is reborn
and finds Me, once again.

§

Text 47

yogināṃ api sarveṣāṃ mad-gatenāntar-ātmanā
śraddhāvān bhajate yo māṃ sa me yuktatamo mataḥ

-

Those who know Me completely
journey with the sun –
they enjoy the strength of the wind
and worship me in devotion and faith;
one who has been yoked to Me
leaves this lifetime
with praise in the funeral pyre –
he journeys into darkness
towards the next lifetime, consumed by Agni.

-

Commentary

This text relates very much to Text 18 from the Śrīśopaniṣad:

Agni – lead us on the path
to virtue and understanding –
please remove
our misfortunes and unhappiness –
we want to worship the Highest
by the light of His moon.

Chapter Seven

Text 1

śrī-bhagavān uvāca
mayy āsakta-manāḥ pārtha yogaṃ yuñjan mad-āśrayaḥ
asaṃśayaṃ samagraṃ māṃ yathā jñāsyasi tac chṛṇu

-

Śrī-Bhagavān said:

Pārtha –
one who applies discrimination
finds yoga through Me –
one requires complete certainty and faith –
you will understand
if you listen to Me.

§

Text 2

jñānaṃ te 'haṃ sa-vijñānam idaṃ vakṣyāmy aśeṣataḥ
yaj jñātvā neha bhūyo 'nyaj jñātavyam avaśiṣyate

-

I will tell you,
so that you can improve in wisdom
and understanding of the world,
as you have committed completely
to knowing Me –
one should always desire to worship.

§

Text 3

manuṣyāṇām sahasreṣu kaścid yatati siddhaye
yatatām api siddhānāṃ kaścin māṃ vetti tattvataḥ

-

One who wants to provide for humanity
must remain close
to those who have already found accomplishment;
he knows Me through understanding Truth.

§

Text 4

bhūmir āpo 'nalo vāyuḥ khaṃ mano buddhir eva ca
ahaṅkāra itīyaṃ me bhinnā prakṛtir aṣṭadhā

-

Prakṛti has eight parts –
earth, water, fire, air, space,
mind and the intellect –
as well as the ātman;
they are both separate from
and a part of Me.

-

Commentary

Kham is frequently translated as ether; however, it is better translated as space. This refers both to outer space and space-time. The five physical elements correspond to the matter of the universe, as well as the three-dimensions – and kham represents that which exists outside of the Earth (it is associated with the void and the Sun, and is part of what the ancient Hindus associated with the blackness of Kṛṣṇa), and it also encompasses the fourth dimension, which modern scientists believe to be part of the fabric of physical reality which we call Prakṛti. Ahaṅkāraḥ has negative associations in some translations; however, generally the ego is part of our own presence of Kṛṣṇa within the mind, and it is the force through which our perception of reality arises, in combination with the senses. It is intimately linked to the power of reason, as well as the brain and our ability to have thought. It is a fundamental component of what is known as the ātman from the microcosmic perspective.

§

Text 5

apareyam itas tv anyāṃ prakṛtiṃ viddhi me parām
jīva-bhūtāṃ mahā-bāho yayedaṃ dhāryate jagat

-

Understand that for one who returns,
Prakṛti is infinite, and not distant –
the jīva is reborn as a part
of the divinity of this world,
which is preserved for Me

through procreation.

-

Commentary

Prabhupāda likely associated dhāryate with "exploiting" due to his association with "using" or "employing." However, dhṛ refers to living – as well as creation. Its primary definition is preservation – which includes the preservation of one's own life (action and breathing), as well as preservation of the human race, through procreation. Human reproduction, as well as the various forms of love shared between soulmates, mirrors the Divine process of the creation, preservation and enjoyment of the universe, as experienced between Rādhā and Kṛṣṇa.

No one can completely understand the universe – the concept of male and female corresponds to His/Her creative aspect, as well as preservation – and like humanity, the universe dissolves and experiences rebirth. That is the original Vedic viewpoint and is consistent with modern theories of cosmology. God represents unity – and many modern scientists believe that both time and space are an illusion, which is created through our perception. The below texts from the Brahma Saṃhitā discuss (in particular, in the original Sanskrit) the process of God's ability to continually give birth to His universe, as well as the enjoyment He takes in it. These are Texts 6 and 7:

Prakṛti is eternally reborn through Rāma –
His existence is pure joy;

the ātman is pleasurable to Him,
even in separation.

He who does not rest
enjoyed creating the lack of separation
for the souls of His lovers,
who are in māya –
you who are abandoned in the darkness,
take comfort.

§

Text 6

etad-yonīni bhūtāni sarvāṇīty upadhāraya
ahaṃ kṛtsnasya jagataḥ prabhavaḥ pralayas tathā

-

All are reborn through the yoni –
I am the source of all of creation,
the waters of the universe, and its belly –
and I am its dissolution.

§

Text 7

mattaḥ parataraṃ nānyat kiñcid asti dhanañjaya
mayi sarvam idaṃ protaṃ sūtre maṇi-gaṇā iva

-

Arjuna, conqueror of wealth –
one who has been intoxicated with passion

is non-different from the other
and knows the Highest –
the jewel of humanity
are the two threads
woven between the two
who are with Me, together.

-

Commentary

Maṇiḥ means jewel and also refers to two parts of the body (both male and female) which relate to pleasure. It is also a name for the very famous mantra: oṃ maṇi padme hūṃ.

Padme is the locative of padma and refers to being near or in the lotus flower – however, it is also the dual vocative.

Hūṃ is a bīja mantra associated with Śiva and Śakti, primarily Śiva. It is also associated with the call and response portions of chanting in a yajña – with prastāva referring to "beginning" and pratihāra referring to "contact" – this is contact in terms of that which occurs in speech, as well as in physical touch – and also refers to singing and the door to a temple.

There are some similar meanings between this text and Text 17 of the Brahma Saṃhitā:

Those who rest in the union of Śrī
are annihilated by Śiva.

And the concept of music, as well as the current dialogue from Kṛṣṇa with respect to the unity of the universe, also relates to Text 4 from the Brahma Saṃhitā:

Those petals of the aṃśa svara
lay upon the leaves of Śrī.

§

Text 8

raso 'ham apsu kaunteya prabhāsmi śaśi-sūryayoḥ
praṇavaḥ sarva-vedeṣu śabdaḥ khe pauruṣaṃ nṛṣu

-

I am Oṃ – the essence
of the waters of creation,
Kaunteya –
I am like the moon
in all seasons – and all phases;
Oṃ is the entirety of the Vedas,
the music of the universe –
all are sacred to Me.

-

Commentary

Rasaḥ refers to nectar and the essence of anything – and also refers to Oṃ. While āpaḥ refers to water, it has specific connotations related to either the element of water, or the waters of creation – and is only declined in the plural. The word can be used to represent all of the sacred rivers of India, which not only represent purification and life (both sustaining life, as well as our journey through all lifetimes), but they also represent the waters of creation, from which we and the universe flow.

Śaśi-sūryayoḥ is a reference to an older expression concerning the path of the sun throughout the year. It is a reference to the two most extreme seasons – while Prabupāda seems to have assumed that the dual applied to sūryaḥ due to the compound reference of both the sun and moon, this is in fact a reference to the moon within the principle seasons – it is later referenced again with respect to the dual applied to kham, which represents space, or the void. These two concepts, the two suns and the two "voids," as well as the reference to the moon, refers to the sun in its various seasons and the moon in its various phases. The notion of the moon being a principle part of this text is very relevant to the reference from Kṛṣṇa identifying Himself with the waters of creation, and previous references to His identification with the cosmic and human yoni.

Oṃ of course represents the entire universe – the sun, the moon, the music of the universe, the Trimūrti – and of course man, including his journey through each lifetime and each day.

§

Text 9

puṇyo gandhaḥ pṛthivyāṃ ca tejaś cāsmi vibhāvasau
jīvanaṃ sarva-bhūteṣu tapaś cāsmi tapasviṣu

-

I am the fragrance of candan
permeating the universe;
I am the fire
of the yajña – I burn
and provide illumination
and carry the offering –
I am present in the breath of life –
the sun, the moon and the wind;
I am in all who have lived –
and I am springtime,
the warmth between two loved ones.

-

Commentary

While tapaḥ can refer to one who burns himself in austerity – it can also refer to one who burns. It also relates to the Vedic month of Tapas, which in the Hindu calendar overlaps with the month of Phalguna, in which Holi falls, which corresponds to the last full moon of winter. Kumbha or Tapas, relates to the Vedic astrological sign representing the water-bearer (known in the West as Aquarius).

§

Text 10

bījaṃ māṃ sarva-bhūtānāṃ viddhi pārtha sanātanam
buddhir buddhimatām asmi tejas tejasvinām aham

-

Pārtha –
know that I am the seed
within all people, and all actions –
those who are wise and rational
know that I am eternal;
I am the fire in the eyes
of the noble, the powerful –
one who is beautiful, full of splendor
and carries the sword.

§

Text 11

balaṃ balavatāṃ cāhaṃ kāma-rāga-vivarjitam
dharmāviruddho bhūteṣu kāmo 'smi bharatarṣabha

-

I am the power and strength
of the mighty and the passionate;
the color, beauty and music
of those who live in yoga
and enforce the dharma of the people;
I am desire and passion –
Arjuna – prince of the spring showers
and cows of Bhārata.

-

Commentary

All who read the Vedas must filter the words through their own perspective on life. Dharmāviruddhaḥ means either "compatible with dharma" or "one who does not obstruct or impede dharma." Some who have translated this text have added content and meaning that is not actually present in the Gītā to further their own aims and message – the Vedic message not only embraces Viṣṇu's desire for the preservation of the human race, but that we also engage in a variety of forms of yoga, which includes using Rādha-Kṛṣṇa as an example of how we can experience love of the Divine together. Note that the prefix vi can have many meanings depending on context – it can provide a form of negation or it can strengthen the base word, but depends on both the base word, as well as the context in which it appears. Note that Prabhupāda was quoted as trying to destroy the West by introducing them to his form of Kṛṣṇa consciousness – instead of destroying the West, we should try and use it to our advantage and bring about an age of Vedic culture world-wide, using all resources available – while this comment makes this particular commentary mostly relevant to the age in which it is written, it is necessary to reinforce the notion that destroying Western culture is not necessary, but instead that we find ways to transcend it, no matter in which country it appears, and that the ample resources available (currently) in the West will be useful in establishing world peace and financial prosperity.

§

Text 12

ye caiva sāttvikā bhāvā rājasās tāmasāś ca ye
matta eveti tān viddhi na tv ahaṃ teṣu te mayi

-

I am with those
who have spirit and passion
in existence,
those who are enshrouded in darkness –
I am intoxication and joy –
know them,
for I am with those
who are near Me
and dear to you.

§

Text 13

tribhir guṇa-mayair bhāvair ebhiḥ sarvam idaṃ jagat
mohitam nābhijānāti mām ebhyaḥ param avyayam

-

All enter into and live in this world
with the guṇas;
even in realizing that each lifetime
is short –
one falls in love
with the knowledge
that this world is a part of Me
and that I am eternal.

-

Commentary

The word maya creates a fair bit of confusion for translators. It can refer to being composed of something – it also refers to horses. While it is also the name of a later character in mythology, the Āsuras refer both to a lesser form of mythological being, as well as being an original name associated with the Vedic gods. While the Rāmāyaṇa is a later work, the concept of rāmaḥ is very old – and is associated with one of the aspects of Kṛṣṇa of which the universe in its entirety is created. And of course, the horse is a symbol of man and each lifetime – and has a number of Vedic references (in particular in the Gītā), as Kṛṣṇa is our charioteer and we are His chariot.

Incidentally, the word na also creates a great deal of confusion and it is impossible for anyone to completely explain how it, or any other particle in Sanskrit, is used – it simply requires experience reading the texts and reviewing all possible uses to determine the best meaning based on the context from a traditional Vedic perspective (and of course, specific context). It is a well-known fact that one requires an education in the religion in order to read the Vedas, which is why so many traditions have existed.

§

Text 14

daivī hy eṣā guṇa-mayī mama māyā duratyayā
mām eva ye prapadyante māyām etāṃ taranti te

-

All of life and this universe
are divine and come from Kṛṣṇa –
it can be difficult to find Me,
but those who fall before My feet
help others across the river.

-

Commentary

Tṝ can refer to attainment or crossing the river, as well as living – but it can also refer to carrying someone, as well. Interpreting the text as finding Kṛṣṇa with ease is really not consistent with life experience for many, either in their own lives or in observing those of others.

§

Text 15

na māṃ duṣkṛtino mūḍhāḥ prapadyante narādhamāḥ
māyayāpahṛta-jñānā āsuraṃ bhāvam āśritāḥ

-

Those who have not seen past māya
find it difficult to find attainment
and to worship Me –
one who drinks the milk
poured by one who has been ravished
by jñānam

can share in understanding.

§

Text 16

catur-vidhā bhajante māṃ janāḥ sukṛtino 'rjuna
ārto jijñāsur arthārthi jñānī ca bharatarṣabha

-

Arjuna –
the society of the righteous
is divided into four varṇas –
the virtuous jñānī
who understands the Vedas
is kind to one who is oppressed,
sick or unfortunate –
and to one who longs to find Me.

-

Commentary

While there is potentially a list of four kinds of people in the second half of this śloka, it makes most sense to interpret catur-vidhā as a reference to both the four varṇas, as well as understanding the four Vedas. Vidhā refers both to division, as well as understanding with the intellect. The list that Prabhupāda provides really has no relationship to the "pious" – one who knows Kṛṣṇa provides for his or her family but has no need to actually desire material gain. One can certainly experience hardship and still be faithful; however, despite life circumstances, one may still be considered fortunate, regardless. Arthārthi refers more to one who is committed to his artha, or to someone seeking marriage. Instead, jijñāsuḥ can be paired with the accusative of arthārthi.

One is not excluded from seeking or finding Kṛṣṇa based on one's position in society – instead one must desire to know Him/Her and have the capacity for understanding; and of course, those who are fortunate enough to find Kṛṣṇa's grace have an obligation to help others.

§

Text 17

teṣāṃ jñānī nitya-yukta eka-bhaktir viśiṣyate
priyo hi jñānino 'tyartham ahaṃ sa ca mama priyaḥ

-

A jñānī who works for the people
and is yoked to Me
is particularly dear –
he works with devotion
and administers dharma;
measure one's self against both him
and Me.

§

Text 18

udārāḥ sarva evaite jnānī tv ātmaiva me matam

āsthitaḥ sa hi yuktātmā mām evānuttamām gatim

-

The various choices and actions of the jñānī
are exalted –
he stands firm and is considered by Me
to be yoked to the Self –
he is accepted by Me
and is fearless on the path to Kṛṣṇa.

§

Text 19

bahūnāṃ janmanām ante jñānavān māṃ prapadyate
vāsudevaḥ sarvam iti sa mahātmā su-durlabhaḥ

-

One who knows that life is eternal
but reaches each end –
is wise
and worships Me –
such a one is difficult to find,
but extraordinary.

§

Text 20

kāmais tais tair hṛta-jñānāḥ prapadyante 'nya-
devatāḥ
taṃ taṃ niyamam āsthāya prakṛtyā niyatāḥ svayā

-

Those who worship
are enraptured with desire –
they live and enjoy the divinity
of the senses –
and in inward aspiration
they live in union
with Prakṛti and their own.

-

Commentary

Prabhupāda was frequently confused by the concept of "taken away" and "seized." Hṛta refers to having one's heart stolen – it refers to fascination, charm, being ravished, as well as that to which we are devoted.

Devataḥ refers both to divinity and the organs of sense. Anya in this context refers to continual breathing and living and is a result of worship. There is actually no such thing as a demigod – we are all divine and a part of Kṛṣṇa, and the names of the devas are simply the various names of God and or, depending on context, simply myths. The concept Prabhupāda frequently refers to with respect to worshipping the devas is tied to requests for material gain – however, he failed to understand that most worship God in devotion and praise, rather than asking for material things. This is something that parents try to teach their children when they are young – and if not, they generally end up learning that at their local temple.

§

Text 21

yo yo yāṃ yāṃ tanuṃ bhaktaḥ śraddhayārcitum icchati
tasya tasyācalāṃ śraddhāṃ tām eva vidadhāmy aham

-

One longs for the body and soul
of his beloved –
he sings to her in praise and devotion,
with faith and certainty in both her
and Me –
as he sees himself and Kṛṣṇa in her;
she presents herself
to him, as a gift –
her faith and affection
rise and meet him, as tulasi in springtime –
and I provide for both
and exist together in their separation and union.

-

Commentary

In this particular case, Prabhupāda's translation does acknowledge one of the correct terms of deva, which can refer to people – and of course, when in the feminine, devī rarely refers to what are known as the devas, but instead Devī. Prabhupāda's purport for this text also seems to indirectly – whether intentional or not – reference one of the meanings associated with calam, which is a young plant reaching for the sun – in this text, either acalam or ācalam can appear. However, despite the fact that Prabhupāda references material gain in his purport, he attributes the wrong meaning to the concept of prosperity – and he continually encouraged devotees to reject the material and never taught them to actually seek Lakṣmī, and in fact highly discouraged that pursuit other than a very few isolated occurrences in his various works and quotes. Given the above, it is likely that his references to enjoying the affection of Rādhā and her various gifts is an accident. We should all understand the traditional Vedic concept of wealth – our loved ones, in particular our soulmate, as well as our children – and the Vedas teach us to actually enjoy our time together and to acknowledge the divinity of all existence, and all experience. In terms of gifts from Kṛṣṇa and wealth – the root verb of vidhā refers to conception.

§

Text 22

sa tayā śraddhayā yuktas tasyārādhanam īhate
labhate ca tataḥ kāmān mayaiva vihitān hi tān

-

He seeks her favor
with faith – and finds
pleasure and union, with her;
the father seeks conception
with desire, in companionship with Me –

they exist together,
in the friendship of marriage.

-

Commentary

Most, if not all, of Prabhupāda's works are highly irrational. In the preceding text, Prabhupāda indicates that Kṛṣṇa provides one with the ability and desire to successfully seek fortune and prosperity through a particular chosen demigod, and then in Text 22 indicates that it is foolish to seek Devī (or from a female perspective, her husband).

§

Text 23

antavat tu phalaṃ teṣāṃ tad bhavaty alpa-medhasām
devān deva-yajo yānti mad-bhaktā yānti mām api

-

The fruit one experiences together
in this lifetime is perishable –
but one easily enjoys shared worship
of each other –
in living together in devotion,
one moves towards Me, because of Me.

-

Commentary

In this text, the word deva is used reflexively. As the Padma Purāṇa teaches, the best form of worship is that of other human beings. We all hopefully find a special someone in our lives – whether male or female – who we can experience companionship with and raise a family, but this also extends to others, whether devotees or not. A traditional greeting in India is "namaste," and traditionally reflects this concept. A text quoted from the Padma Purāṇa in the purport for Prabhupāda's translation of the Bhāgavatam is:

The most sacred form of adoration
apart from that of Viṣṇu – Devi –
is the worship of those who belong to the breath.

§

Text 24

avyaktaṃ vyaktim āpannaṃ manyante mām abuddhayaḥ
paraṃ bhāvam ajānanto mamāvyayam anuttamam

-

Those who value the fruit
of those who do not know Me
lack intelligence and are not likely
to understand the Highest.

§

Text 25

nāhaṃ prakāśaḥ sarvasya yoga-māyā-samāvṛtaḥ
mūḍho 'yaṃ nābhijānāti loko mām ajam avyayam

-

One who does not know Me
does not perceive my light
shining through the unity of existence –
he is confused
and does not understand the world;
he is not likely to change
and attempts to mislead others.

§

Text 26

vedāhaṃ samatītāni vartamānāni cārjuna
bhaviṣyāṇi ca bhūtāni māṃ tu veda na kaścana

-

Arjuna –
I have known those who are gone,
and those who live –
that which will come to be,
and that which has already happened –
I have known Myself,
as I am all of existence.

§

Text 27

icchā-dveṣa-samutthena dvandva-mohena bhārata
sarva-bhūtāni sammohaṃ sarge yānti parantapa

-

Delusion and ignorance
are a problem for those who want
to live together and ascend
as a pair – Bhārata –
all live in māya
but can find enlightenment
in love and the process of creation.

-

Commentary

Icchā-dveṣa-samutthena means "the problem for those rising together." While mohaḥ can refer to confusion, it also refers to falling asleep, the infatuation of lovers and wonder. Sammohaḥ refers to the conjunction of planets, as well as battle (which in Hindu tradition, is considered auspicious and is associated with fortune). Sarga refers to procreation and childbirth, as well as that which is natural. Dvandvaḥ can refer to duality, but it also refers to a pair.

§

Text 28

yeṣāṃ tv anta-gataṃ pāpaṃ janānāṃ puṇya-karmaṇām

te dvandva-moha-nirmuktā bhajante māṃ dṛḍha-vratāḥ

-

For those committed to monogamy
and who pour forth their love for one another
in devotion to Me –
their actions are pure
and they find an end to misfortune.

-

Commentary

Pāpam is not translated as "sin" – it refers to either misfortune, that which is not desirable or those who violate dharma (and their actions). This is not the same concept that exists in Western culture (at least within Christianity).

Vrātaḥ refers to one committed to learning the Vedas, as well as drinking milk and eating the same food – which is a reference to monogamy and marriage.

Puṇyaḥ does not refer to "piety," but instead the auspicious and that which is pleasant, pure and sacred, as well as good work.

§

Text 29

jarā-maraṇa-mokṣāya mām āśritya yatanti ye

te brahma tad viduḥ kṛtsnam adhyātmaṃ karma cākhilam

-

Those reaching old age and death
take comfort in Me –
they know that I am the entirety of the ātman –
and that they will find rebirth.

§

Text 30

sādhibhūtādhidaivaṃ māṃ sādhiyajñaṃ ca ye viduḥ
prayāṇa-kāle 'pi ca māṃ te vidur yukta-cetasaḥ

-

One offers the greatest praise to Me –
as I am the entirety of existence, the universe and God;
those who are nearing the beginning
are near Me –
I am time – I am the darkness of the night sky –
and I am death –
those who find yoga with Me
know the splendor and beauty
of the ātman.

Chapter Eight

Text 1

arjuna uvāca
kiṃ tad brahma kim adhyātmaṃ kiṃ karma puruṣottama
adhibhūtaṃ ca kiṃ proktam adhidaivam kim ucyate

-

Arjuna said:

It has been said that Kṛṣṇa is the Highest,
that He is everything,
the law of karma –
and the best in man, if he is anointed by You.

§

Text 2

adhiyajñaḥ kathaṃ ko 'tra dehe 'smin madhusūdana
prayāṇa-kāle ca kathaṃ jñeyo 'si niyatātmabhiḥ

-

Kṛṣṇa –
I find pleasure and amazement
in the idea of the Highest yajña –
for one starting in life –
or approaching death –
how are we to know how to reach You?

§

Text 3

śrī-bhagavān uvāca
akṣaraṃ brahma paramaṃ svabhāvo 'dhyātmam ucyate
bhūta-bhāvodbhava-karo visargaḥ karma-saṃjñitaḥ

-

Śrī-Bhagavān said:

It has been said that I am Brahman –
that everything flows from Me
and I am the Self –
I am everything which has lived
and all who are living –
I am existence, birth, procreation –
I am the doer –
I am light, life, the sun and death –
and together we act, live and know one another.

§

Text 4

adhibhūtaṃ kṣaro bhāvaḥ puruṣaś cādhidaivatam
adhiyajño 'ham evātra dehe deha-bhṛtāṃ vara

-

All of Prakṛti is perishable – and eternal;
the Puruṣa is the source
of all living things, and the substance of the universe
flows from Her waters;

the world comes from the Divine Mother
and is borne and nurtured in Her heart eternally,
as a child in the womb.

Commentary

Deha-bhṛtām is in the plural genitive and refers to the body of all mothers. The Adhiyajñaḥ is the Nāciketa sacrifice, and the loving mother who knows Kṛṣṇa provides love and affection for her children, starting in the womb – which is the shared love between her and the child, as well as that between the mother and the father. Varaḥ refers both to that which fully encircles or encompasses, as well as a bridegroom. Kṣaraḥ refers to the perishable – that which melts away and refers to both water and the clouds. This text overall references the impermanent nature of physical reality – as well as its eternal nature and overall references the concept of Kṛṣṇa from the perspective of Rādhā in Her role as the Divine Mother.

This text relates to Text 23 from the Brahma Saṃhitā:

Bhagavān-Śakti gave birth
through the prayer of the cakra
and the first saṃskāra;
They comprehended each other in the indigo night
of time – They are alone, undifferentiated
and the mantra of the universe.

§

Text 5

anta-kāle ca mām eva smaran muktvā kalevaram
yaḥ prayāti sa mad-bhāvaṃ yāti nāsty atra saṃśayaḥ

-

As one approaches the end of life,
one lays down, as if to sleep –
he remembers Me – and that we are the same –
and is released into the next lifetime.

§

Text 6

yaṃ yaṃ vāpi smaran bhāvaṃ tyajaty ante kalevaram
taṃ tam evaiti kaunteya sadā tad-bhāva-bhāvitaḥ

-

In death, one remembers life, Kaunteya –
one flows from lifetime to lifetime
and is reborn, eternally.

§

Text 7

tasmāt sarveṣu kāleṣu mām anusmara yudhya ca
mayy arpita-mano-buddhir mām evaiṣyasy
asaṃśayaḥ

-

At all times remember life with Me, fondly –
if you approach Me in prayer
and fix the mind and intellect on Me
then one will achieve faith and certainty.

§

Text 8

abhyāsa-yoga-yuktena cetasā nānya-gāminā
paramaṃ puruṣaṃ divyam yāti pārthānucintayan

-

I am the Puruṣa – the Highest –
and one can always reach Me;
I am the sky, the heavens –
and all divinity;
striving for attainment is no way to live.

§

Text 9

kaviṃ purāṇam anuśāsitāram
aṇor aṇīyāṃsam anusmared yaḥ
sarvasya dhātāram acintya-rūpam
āditya-varṇaṃ tamasaḥ parastāt

-

Words written by men
may contain the essence of truth,
but they are less than My words –

My form is inconceivable –
but beautiful –
I am Kṛṣṇa – the music
and face of the darkness
of the beyond.

-

Commentary

All must determine for themselves whether śāstras are śruti or smṛti literature. All tend to agree that the original four Vedas are śruti, but many accept a variety of later documents, such as the Gītā, as being considered śruti, as well. In this text the reference to the words written by men are the Purāṇas, which are primarily tales of mythology. While Prabhupāda was quoted as indicating the Bhāgavatam was the ultimate wisdom of the Vedas, many tend to assume that is because it is eighteen volumes long and contains a verbose description of of his own personal ideas on life – much of which is incredibly negative and disrespectful to Kṛṣṇa's gift of life that She/He provided to humanity.

§

Text 10

prayāṇa-kāle manasācalena
bhaktyā yukto yoga-balena caiva
bhruvor madhye prāṇam āveśya samyak
sa taṃ paraṃ puruṣam upaiti divyam

-

One who is moved
in devotion and affection for Me,
has the strength of vision to see past māya –
we live and seek together
and aspire towards the beauty of the heavens.

§

Text 11

yad akṣaraṃ veda-vido vadanti
viśanti yad yatayo vīta-rāgāḥ
yad icchanto brahmacaryaṃ caranti
tat te padaṃ saṅgraheṇa pravakṣye

-

I have poured Myself out
within the Vedas –
they praise life and humanity
and provide wisdom –
approach them with passion and desire,
study them and practice what they teach;
I enjoy those who understand
their light and glory.

-

Commentary

The word brahmacarya simply refers to following Kṛṣṇa. While there is an ancient āśrama related to a specific stage of life, the purpose of this stage was study of the Vedas and saving oneself for marriage in preparation for having a family.

Vīta-rāgāḥ means "approaching with love, affection and desire" and also relates to music, royalty and God.

While akṣaram can refer to the syllable Oṃ, it literally refers to the process of emanation from Godhead and refers to most of the primary definitions of the term Brahman. It is the first-person imperfect of pouring out or flowing. In this text it is not an instruction to actually chant Oṃ, but instead refers to the one who is identified as actually being Oṃ and is a part of the dialogue of the Gītā.

§

Text 12

sarva-dvārāṇi saṃyamya mano hṛdi nirudhya ca
mūrdhny ādhāyātmanaḥ prāṇam āsthito yoga-
dhārāṇām

-

All who understand the path
to attainment within their heart and mind
provide the knowledge of the Vedas
to others;
one who hears and understands the Self
will continually enjoy
breathing in unison with Me.

-

Commentary

Very few words in Sanskrit are actually literal in meaning, which some find confusing – as are some of the definitions acquired in English over the last several hundred years. And sometimes references to the body relate to the concepts they are associated with, rather than the actual physical body parts.

There are many misconceptions related to the word yama, which is found within a number of terms associated with what those in the West consider to be yoga. It is of course related to death, but death is not seen in a negative light, as it is also the beginning of the next lifetime – while it is associated with the concept of restraint, it really refers to determination, which is not the same thing. Yama refers to the reins of a horse and has an association with the mind but refers to movement in life and aspiration towards the Divine – in doing so, one requires determination and purity of thought, but that is not equivalent to mental exercise or attempting to eliminate thought. Yama also – of course – relates to the concept of the twin. Saṃyamya refers to one of the key messages of the Vedas, rather than the concept of "controlling."

Ādhāya refers both to giving and receiving.

Both dhāraḥ and dhārā refer to a stream or flow of water; dhārā also refers to rain or a downpour and can be applied to objects such as a "rain of arrows" or a "rain of flowers" – and also refers to eternity, sacred bathing, the Highest and the night.

§

Text 13

oṃ ity ekākṣaraṃ brahma vyāharan mām anusmaran
yaḥ prayāti tyajan dehaṃ sa yāti paramāṃ gatim

-

I am Oṃ – who is the unity
of all existence;
the flowing stream of time,
matter and spirit –
I am divided and separate
so that I may know Myself –
one who seeks Me
will find union, once again,
in the yajña of the heart.

-

Commentary

This is another text in the Gītā that outlines one of the core messages associated with the Gaudiya tradition, but is commonly misinterpreted, both by devotees and their various gurus, but is a fundamental Vedic point of view which is captured in all śruti literature going back to the original Vedas.

Many Western definitions of words in Sanskrit either represent the common perception of those who engage in the practice of renunciation of life (or make a show of it in order to mislead the youth) – and or, in particular in today's age, the instruction that is commonly provided to those from the West (by individuals originating from similar traditions as those referenced above). Tyajan relates to aspiration, providing for humanity and yajña – as well as having the connotation of one who is suffering from spiritual death.

§

Text 14

ananya-cetāḥ satataṃ yo māṃ smarati nityaśaḥ
tasyāhaṃ sulabhaḥ pārtha nitya-yuktasya yoginaḥ

-

Pārtha –
one who has continual affection and devotion
for Me, remembers that I am the eternal
splendor of thought – and the consciousness
of the universe;
and that I am one with him.

§

Text 15

mām upetya punar janma duḥkhālayam aśāśvatam
nāpnuvanti mahātmānaḥ saṃsiddhiṃ paramāṃ
gatāḥ

-

One approaches Me on the journey home –
through eternity, into each lifetime;

the thought of not being born
is a source of pain and sorrow –
time passes by, as if in death,
for those who do not attain the Highest.

-

Commentary

Many concepts in Sanskrit are expressed as phrases (as with all languages) and cannot be translated word by word. Those trained in translation of course understand the structure of language and a key component of linguistic education is exposure to theory (generally speaking), as well as exposure to many languages. While this is an obvious fact, it is merely mentioned here as some of the current translations of the Gītā have made their way into both popular culture and academia and seem to have contributed to inaccurate reference materials being used today. While inaccurate translations of Sanskrit literature have existed for at least several centuries, due to the fact that so many translations have originated from the West and have in turn influenced education in India (starting with the British occupation), the translations produced by the author referenced below (as well as throughout the commentary within this book) are particularly inaccurate – both from a devotional and linguistic perspective.

Duḥkhālayam is the "home or source of misery or unhappiness." Aśāśvatam refers to that which is "not eternal" or that which is "not going to happen in the future." The negation of eternity or the future is not the same thing as "temporary." This should be a logical conclusion – sorrow one experiences in this lifetime could last for a short period of time, or it could last for one's entire life, depending on circumstances and perspective. If something is not going to happen in the future, that merely refers to the lack of a future outcome, rather than referring to the fact that something is fleeting. When interpreted together duḥkhālayam aśāśvatam can mean "the lack of eternity is the source of pain and misery." It could also mean "that which is not going to happen is the home of sorrow and discomfort."

The final part of this śloka refers to "time passes by for those who do not attain the Highest" and includes a reference to death (which is the result of not finding Kṛṣṇa in this lifetime). The first part of this śloka refers to finding one's way home, which is found in birth, life and eternity (with the specific connotation of the eternity of saṃsāra). It truly is a source of sorrow to not find Him/Her in this lifetime – it is a source of comfort that we can either try again in the future, or once again find happiness in the next lifetime. The idea of not finding heaven is truly a source of sorrow for those who experience it.

There are a variety of ways of translating nearly all texts in Sanskrit, but nearly all meanings end up the same but with different specific connotations. Some alternate translations refer to very specific and mundane concepts but have very spiritual meanings which are incredibly obvious. When given the opportunity, Prabhupāda always chose the mundane interpretation and disregarded the very obvious meaning that is consistent with Vedic tradition, including ignoring a variety of terms that are very well-known from "every day" devotional practice. In this text, Prabhupāda associates the idea of accomplishment with death, which is very consistent in all of his translations and purports – and is also consistent with a traditional perception of the devout concerning those who either seek or teach others to seek death and renunciation of life. In this particular text, there is really no way of arriving at his interpretation of the Sanskrit. One can study even Prabhupāda's embarrassing word by word definitions of this text or look at the richer definitions that come from the actual study of Sanskrit and the Vedas – along with his translation of the entire text, for quite a while and never arrive at his conclusion concerning the meaning.

§

Text 16

ā-brahma-bhuvanāl lokāḥ punar āvartino 'rjuna
mām upetya tu kaunteya punar janma na vidyate

-

I create Myself eternally in every moment, Kaunteya.

-

Commentary

In the field of science, any theory is considered simply an assumption, even if based in evidence or reason, until it has been proven. Many aspects of science really cannot be proven – but despite that, they may have a rational basis to them. Current cosmology and physics are starting to catch up with the original Vedic view of the universe – for example, the notions that what we perceive as reality is actually an illusion, as well as the Vedic concept of cosmology and time. Many theories in modern physics and cosmology state that the universe continually experiences rebirth and that time and space are illusions. That said – the concept of māya actually refers to our perceived separation from God. Piercing the veil of māya refers to attaining the intuitive knowledge that we are all one with Kṛṣṇa – once we can perceive that fact, then we will have transcended the concept of māya. Despite that, it could still take some time to actually "leave" the material world. But that is an opportunity we have in every lifetime – and as humanity has no real means of completely understanding Truth, if we really only have one lifetime, then we should also just make the best of the one we have right now.

§

Text 17

sahasra-yuga-paryantam ahar yad brahmaṇo viduḥ
rātriṃ yuga-sahasrāntāṃ te 'ho-rātra-vido janāḥ

-

I am eternal – and I am the night sky –
the universe is reborn continually,
and I delight in My existence, and you have, as well.

-

Commentary

Prabhupāda believed a number of bedtime stories which are told to Hindu children while growing up – although his source for many is really not very traditional. Brahmā does not actually appear in this text. Brahmā is an alternate declined form of Brahma and is used when distinguishing the personified aspect of the universe's creative force from that of its unknowable aspect. Brahmā is not worshipped that much on His own in Hinduism and that may be because those from a traditional background understand that there is really only one God and may understand enough of their sacred language to realize that Brahmā represents the original creative force of the universe, rather than that which continually sustains the human race within our perception of time (Viṣṇu).

§

Text 18

avyaktād vyaktayaḥ sarvāḥ prabhavanty ahar-āgame
rātry-āgame pralīyante tatraivāvyakta-saṃjñāke

-

All are born into māya –
but all can rejoice –
as anyone who approaches the night sky
can find Me and will be anointed
with the knowledge of Kṛṣṇa.

Commentary

Prabhupāda associates vyaktaḥ with the concept of the living and avyaktaḥ with that which is not living. This is an interesting association as it is an appropriate definition to use but one can follow his train of thought which reinforces his general perception of humanity. Vyaktaḥ can refer to one who is anointed by Kṛṣṇa. However, using Prabhupāda's understanding of the word, he likely associates this word with one who is not anointed. His institution teaches that man is born into a state of sin which must be absolved by joining his organization – but in fact, the word is a reference to our divinity which we clearly have as a basic state of existence, as the entirety of the universe is part of Him/Her. Regardless, even if he did somehow acknowledge the notion that man is divine and well-loved by God, interpreting avyaktaḥ as "unmanifest" with respect to some supposed state of the universe does not really follow from his association of vyaktaḥ as the "living entity."

Āgama has an interesting set of meanings. While it refers to reading and study, as well as seeking or finding attainment and study of the Vedas, it also refers to something that is added to a meaningful text but has no actual meaning of its own. While not a primary definition associated with āgama, that note reinforces some of Kṛṣṇa's previous statements in the Gītā differentiating between the value of what would be considered man's knowledge vice that which

Kṛṣṇa provides. Of course, all knowledge provided by God is filtered through the human brain – but we have to evaluate what we read or hear to determine for ourselves how close it seems to God's message. One of my theories on why āgamic texts are so popular is that they are often easier to read than the Vedas. They also reinforce a number of doctrines determined by those who may have had an agenda and would therefore be endorsed by the institution. The most efficient means of studying Sanskrit is with the help of modern technology – and anyone who does so and has the appropriate understanding of linguistics and the fundamentals of Hinduism will realize just how sophisticated the human brain is and how sophisticated early man was – for the entirety of human history that is either known or recorded (or even not known) we have always been *homo sapiens sapiens*.

§

Text 19

bhūta-grāmaḥ sa evāyaṃ bhūtvā bhūtvā pralīyate
rātry-āgame 'vaśaḥ pārtha prabhavaty ahar-āgame

-

You should long for home –
two existing and becoming together,
attached to one another and one with the night
in mutual study of the sacred –
without any need for obedience to one another
and living together in mutual respect and worship –
that form of study is a true cause for celebration –

it is a victory for all
when the lotus of the heart opens and flowers.

-

Commentary

This text focuses on the happiness that two can achieve together along with Kṛṣṇa. It refers to study of the Vedas (expressed in the dual), includes references to having no need for power or control, the concept of living life with references to the divinity and regality of both a man and women – as well as multiple references to victory, surpassing the ordinary, excelling and rejoicing – as an individual, as a couple and as a community.

The text also includes a reference to the ambiguity of time and action, including a reference to desire.

§

Text 20

paras tasmāt tu bhāvo 'nyo 'vyakto 'vyaktāt sanātanaḥ
yaḥ sa sarveṣu bhūteṣu naśyatsu na vinaśyati

-

Together we are radiant beings
and achieve the Highest together –
we are not separate
because of our eternal nature
and divinity –

nothing is lost in death,
as we are always together.

§

Text 21

avyatko 'kṣara ity uktas tam āhuḥ paramāṃ gatim
yaṃ prāpya na nivartante tad dhāma paramaṃ
mama

-

I am Oṃ, the imperishable –
Kṛṣṇa is the sword, the yajña and the waters of
creation –
I am attainable and those who seek
and find Me consider me the Highest –
those who seek Me within themselves
find their home with Kṛṣṇa.

§

Text 22

puruṣaḥ sa paraḥ pārtha bhaktyā labhyas tv ananyayā
yasyāntaḥ-sthāni bhūtāni yena sarvam idaṃ tatam

-

Pārtha –
I am Puruṣa, the Highest –
one who seeks attainment
without devotion to another
seeks the end

and is focused on that which has happened –
but I am Brahman
and everything in this world
comes from and is a part of Me.

-

Commentary

There is another reading of this text that is closer to Prabhupāda's translation – however, interpreting the text in this fashion actually indicates that Kṛṣṇa (who is speaking) is advocating the "impersonalist" view of the universe. Many traditions that Prabhupāda associated with his term the "impersonalists" are actually consistent with traditional Vedic thought, despite any assumptions that a few have concerning their teachings; those who would properly be considered impersonalists are the Sāṅkhya philosophers and the Buddhists, both of which are essentially atheist and opposed to traditional Hindu thought (outside of theistic Buddhists who are more prevalent outside of India). Note that word order can have significance but that many words in Sanskrit are optional, including verbs (such as "to be") and pronouns (every word outside of the simpler form of conjugated verbs can be a form of pronoun), many words have to be read together in phrases in order to determine the meaning – and clearly, outside of language features, one has to also look at the overall meaning of the text to determine whether it is consistent with Hindu tradition and the intent of the original author. Note that despite a variety of instructions and supposed doctrines within the Gaudiya tradition, that the general interpretation of their teachings is actually consistent with the impersonalist view of the universe, despite any commentaries or descriptions provided by their gurus – one can of course read into many of their teachings and arrive at a traditional view of the universe and our goals in life (which is to find Gokula and or Goloka in each lifetime, in perceived separation while seeking union with God), but the practices endorsed and enforced by the organization are contrary to these goals.

§

Text 23

yatra kāle tv anāvṛttim āvṛttiṃ caiva yoginaḥ
prayātā yānti taṃ kālaṃ vakṣyāmi bharatarṣabha

-

Two who come together in union –
and feel joy, pleasure
and shed tears of devotion for one another –
they journey in life together
and I call them My own –
even from their very beginning in marriage,
and I accompany them on their journey –
Arjuna – prince of the spring showers
and cows of Bhārata.

-

Commentary

Kāla (which refers to time, as well as the color of Kṛṣṇa) is in the locative or in the dual. Either interpretation works with the text but the Sanskrit for this śloka suggests the actions of two individuals. Anāvṛttim includes a double negative, which yields a positive and is commonly found in Sanskrit. It has a variety of meanings, but does refer to bhakti, as well as tears which roll down the cheek. Āvṛttim means the same thing but indicates an emphasis on being close. The rest of the text for the most part refers to beginning a journey, as well as continuing a journey.

Vakṣyāmi is the first-person future of two verbs (vac and vah). Vac refers to speech, perception and recognition – and vah refers to leading, guiding, carrying, experience, feeling, driving a chariot, shedding tears and marriage.

This text has a relationship to the following text from the Brahma Saṃhitā (Text 32) – note that this is one of the few verses from the Song of Gāyatrī in the Brahma Saṃhitā that appears in the popular song played at the beginning of at least many ārati services in ISKCON temples – in the "official" translation of this book, Bhaktisiddhānta Ṭhākura had a very difficult time understanding the Sanskrit, including the title of the book, as well as who is speaking for much of the śāstra. The song which appears in the Brahma Saṃhitā is actually sung by Gāyatrī, who is considered to be the author of the Vedas.

Rādhā cries eternal tears of devotion in prayer
for the limbs of the wind –
those in separation
perceive and drink

the luminous joy and bliss of spiritual being.
I worship Govinda, the Puruṣa who existed
in the beginning.

§

Text 24

agnir jyotir ahaḥ śuklaḥ ṣaṇ-māsā uttarāyaṇam
tatra prayātā gacchanti brahma brahma-vido janāḥ

-

Agni offers his blessing to the coming harvest
and accompanies Sūrya on his journey
by Her left hand –
those who seek Me
find Us in love, procreation and their own people.

-

Commentary

This text does of course reference the moon – as the moon accompanies the sun on its travels and does represent light and purity. The north is considered sacred and is found on the left when facing the east in prayer – and the left hand is sacred to Lakṣmī. The text references the season following spring-time and references the flowering of the lotus blossom, as well as celebration. Prayātā refers to one who is beginning or on a journey.

§

Text 25

dhūmo rātris tathā kṛṣṇaḥ ṣaṇ-māsā dakṣināyanam
tatra cāndramasaṃ jyotir yogī prāpya nivartate

-

One seeking union with Me
finds Us within –
in the harvest, the heart –
and Her song.

-

Commentary

Dakṣina refers to the south or the right hand – the south also corresponds to anāhata. This text references the harvest season – the summer solstice and Viṣṇu's repose upon Śeṣa in the yoganidrā. It also discusses the joint path of the sun and the moon.

§

Text 26

śukla-kṛṣṇe gati hy ete jagataḥ śāśvate mate
ekayā yāty anāvṛttim anyayāvartate punaḥ

-

Two moving together in life
towards Me, in eternity –
sharing each other's thoughts
and seeking union –

leads to self-discovery in the other,
tears of joy and devotion
and enjoyment in the light of both the sun and the moon.

§

Commentary

This particular text is generally translated as corresponding to the paths of light and darkness – and is typically associated with the notion of leaving saṃsāra. However, most translating the text were guided by sannyāsins and were not aware of the associations in the preceding texts to the harvest season. There are multiple references within the text to saṃsāra, which is referred to as an "inexhaustible supply of precious milk and amṛtam." One lesson to be learned from the concept of saṃsāra – life is joyful, and if not, there is always another try in the future – we should all make the world a better place for future generations – and just in case humanity has no idea what happens in the next lifetime, one should live life to its fullest, as this may be the only lifetime that one actually has. Not all are aware of this but amṛtam refers both to immortality and nectar (despite the fact that these are both basic definitions of the word).

§

Text 27

naite sṛti pārtha yogī muhyati kaścana
tasmāt sarveṣu kāleṣu yoga-yukto bhavārjuna

-

Two travel together through life
in pursuit of yoga –
one can experience hardship
and still remain yoked to Me.

§

Text 28

veduṣu yajñeṣu tapaḥ su caiva
dāneṣu yat puṇya-phalaṃ pradiṣṭam
atyeti tat sarvam idaṃ viditvā
yogī paraṃ sthānam upaiti cādyam

-

The warmth of spring is
found within the yajña of sacred knowledge –
in marriage one seeks to share
life – that of the ordinary and that of the Highest –
and the fruit of spiritual communion;
one approaches in prayer
with the knowledge
that everything in this world is sacred –
in particular sitting near the feet of one who is dear –
I am Bhūmi –
and provide everything to you.

-

Commentary

Most of the words in this text relate to marriage, parenting, children, bhakti, prayer, the sanctity of existence, saṃsāra and Mother Earth, who is known as the provider who has existed since the beginning.

Chapter Nine

Text 1

śrī-bhagavān uvāca
idaṃ tu te guhyatamaṃ pravakṣyāmy anasūyave
jñānaṃ vijñāna-sahitaṃ yaj jñātvā mokṣyase 'śubhāt

-

Śrī-Bhagavān said:

I will explain a mystery to you –
one who knows Me
will have learned how to endure –
and the yajña also exists
to provide liberation for those
who are fallen.

-

Commentary

Mokṣyase is a conjugated form of two related verbs which both relate to liberation – while liberation can refer to self-realization, it also has a strong relationship to capital punishment and war.

§

Text 2

rāja-vidyā rāja-guhyaṃ pavitram idam uttamam
pratyakṣāvagamaṃ dharmyaṃ su-sukhaṃ kartum avyayam

-

A philosopher-king has the qualities of a rāja –
he is radiant and illuminated
by esoteric knowledge –
and well-versed in devotion –
he stands above others
and I accompany him,
in action and understanding –
he enforces dharma
for the good and happiness of the people.

§

Text 3

aśraddadhānāḥ puruṣā dharmasyāsya parantapa
aprāpya māṃ nivartante mṛtyu-saṃsāra-vartmani

-

Those who are not faithful
to dharma, Arjuna – conqueror of your enemies –
cannot find Me –
but they will meet Mara and Yama
and be reborn.

-

Commentary

One literal meaning of mṛtyu-saṃsāra-vartmani is that "saṃsāra is a justification for death," which is a very historic message within Kṛṣṇa's explanation to

Arjuna in the Gītā. Some over the centuries have tried to explain the Gītā's message as being an allegory – the instructions from Kṛṣṇa are very literal and war has long been considered auspicious within Hindu society and culture. The Gītā provides a rationale for war – which is protecting one's family. Kṛṣṇa expects the virtuous to enforce His law – in the modern era, there are also other ways of ending conflict. Unfortunately, much of Western culture is opposed to efficient warfare, due to a variety of concepts that have been popularized – but targeted elimination of an enemy followed by occupation and instituting a government suited to the culture of the people and providing education to help in leadership and governance is far less expensive in many ways, such as in the loss of human life. Fewer weapons are needed, as well. However, Western culture tends to try and improve the economy using more expensive means of warfare and assassination is considered incredibly unpopular, despite the fact that elimination of those in leadership and offering changes within the country that are sympathetic to the people is faster, potentially has a lower cost in terms of the loss of human life – and has a stronger chance of establishing longer term peace. At the time of the writing of this book, elimination of tyranny in the Middle East and the institution of one government embracing fundamental Islam according to Sufi principles that spans the entire Middle East with a capital in Damascus, encouragement of China to adopt greater respect for human rights and the overthrow of a handful of regimes would bring about greater world peace and prosperity, in particular if the prosperous nations of the world engage in effective charity – and in the case where a government is not reformable (such as Russia), then there are always weapons of mass destruction – and we know from human history, that fallout does not last forever. China has an appropriate strategy for warfare, at least as understood by those in the West in studying the work of their academic community – which is to plan to overthrow the enemy once they believe it is possible to do this very quickly and immediately. There is also a subtext running throughout the Gītā that indicates if the population level is reduced, then the world may be repopulated with those of a purer heart – potentially, although no one really knows for sure.

This text and commentary have a relationship to a poem published in the West in the English language:

we came so far
on the escalating upwards crescendo of spent fantasies
inscribed with neon runes
grinding to a halt
that night when the horsemen
came, in the bedrooms
locked behind doors of dreams become some other man's sweaty desire – violence and rage.
we fell into tomorrow.

corpses of black twisted metal and vaporized
metropolises sing from their grave. Calls out
for reclamation. We are
riding on the back
of a leper leading us to an event horizon, the
moment of becoming; a phoenix
to rise and fulfill destiny.

§

Text 4

mayā tatam idaṃ sarvaṃ jagad avyatka-mūrtinā
mat-sthāni sarva-bhūtāni na cāhaṃ teṣv avasthitaḥ

-

Everything comes from and is a part of Me –
the universe, wind, people, cows, water
and the crops –
even those who manifest in this lifetime
and do not find my blessing or disregard it;
one who finds Me
will lead – in action, for the people –
I exist with all
but am particularly devoted to those
who are committed to action and devotion.

§

Text 5

na ca mat-sthāni bhūtāni paśya me yogam aiśvaram
bhūta-bhṛn na ca bhūta-stho mamātmā bhūta-
bhāvanaḥ

-

One who achieves a high position –
does not do so because of Me;
all of his actions are due to understanding
and looking upon My face;

he pursues yoga with Me, for Me –
everything he does comes from Viṣṇu,
as he is a chosen rāja;
his actions are not due to others, but himself –
he provides for the people, for their welfare
and in providing instruction.

-

Commentary

Karma is defined essentially as action – and we all have free will.

§

Text 6

yathākāśa-sthito nityaṃ vāyuḥ sarvatra-go mahān
tathā sarvāṇi bhūtāni mat-sthānīty upadhāraya

-

At the same time –
he lives and acts continually
with Indra and Gaṇeśa –
his greatness and all that he accomplishes
are also due to Me –
he is virtuous and a provider –
and offers everything at My feet.

§

Text 7

sarva-bhūtāni kaunteya prakṛtiṃ yānti māmikām
kalpa-kṣaye punas tāni kalpādau visṛjāmy aham

-

One who seeks everything that is pure
within existence – Kaunteya –
is equivalent to Me – and has a sacred duty
to provide safety and purity
for home and family –
we enjoy our sacred duty and purpose, together –
I provide accomplishment for My family –
brothers, sisters – and the rāṇī.

-

Commentary

There are terms within this text that are related to the various yugas – however, the above translation is quite literal and also is more consistent with the dialogue of the Gītā.

§

Text 8

prakṛtim svām avaṣṭabhya visṛjāmi punaḥ punaḥ
bhūta-grāmam imaṃ kṛtsnam avaśaṃ prakṛter vaśāt

-

I sustain the heavens
and descended into matter –
I pour myself forth and rise to meet Myself –

again and again;
I longed for all of humanity – I am the source,
and all of creation – and I created you
through My desire for the Divine Mother.

-

Commentary

This is Kṛṣṇa's message, which is at odds with that commonly found within Christian culture. Christians – and potentially only Christians – teach that man is born into a state of sin and requires redemption. The Jewish version of this story, as told through the story of the Tetragrammaton (commonly referenced in English as either Jehovah or Yahweh), teaches that the male and female halves of God came together and emanate into physical reality, and that man is created in the image of God. While Muslims have their own scripture, they tend to point back to their original lineage from Abraham. While the story of Adam and Eve is present in the Hebrew Bible, instruction is typically provided (even to children) which demonstrates that this was part of an old myth – the opening of Genesis was written by multiple authors, in different time periods and in different dialects. Jews are taught – especially those who are educated in their mystical tradition, Kabbalah – that God represents love and unity. And of course, the mystical tradition found within Islam – Sufism – teaches joy in life, including finding God through music, dancing – and of course, the Divine Feminine.

Prakṛti refers to physical matter, as well as the divine nature of Kṛṣṇa which infuses it. It also represents the Mother and all women, in addition to God's will.

§

Text 9

na ca māṃ tāni karmāṇi nibadhnanti dhanañjaya
udāsīna-vad āsīnam asaktam teṣu karmasu

-

Arjuna – conqueror of wealth –
those who unite with Me, within themselves,
in all action –
stand apart,
and are unhindered in all of their actions.

§

Text 10

mayādhyakṣeṇa prakṛtiḥ sūyate sa-carācaram
hetunānena kaunteya jagad viparivartate

-

I gave birth to Prakṛti –
and imbued Her with life,
in the form of the cakra –
as I am the life of the universe –
I created Her, as She is Myself –
all live in this world in separation
and unity.

-

Commentary

While acaram could potentially mean "nonmoving" it is actually the first-person imperfect for a word which means "living," and like most words in Sanskrit related to life, it also has a relationship to the wheel, which also applies to adhyakṣeṇa, as well. Adhyakṣeṇa also refers to eternity.

§

Text 11

avajānanti māṃ mūḍhā mānuṣīṃ tanum āśritam
paraṃ bhāvam ajānanto mama bhūta-maheśvaram

-

Those who do not understand Me
are led astray in their actions –
they do not know
the highest state of being,
which is continually aspiring towards Maheśvara.

§

Text 12

moghāśā mogha-karmāṇo mogha-jñānā vicetasaḥ
rākṣasīm āsurīṃ caiva prakṛtiṃ mohinīṃ śritāḥ

-

The hope and actions of a demon
are vain and fruitless –
they are without wisdom
and divided in heart and mind –
they are attached to delusion
and cannot see Prakṛti.

Commentary

The concept of a demon that is popular in fiction does not of course exist – instead, demons are human beings who have lost their way and have allowed themselves to be consumed by evil. While people can change, some are so twisted and broken – whether due to not having the intellectual capacity to properly process the events of their lives or due to mental illness – that they are incapable of changing. For example, certain kinds of criminals (rapists) tend to be repeat offenders – modern studies have shown that for many there is no form of punishment or therapy that helps them overcome this weakness and they tend to repeat the crime over and over again.

Moghā, in addition to referring to that which is vain or fruitless (or useless) also refers to the fence – there is a fence surrounding humanity, which is the law, and it serves to keep the criminals and demons outside the fence. While permanent imprisonment is a possibility for dealing with demons, it is also true that it is very expensive and a burden on society. For crimes that have no hope of rehabilitation and which hurt humanity, the Gītā does teach us (through

Kṛṣṇa's words) that the death penalty exists for a reason and has a long history within the language of the Vedas with respect to many terms related to mokṣa (which refers both to self-realization and "liberation"). One concept that has been introduced into Western culture via Christianity is the concept of forgiveness – while we always forgive the ones we love for their actions, there are some for whom no forgiveness is warranted and Kṛṣṇa instructs humanity to deal with those individuals appropriately. In fact, many Christians teach that one should allow oneself to be abused – which is the wrong message to send to humanity, and very wrong to teach children. Christians attempt to teach others to love everyone – of course, they do not themselves engage in that delusion – and that teaching serves, along with the command to "turn the other cheek" to continue to propogate and preserve their culture of rape.

§

Text 13

mahātmānas tu māṃ pārtha daivīṃ prakṛtim āśritāḥ
bhajanty ananya-manaso jñātvā bhūtādim avyayam

-

Pārtha –
those who are great
are sacred – they are attached
to Prakṛti;
they offer worship and devotion –
especially to the one who offers completion –

I am imperishable
and have existed from the beginning.

§

Text 14

satataṃ kīrtayanto māṃ yatantaś ca dṛḍha-vratāḥ
namasyantaś ca māṃ bhaktyā nitya-yuktā upāsate

-

Continual conversation with Kṛṣṇa
leads one to establish beauty through
the dominion of law, which serves
to protect My people –
one will find yoga
in devotion to those who are dear, and to Me.

§

Text 15

jñāna-yajñena cāpy anye yajanto mām upāsate
ekatvena pṛthaktvena bahudhā viśvato-mukham

-

Through the wisdom of the yajña
one draws close to the other –
in their offering to Me,
two live together in union, as one –
the entirety of the universe
flows from the mouth of Gāyatrī,
in both separation and unity.

§

Text 16

ahaṃ kratur ahaṃ yajñāḥ svadhāham aham auṣadham
mantro 'ham aham evājyam aham agnir ahaṃ hutam

-

I am resolution – I am power, intelligence,
understanding, inspiration – and sacrifice –

I am the yajñas,
and I am self-reliance –

I am the cure –
I am the mantra, and thought –

I am ghee – I am the stotra and I am the sword –
I am Agni – I am the oblation
and the one to whom it is offered.

§

Text 17

pitāham asya jagato mātā dhātā pitāmahaḥ
vedyaṃ pavitram oṃkāra ṛk sāma yajur eva ca

-

I am the Father
and created all that is living

with the Mother –
I am Viṣṇu – the Preserver –
and Prajāpati –

I am sacred knowledge and praise –
and am found in marriage and
all of the Vedas –

I am the music of the universe, I am Oṃ.

§

Text 18

gatir bhartā prabhuḥ sākṣī nivāsaḥ śaraṇaṃ suhṛt
prabhavaḥ pralayaḥ sthānaṃ nidhānaṃ bījam
avyayam

-

One who preserves – is a lord and master
and is a match for his beloved –
he is pierced by the arrows of Kāma
and makes his home in the cycle of the sun –
I am Viṣṇu – I am Kāma –
I am existence, aspiration, wealth and rest –
and I am the seed of existence, the eternal mantra
of the universe – Oṃ.

§

Text 19

tapāmy aham ahaṃ varṣaṃ nigṛhṇāmy utsṛjāmi ca
amṛtam caiva mṛtyuś ca sad asac cāham arjuna

-

Arjuna –
I shine like the sun – and
provide warmth –
I am the rain – I enjoy Myself
and My existence is like the flowing
of the tears of devotion –
I am saṃsāra – I am nectar and immortality –
I am the twins and I am love –
and I am present in existence and with those
who no longer exist.

§

Text 20

trai-vidyā māṃ soma-pāḥ pūta-pāpā
yajñair iṣṭvā svar-gatiṃ prārthayante
te puṇyam āsādya surendra-lokam
aśnanti divyān divi deva-bhogān

-

One who drinks the soma of the Vedas
protects humanity in cleansing
the wicked and the demons
through yajña –
in seeking the soulmate
one strives for the stars
and finds heaven in the serpent –
wisdom and eternity
and enjoyment of the Divine.

-

Commentary

The serpent has long been a symbol of wisdom and the feminine throughout human history. Christians associate the serpent (and women) with evil – but it is in fact a symbol not only of the eternal and saṃsāra, but also the holy and sacred, including knowledge of the Divine. Hindus have long worshipped women and in fact, women are probably the original authors of the Vedas. While no one knows for sure what soma actually was, as there are many theories related to a variety of possible substances used as a sacrament – based on linguistic analysis of Hindu scripture, soma (which is also associated with the moon) likely refers to women, and if one considers one of the meanings associated with phalam and the fact that the soma strainer was made of wool, that it should be reasonably obvious that soma is a reference to the wisdom and beauty of women, the sanctity of existence, the motivation for war and the joy of raising a family.

§

Text 21

te taṃ bhuktvā svarga-lokaṃ viśālaṃ
kṣīṇe puṇye martya-lokaṃ viśanti
evaṃ trayī-dharmam anuprapannā
gatāgataṃ kāma-kāmā labhante

-

Those who engage in devotion,
worship and enjoyment
reach heaven –
one who wastes away or dies
will be reborn;
the wisdom of dharma serves
to protect family – the parents and children –
and life together in aspiration towards Me
leads to the Highest Desire –
and one of My gifts to you – conception and birth.

§

Text 22

ananyāś cintayanto māṃ ye janāḥ paryupāsate
teṣām nityābhiyuktānāṃ yoga-kṣemaṃ vahāmy aham

-

Those who comprehend and know
the soulmate –
live continually in devotion
with the other and share the Highest yajña –
and I carry them to peace and happiness.

-

Commentary

Ananyā refers to one who is "not the other," "not another" or "not different." While not are all as lucky as others in each lifetime, we all have the possibility of experiencing the joy of meeting that other person who is our other half and twin.

§

Text 23

ye 'py anya-devatā-bhaktā yajante śraddhayānvitāḥ
te 'pi mām eva kaunteya yajanty avidhi-pūrvakam

-

Those who are close to the divinity
of the other –
those who worship in faith and certainty, Kaunteya –
sacrifice with understanding of the one who is First.

§

Text 24

ahaṃ hi sarva-yajñānāṃ bhoktā ca prabhur eva ca
na tu mām abhijānanti tattvenātaś cyavanti te

-

I am all in all of the yajñas –
one who has worshipped Me
is powerful and a lord –
the Truth is that the might and glory
of the intellect comes from Me –
you have continually lived and aspired
to the knowledge of the Highest –
and they fall away.

§

Text 25

yānti deva-vratā devān pitṝn yānti pitṛ-vratāḥ
bhūtāni yānti bhūtejyā yānti mad-yājino 'pi mām

-

Those who follow God's law –
bring about change
and establish man's law –
life and family
are My gift –
one seeks, worships and sacrifices
because of Me and to Me.

-

Commentary

God only provides one law to humanity – dharma.

Dharma indicates only one absolute sin and law – "thou shalt not rape." Everything else is relative, based on the situation. For crimes serious enough to be considered sin, there is really only one appropriate punishment, and that is the death penalty (administered by the government in a manner consistent with the concept of ahiṃsā).

In a society established according to Vedic principles, then there is no need for prisons. There is really one true law, which carries a death sentence on the first offense. All other crimes must be evaluated according to the situation (for example, people are entitled to defend themselves). Theft may be warranted in some situations given the lack of charity in the world today. All "crimes" we know of today, other than rape, may have financial penalties, instead (for example, ethics breaches in business) – and in the case of serial killers and other cases of murder in the first degree, then there is also the death penalty.

Rather than the inefficient judicial system known today, decisions will be made based on the situation and will be made by enlightened philosopher-kings who have the proper intellectual and moral education to make the right decision concerning the welfare of the alleged criminal. There will be few trials given the fact that there would be so few actual laws, other than a variety of guidelines with financial value associated with them if convicted (mostly just theft and unethical business conduct) and the ever-declining incidents of rape and murder.

A variety of other issues (such as discrimination, et cetera) will eventually have less of a need for a legal basis if the citizens of a Vedic society are provided with proper moral and intellectual education.

As mentioned in the foreword, this book taken in its entirety provides the guidelines as defined in the original śāstras to bring about world peace and prosperity.

§

Text 26

patraṃ puṣpaṃ phalaṃ toyaṃ yo me bhaktyā prayacchati

tad ahaṃ bhakty-upahṛtam aśnāmi prayatātmanaḥ

-

Whoever offers a leaf, flower, fruit or water
to Kṛṣṇa with love and affection
and strives in devotion to the ātman –
I accept and consume him
as a part of Me.

§

Text 27

yat karoṣi yad aśnāsi yaj juhoṣi dadāsi yat
yat tapasyasi kaunteya tat kuruṣva mad-arpaṇam

--

You reach your goal in action, Kaunteya –
offer ghee into the homam fire –
provide sacrifice to Kṛṣṇa and enjoy marriage –
fire provides warmth,
which you in turn will provide –
act in My name.

-

Commentary

The eyes of those whose hearts are consumed by the flames of bhakti are anointed and opened by Kṛṣṇa – and everything is offered at His/Her feet. Within this text there are references to the one absolute sin defined by dharma (which is that we offer ourselves and provide permission – no one is entitled to abuse or take) – and the various references to action, austerity, sacrifice, providing, giving back, offering and delivering also reference an ongoing theme within the Gītā concerning the other definition of liberation (related to capital punishment and warfare).

§

Text 28

śubhāśubha-phalair evaṃ mokṣyase karma-bandhanaiḥ
sannyāsa-yoga-yuktātmā vimukto mām upaiṣyasi

-

The morally superior are beautiful –
they are versed in the Vedas
and enforce dharma – they provide
prosperity and uphold the law
through the fruit of their actions;
therefore, provide liberation
for those who renounce life
and union with the Self –
you will approach Me in prayer
and set them free.

-

Commentary

Mokṣyase indicates providing liberation for another and at the same time also refers to the future –

through two verbs related to the concept of mokṣa which have the same conjugated form.

Those who cannot perceive Prakṛti and reject the notion of the sanctity of our existence on this Earth may lead unhappy lives – but in some cases, they may become so consumed with evil that they become demons – and Kṛṣṇa provides instruction to humanity throughout the Gītā on how to deal with and treat them. This text has some associations with the traditions of both Halal and Kosher (in Islam and Judaism) and also indicates that we may be unhappy about the obligation (and may shed tears for the individual) – but that it is our moral imperative to enforce dharma for the happiness of the people and the harmony of society.

§

Text 29

samo 'haṃ sarva-bhūteṣu na me dveṣyo 'sti na priyaḥ
ye bhajanti tu māṃ bhaktyā mayi te teṣu cāpy aham

-

I am the flame of Agni
kindled between soulmates –
the couple and their children
are sacred –
the enemy does not love Kṛṣṇa;
I am with those who worship Me
and their families in devotion.

-

Commentary

Samo 'ham sarva-bhūteṣu indicates a variety of concepts – it refers to the pair, the Nāciketa sacrifice – justice, compensation and that which is right – unity, people and children.

The rest of the text is quite simple and is elementary Sanskrit. It does not reflect any favor or indifference given towards those who are evil – instead it indicates that those who do not know Kṛṣṇa's love are despised by Him/Her. And then simply concludes in simple language that those who practice bhakti are well-loved by Kṛṣṇa and He is present in their lives.

§

Text 30

api cet su-durācāro bhajate mām ananya-bhāk
sādhur eva sa mantavyaḥ samyag vyavasito hi saḥ

-

The righteous share each other
in worship and devotion to Me –
they cast judgment together on the wicked,
and are of one accord.

-

Commentary

There is an old saying in the West that is very popular – "let he who is without sin cast the first stone." If one reads the words of Kṛṣṇa and understands the concept of dharma, then all who listen to His/Her words should consider picking up a stone, when necessary – and in those cases when one does encounter a "demon," then society should work together in providing the needed liberation.

§

Text 31

kṣipraṃ bhavati dharmātmā śaśvac-chāntiṃ nigacchati
kaunteya pratijānīhi na me bhaktaḥ praṇaśyati

-

Kaunteya –
one who follows the Sanātana Dharma within provides peace
through aspiration and decisiveness –
and know that those who are not
devoted to Me will fall and perish.

§

Text 32

māṃ hi pārtha vyapāśritya ye 'pi syuḥ pāpa-yonayaḥ
striyo vaiśyās tathā śūdrās te 'pi yānti parāṃ gatim

-

Pārtha –
A man who cultivates the soil
should provide rest to those
who are the enemies of our women –
those born at the feet of Puruṣa
are My army
and seek the Highest.

§

Text 33

kiṃ punar brāhmaṇāḥ puṇyā bhaktā rājarṣayas tathā
anityam asukhaṃ lokam imaṃ prāpya bhajasva mām

-

One who is devoted to the Divine –
Agni, yajña and soma – continually enjoys drinking
amṛtam –
he is a ruler and radiant, provides illumination
and enjoys the light
and song of the Moon;
those who are not devoted to Me
are not happy in this world –
worship Me
and find attainment.

§

Text 34

man-manā bhava mad-bhukto mad-yājī māṃ
namaskuru
mām evaiṣyasi yuktvaivam ātmānaṃ mat-parāyaṇaḥ

-

You are born into this world
through My devotion and desire
to see you live –
we worship together, as I have provided
food and enjoyment –
bow before Me;
you will offer prayer in sacrifice to the Self
and devotion to Kṛṣṇa.

Chapter Ten

Text 1

śrī-bhagavān uvāca
bhūya eva mahā-bāho śṛṇu me paramaṃ vacaḥ
yat te 'haṃ prīyamāṇāya vakṣyāmi hita-kāmyayā

-

Śrī-Bhagavān said:

We should listen to one another – I will teach you
the Highest song –
I provide comfort
and desire you –
in the devotion of thought
I swell and provide the desire
to meet Destiny
and provide children for the Earth.

§

Text 2

na me viduḥ sura-gaṇāḥ prabhavaṃ na maharṣayaḥ
aham ādir hi devānāṃ maharṣīṇāṃ ca sarvaśaḥ

-

One who understands Me
stands above the crowd –
even that of the intelligent –

I am the light and splendor

of the poets and the moon –
I existed in the beginning
and am Her song.

§

Text 3

yo mām ajam anādiṃ ca vetti loka-maheśvaram
asammūḍhaḥ sa martyeṣu sarva-pāpaiḥ pramucyate

-

One who understands Me, that I am the beginning –
that I am Pūṣan, Agni – that I am
He who drives the chariot
and Maheśvara –
is intelligent and remains on his course;
those who must die
are consumed by evil –
they must be liberated –
and I will slacken the reins.

§

Texts 4 and 5

buddhir jñānam asammohaḥ kṣamā satyaṃ damaḥ śamaḥ
sukhaṃ duḥkhaṃ bhavo 'bhāvo bhayaṃ cābhayam eva ca

ahiṃsā samatā tuṣṭis tapo dānaṃ yaśo 'yaśaḥ
bhavanti bhāvā bhūtānāṃ matta eva pṛthag-vidhāḥ

-

One who knows and understands Truth
is confident, patient, calm
and has self-control and happiness –
misfortune is born
from those who are impure
and diseased –
the healthy are impartial and fair
and practice ahiṃsā –
in their beauty they provide for those
who are unworthy –
and in their passion for family
they offer division and purification.

§

Text 6

maharṣayaḥ sapta pūrve catvāro manavas tathā
mad-bhāva mānasā jātā yeṣāṃ loka imāḥ prajāḥ

-

All existence flows from Me
and Her song –
it is Our shared thought
and you are the elements of Her mantra
and praise – man is created
in Our image and is born
into this world through the act of creation.

-

Commentary

There are of course numerous terms for both God and man found in Sanskrit. Manu refers to one who is capable of thought – and can also refer to both Viṣṇu and Manu's wife, as well.

This text has a relationship to Text 35 of the Brahma Saṃhitā:

The universe is one with His breath;
the Brahmaṇḍa moves with Śakti
through the yugas –
you are the paramāṇu,
the elements of His mantra
engaged in eternal devotion.
I worship Govinda, the Puruṣa who existed
in the beginning.

§

Text 7

etāṃ vibhūtiṃ yogaṃ ca mama yo vetti tattvataḥ
so 'vikalpena yogena yujyate nātra saṃśayaḥ

-

One who understands
that he is part of the True Reality –
seeks yoga with Me – in the glory
of Her music – there is no difference
between the other in yoga
and one finds comfort and certainty.

§

Text 8

ahaṃ sarvasya prabhavo mattaḥ sarvaṃ pravartate
iti matvā bhajante māṃ budhā bhāva-samanvitāḥ

-

Everything comes from Me –
the mighty and glorious are consumed
with passion and desire –
and the intoxication
of an elephant in love on the rampage –
those who worship Me in devotion
continually think of Me
and awaken to the purpose of existence
in their hearts and mind –
living together, united in breath – thought –
and pursuit of the Divine.

§

Text 9

mac-cittā mad-gata-prāṇā bodhayantaḥ parasparam
kathayantaś ca māṃ nityaṃ tuṣyanti ca ramanti ca

-

One passes time in life
in contemplation of the other –
in mutual breath and conversation –
and satisfy and delight one another
in song and prayer to Me.

-

Commentary

This text has a relationship to Text 13 of the Śrīśopaniṣad:

Those who are intelligent
tell us that some will experience yoga
and that others will not –
one must seek union with each other –
the intimacy of conversation is eternal.

§

Text 10

teṣāṃ satata-yuktānāṃ bhajatāṃ prīti-pūrvakam
dadāmi buddhi-yogaṃ taṃ yena mām upayānti te

-

I provide pleasure and joy
to those who continually worship
in devotion and yoga – the intellect
moves and seeks yoga with Me
and attainment
at My feet – and yours.

§

Text 11

teṣām evānukampārtham aham ajñāna-jaṃ tamaḥ
nāśayāmy ātma-bhāva-stho jñāna-dipena bhāsvatā

-

I am with those who seek
pleasure and submission to one another
and to Me, Pārtha –
all are born into darkness and ignorance
and cannot see the light of the stars –
but I cause them to seek and enjoy
the Self –
they find their home
and shine like the sun and the moon –
and provide the illumination of wisdom.

§

Texts 12 and 13

arjuna uvāca
paraṃ brahma paraṃ dhāma pavitraṃ paramaṃ bhavān
puruṣaṃ śāśvataṃ divyam ādi-devam ajaṃ vibhum

āhus tvām ṛṣayaḥ sarve devarṣir nāradas tathā
asito devalo vyāsaḥ svayaṃ caiva bravīṣi me

-

Arjuna said:

They have said, that one who
seeks the highest – Brahman, the Puruṣa –
finds heaven and eternity
and the highest home
in the forest of light and bliss, and enjoys soma –

and that all come from You.

And you say that those who sing praise
find each other to be one – even though
they are two –
and that you are Kṛṣṇa,
the eternal darkness of the night sky – the ātman.

-

Commentary

This text has a relationship to Text 5 in the Brahma Saṃhitā:

The extraordinary forest of bliss
has four āśramas and four beautiful forms –
which are four-times enough.

Four puruṣārthas – four impulses;
ten spears beat the drum –
as above, so below.

Eight kalaśa for Lakṣmī – eight means of attainment;
ten cowherds protect
the beautiful form of man.

Black, indigo – white – red – brilliant gold –
these are colors of Viṣṇu and Sarasvatī;
the yajñas are adorned
and surrounded by
extraordinary Śaktis.

And also has a relationship to Text 26 in the Brahma Saṃhitā:

Govinda, the immortal lord
of indigo Śvetadvīpa,
has always existed blissfully in Goloka
of which Gokula is a reflection.

Prakṛti has the form of a guṇa,
seated in time and space –
amid the golden filaments of the thousand-petaled
lotus,
growing and nourished
by the roar of the elephant.

Bhūmi exists
near the center of the lotus,
seated in the highest āsana –
near the radiant, eternal form of the
bliss of consciousness.

His gopis worship Kṛṣṇa-Rāma
by weaving water with a portion of Himself –
He enjoys playing Oṃ – the sound of Brahman –
for His Rādha-Sīta.

§

Text 14

sarvam etad ṛtaṃ manye yan māṃ vadasi keśava
na hi te bhagavan vyaktiṃ vidur devā na dānavāḥ

-

Keśava, you do not love those who are evil,
but instead praise those

who find themselves to be one in both
thought and body, even as they are two –
the adorable one provides fortune and happiness
and her husband is attentive to her needs and
thoughts.

-

Commentary

Kṛṣṇa is also known as "the Adorable One."

§

Text 15

svayam evātmanātmānaṃ vettha tvaṃ puruṣottama
bhūta-bhāvana bhūteśa deva-deva jagat-pate

-

You are the Highest – the Puruṣa –
and you have known Yourself –
you are all that lives, you are heaven
and you are prosperous, as you are
married to Her – Prakṛti.

§

Text 16

vaktuṃ arhasy aśeṣeṇa divyā hy ātma-vibhūtayaḥ
yābhir vibhūtibhir lokān imāṃs tvaṃ vyāpya tiṣṭhasi

-

You are the other half –
and are worthy as Her husband –
Kṛṣṇa is all that is beautiful
and pervades reality –
You are the glory and splendor
of all – and You penetrate
and fill all of existence, as You
are penetrable and Her friend.

-

Commentary

One could potentially interpret the beginning of this text as a request, as one use of arhasi indicates permission – but it also indicates that one has worth or that one is a counter-balance. We can all find heaven on this Earth if we find that special someone who is our other half and compliments ourselves – both in similarity and difference.

§

Text 17

kathaṃ vidyām ahaṃ yogiṃs tvāṃ sadā paricintayan
keṣu keṣu ca bhāveṣu cintyo 'si bhagavan mayā

-

Bhagavān –
I want to know how two
exist together as one –
merging in thought and comprehension

of the other in yoga.

§

Text 18

vistareṇātmano yogaṃ vibhūtiṃ ca janārdana
bhūyaḥ kathaya tṛptir hi 'śṛṇvato nāsti me 'mṛtam

-

In extension, the ātman
penetrates all – and Lakṣmī
touches the heart of passionate men
and increases our greatness –
You provide satisfaction and contentment –
but those who do not listen and understand
do not know the nectar of living.

§

Text 19

śrī-bhagavān uvāca
hanta te kathayiṣyāmi divyā hy ātma-vibhūtayaḥ
prādhānyataḥ kuru-śreṣṭha nāsty anto vistarasya me

-

Śrī-Bhagavān said:

I will explain to you
that the ātman is all-pervasive
and diffuse – the heart
is the Highest object of attainment –

but there is a border
surrounding humanity, which keeps
our loved ones near – and the demons
outside the fence.

§

Text 20

aham ātmā guḍākeśa sarva-bhūtāśaya-sthitaḥ
aham ādiś ca madhyaṃ ca bhūtānām anta eva ca

-

I am the ātman – I am Śiva –

I am all that has happened
and all that exists –

I rest on Śeṣa in the yoganidrā –

I am the beginning and I am Her belly –

one can be judged based on one's actions
and I therefore also provide a limit.

§

Text 21

ādityānām ahaṃ viṣṇur jyotiṣāṃ ravir aṃśumān
marīcir marutām asmi nakṣatrāṇām ahaṃ śaśī

-

I am Viṣṇu – the light
of the stars and the heavens –

I am the eclipse
and the constellations through
which the moon passes –

I am the light of soma –
the flash of lightning and
those who wield the thunderbolt –

and I am both the sun and the moon.

§

Text 22

vedānām sāma-vedo 'smi devānām asmi vāsavaḥ
indriyāṇāṃ manaś cāsmi bhūtānām asmi cetanā

-

I am the Divine – and sacred knowledge –

I am Viṣṇu – I am Indra – and I am
that which is suitable for Him –

I am wealth and prosperity – I am the father
and the husband, I am the mother
and I am children –

I am the mind, I am the senses
and I am thought.

-

Commentary

This text has a number of relationships to most, if not all of the texts in the Brahma Saṃhitā – however, it does have a particular relationship to Texts 57 – 62 which appear at the end of the śāstra and are instructions for parents to give their children:

If one provides these five ślokas
to one's children,
then they will have understanding
of Me – the great Viṣṇu, Bhagavān, Brahmā, Brahman
and the process of creation.

Those who experience
the joy and consciousness
of the ātman
and aspire towards Bhagavān
through bhakti
will ascend and experience
enlightenment together.

The most effective means
of understanding the ātman
is with the ātman –
through jñāna and dharma,
as well as bhakti – which is the highest
means of attainment.

Bhakti is the preferred path
to attain the highest bliss
through knowledge of Kṛṣṇa and Śrī.

All must have faith and trust in Kṛṣṇa

and act within dharma –
understanding will make you like Me.

Acting continually while thinking of Me
will enable one to achieve the highest devotion.

I am the entirety
of that which moves –
and that which does not move –
I am the seed of the intellect, Prakṛti and every
human being –
I have provided you with reason
and the ability to achieve jñānam –
you will foster and establish
the world through your offspring.

§

Text 23

rudrāṇām śaṅkaraś cāsmi vitteśo yakṣa-rakṣasām
vasūnāṃ pāvakaś cāsmi meruḥ śikhariṇām aham

-

I am Śiva – who sings the music
of the universe –

I am war and I am the rāga –

I am Agni – I am the lord of wealth,
I am Indra's palace – and I guard
against the demons –

I am the stars, the horse – and I am water –

I am Meru – I am the stronghold –
and I am as sweet as dahi.

§

Text 24

purodhasāṃ ca mukhyaṃ māṃ viddhi pārtha
bṛhaspatim
senānīnām ahaṃ skandaḥ sarasām asmi sāgaraḥ

-

Understand Me, Pārtha –

I am the king and the priest – I am
the mouth of the Vedas, I am prayer and devotion –

I am Kārttikeya, I am the spear – I am the body
and I slay the enemy –

I am rāsa, I am speech
and I flow throughout eternity
as the waters of creation.

§

Text 25

maharṣīṇāṃ bhṛgur ahaṃ girām asmy ekam akṣaram
yajñānām japa-yajño 'smi sthāvarāṇāṃ himālayaḥ

-

I am the great poets
who bring fire and the light of the moon
to My people –

I am the prayer – I am the whisper –

I am single and dual – I am sincere
and truthful –

I am the family, I am stability –
and I am the home.

-

Commentary

Prabhupāda (and those in his tradition who came before) likely associated the concept of japa with the Roman Catholic rosary – which is very consistent with a number of elements of the Gaudiya tradition. Traditionally there is quite a bit of reverence given to the concept of Jesus – despite the fact that his teachings are abhorrent and foster shame in humanity and he did not serve as a good example to others. One of the alternate meanings associated with japa relates to blame (which is done in a whisper by some). Prabhupāda seemed to have wanted to share his hatred of life and humanity, which is a running theme throughout the commentary of this book – he hated women and attempted to teach those who followed him to hate themselves, others and life – other than his chosen disciples, who he indicated (and this is currently still taught by the institution) – can absolve original sin, and that his practice of japa meditation also offsets karma. He also taught the concept of the afterlife, rather than the traditional concept of heaven – which is life on this Earth – and in Hindu tradition, life is eternal.

§

Text 26

aśvatthaḥ sarva-vṛkṣāṇāṃ devarṣīṇāṃ ca nāradaḥ
gandharvāṇāṃ citrarathaḥ siddhānāṃ kapilo muniḥ

-

I am the fig tree, and provide
shelter for My horses –

I am the axe –

I am Agni, and I guard the soma –

I am the chariot, and the charioteer –

I am accomplishment, fulfillment and success
and I provide termination for the unholy –

I am the inward impulse – I am fire, the sun
and I am the devotee.

§

Text 27

ucchaiḥśravasam aśvānāṃ viddhi mām
amṛtodbhavam
airāvataṃ gajendrāṇām narāṇāṃ ca narādhipam

-

Listen to the roar and praise
of the stallions –
and enjoy the nectar of immortality
that flows from the oceans of eternity –
a rāja is a conqueror and hero among men
and is possessed with the might of the elephant –
his eyes are wild with passion – one eye is dedicated to himself
and one to his wife.

§

Text 28

āyudhānām ahaṃ vajraṃ dhenūnām asmi kāmadhuk
prajanaś cāsmi kandarpaḥ sarpāṇām asmi vāsukiḥ

-

I am the thunderbolt and the cakra
and I am the denunciation –

I provide milk and am the mother –

I enflame my husband with passion
and am the king of the nāgas.

§

Text 29

anantaś cāsmi nāgānāṃ varuṇo yādasām aham

pitṝṇām aryamā cāsmi yamaḥ saṃyamatām aham

-

I am Viṣṇu – I am Śeṣa –

I am the serpent and the elephant –

I am the ocean and sun
of the twins –

I am the married couple, I am
their shared mantra –
and I am the yajña used to execute
the wicked.

§

Text 30

prahlādaś cāsmi daityānāṃ kālaḥ kalayatām aham
mṛgāṇāṃ ca mṛgendro 'haṃ vainateyaś ca pakṣiṇām

-

I am joy and excitement –
and I am death for the demons –
both the mother and the father
declare war –

I am Indra and urge both
to contemplate one another –

I am Garuḍa and am by your
side at the time of sacrifice.

§

Text 31

puruṣaḥ pavatām asmi rāmaḥ śastra-bhṛtām aham
jhaṣāṇāṃ makaraś cāsmi srotasām asmi jāhnavī

-

I am the Puruṣa –
and belong to those who purify –

I am Rāma – I am praise
and I am the knife –

I belong to the mothers and those
who nourish –

I am the fish and the grove in the forest –

and I am the stream, I am the torrent
of warfare – I am the senses, I am pleasure
and I am the morally superior –

I am Viśvāmitra – I am Gāyatrī.

§

Text 32

sargāṇām ādir antaś ca madhyaṃ caivāham arjuna
adhyātma-vidyā vidhyānāṃ vādaḥ pravadatām aham

-

I am the rain of arrows – I am the storm –

I am Śiva and I am the resolution
and determination of the warrior –

I am the beginning and I am the limit
of those who stand between My people –

I am the Visarga.

Arjuna –

I am the paramātman and the heart –
and I am science –
those who worship Me
inflict justice on the demons
and cleave with the sword –

I am the song of My flute
and the one who plays it.

-

Commentary

Vidhyānām simultaneously refers to the continual worship of God, affection – attachment and contact from a weapon, opening a vein – as well as being a command directly to Arjuna to do the above. This text also refers again to the fence which surrounds humanity – which is the death penalty for those for whom there is no hope of saving.

§

Text 33

akṣarāṇām akāro 'smi dvandvaḥ sāmāsikasya ca
aham evākṣayaḥ kālo dhātāhaṃ viśvato-mukhaḥ

-

I am eternity and the thunderstorm –

I am language and the compound
and I am the pair –

I am home, I am time – I am death
and the indigo night of the universe –

I am Kālī –

I am the Mother and the milky heavens
flow from Me and sustain the universe.

§

Text 34

mṛtyuḥ sarva-haraś cāham ubhavaś ca bhaviṣyatām
kīrtiḥ śrīr vāk ca nārīṇāṃ smṛtir medhā dhṛtiḥ kṣamā

-

I am Mara and Yama – I am Kāma –

I am the support of the universe – I am ravishing
and I am captivating – I am the stallion and I am fire –

I receive and I destroy –

I provide sustenance and milk, I am the future
and I am life –

I am humanity – I am diffuse
and radiant, I am the glory of the palace
and I am speech –

I am the music of the universe and the
waters of creation –

I am memory and I am dharma –

I am medha and I am intoxicating –

I am Śrī – I am the oblation –
and I drink the blood of the demon
spilled in sacrifice.

-

Commentary

Dhṛti refers both to the wife of Dharma, as well as the final oblation performed on the evening of the Aśvamedha.

This text (and all of the Gītā) also relates to the final śloka in the Śrīśopaniṣad, Text 18, which is associated with traditional Hindu funeral rites:

Agni – lead us on the path
to virtue and understanding –
please remove
our misfortunes and unhappiness –

we want to worship the Highest
by the light of His moon.

§

Text 35

bṛhat-sāma tathā sāmnāṃ gāyatrī chandasām aham
māsānāṃ mārga-śīrṣo 'ham ṛtūnāṃ kusumākaraḥ

-

I make the great strong and mighty –

I am luminous and tranquilizing
and I am the song –

I am wealth and abundance, I am Gāyatrī –

I am sacred desire, I am the moon –

I am the Vedas –

I am the yuga and I am the appointed time –

I am the lotus, I am phalam –

I am flame, I am the Highest –
and I am the womb.

§

Text 36

dyūtaṃ chalayatām asmi tejas tejasvinām aham

jayo 'smi vyavasāyo 'smi sattvaṃ sattvavatām aham

-

I am battle – and I am the dice game of the rāja –

I am the edge of the knife
and the clarity of your eyes –

I am health and spirit – I am fire –

I am beauty and splendor – I am music
and I am Indra –

I am victory and conquest –

I am Resolution and I am karma –

I am the beauty of existence
and the joy of saṃsāra –

I am courage and I am childbirth.

§

Text 37

vṛṣnīnāṃ vāsudevo 'smi pāṇḍavānāṃ dhanañjayaḥ
munīnām apy ahaṃ vyāsaḥ kavīnām uśanā kaviḥ

–

I am Kṛṣṇa, descendant of the Yadus,
Arjuna, conqueror of wealth –
and the ecstasy of the stars –

I am wisdom and I am Lakṣmī
and I am division – the strongest and most intelligent
fight for the soma and care for the herd.

§

Text 38

daṇḍo damayatām asmi nītir asmi jigīṣatām
maunaṃ caivāsmi guhyānāṃ jñānaṃ jñānavatām
aham

-

I am the instrument, and the one who plays it
and I am the sovereignty of the rāja –

I am with those who conquer and defeat the enemy –

I am Punishment, I am the Twins and I am Śiva –
there is wisdom in silence
but I will help the wise
provide it in both speech and action.

§

Text 39

yac cāpi sarva-bhūtānāṃ bījaṃ tad aham arjuna
na tad asti vinā yat syān mayā bhūtaṃ carācaram

-

One who understands Truth –
that I am the entirety of existence, Arjuna –

craves life and acts with Me –
two should become one and join together
in love and companionship –
as I have always enjoyed Myself
and act in accordance with dharma.

§

Text 40

nānto 'sti mama divyānāṃ vibhūtīnāṃ parantapa
eṣa tuddeśataḥ prokto vibhūter vistaro mayā

-

The enemy is not with Me
and their army is large and have lost their divine nature,
conqueror of the enemies –
one has the need to cast judgement –
Lakṣmī is powerful and reigns over your army –
the fondness of your heart will continually increase through Me
and join her with victory.

§

Text 41

yad yad vibhūtimat sattvaṃ śrīmad ūrjitam eva vā
tat tad evāvagaccha tvaṃ mama tejo-'ṃśa-sambhavam

-

The morally superior and powerful
act and seek attainment –
existence is beautiful
and Śrī is venerable and fortunate
and provides Her strength, power and majesty –
aspire towards that –
approach Me
through Her –
and with fire and ardor
you will apply the arrow and knife
and come together
through the act of preservation.

§

Text 42

atha vā bahunaitena kiṃ jñātena tavārjuna
viṣṭabhyāham idaṃ kṛtsnam ekāṃśena sthito jagat

-

Arjuna –
with a storm of arrows
one hastens towards comprehension
of the one who completes you,
the one who is your other half –
stand firmly in battle and with resolve –
act in accordance with dharma
and you will receive your inheritance – home.

-

Commentary

Kim is a pronoun and does not always indicate a question.

Chapter Eleven

Text 1

arjuna uvāca
mad-anugrahāya paramaṃ guhyam adhyātma-saṃjñītam
yat tvayoktaṃ vacas tena moho 'yaṃ vigato mama

-

Arjuna said:

I hear the sound of the birds calling
me home –
the highest self – the one who
shows favor and kindness
and is veiled in mystery –
who provides wonder and amazement,
the one who I am fond of –
and who I am currently separated from.

§

Text 2

bhavāpyayau hi bhūtānāṃ śrutau vistaraśo mayā
tvattaḥ kamala-patrākṣa māhātmyam api cāvyayam

-

Two come together in union
and give birth to life –
two listen to each other
and learn from one another –

the enemy fades away when
the heart stops – and her heart
is one with mine –
the peacock feathers are that of the arrow –
in slaying the enemy and in aspiration towards
the divine – the Highest Self –
she pervades my thoughts, and her mind
and mine are holy and sacred –
as one, and we will anticipate
the first speech of our newborn child.

§

Text 3

evam etad yathāttha tvam ātmānaṃ parameśvara
draṣṭum icchāmi te rūpam aiśvaraṃ puruṣottama

-

One listens to what has been said –
that you – Parameśvara –
are the eternal desire
of the Self –
I long for and desire
Her beautiful form – her regality,
power and might –
Puruṣa – the highest tone
and the music of the universe.

§

Text 4

manyase yadi tac chakyaṃ mayā draṣṭum iti prabho

yogeśvara tato me tvaṃ darśayātmānam avyayam

-

You look forward
to my beholding the beautiful
appearance of the Lord –
who is adept in yoga
and my object of devout contemplation –
I am the father and will always be there
and cherish soma – and I am
fond of the moon and Her face
in both the light and the dark –
and the beauty of the imperishable Self.

-

Commentary

Vedic society long predated Christianity and Judaism – but it is very interesting that avyayam refers both to the soma strainer, as well as an organized body that is unwilling to change. The soma strainer was made of wool and its literal meaning is quite obvious.

§

Text 5

śrī-bhagavān uvāca
paśya me pārtha rūpāṇi śataśo 'tha sahasraśaḥ
nānā-vidhāni divyāni nānā-varṇākṛtīni ca

-

Śrī-Bhagavān said:

Behold Me – Pārtha –

My forms are beautiful and lovely
and My mūrtis are a reflection of the Divine –
I worship Myself continually
in My many forms –
they are all separate and beautiful – they are
the music of praise and those who are pure
and seek and attain Lakṣmī.

§

Text 6

paśyādityān vasūn rudrān aśvinau marutas tathā
bahūny adṛsta-pūrvāṇi paśyāścaryāṇi bhārata

-

Bhārata –
observe, experience and offer praise
for I am Viṣṇu,

I am Sūrya and I am the twin Aśvin –

I am Agni, I am wealth, I am the forest –

I am those who sing and howl – I am
the shining ones
and the herd of horses –

I am the desert and the antelope –

I am the cow, milk and the Earth, and I am
freedom, security, safety and happiness –

I am the great and the mighty, and I am abundant –

I am the rising sun and the ancient rite –

I am sight and right understanding –

I am Dūrga and I consume and devour –

and I provide the solution for those who violate
dharma –

as I am also the Aśvamedha.

§

Text 7

ihaika-sthaṃ jagat kṛtsnam paśyādya sa-carācaram
mama dehe guḍākeśa yac cānyad draṣṭum icchasi

-

Arjuna –
in this world two who are identical
become one –
in devotion they create a home together
and in seeing each other with ājñā
they graze together and are consumed by flame –
I have always lived with Prakṛti –
two fashion new life together
in seeking and finding each other worthy –
and behold the entrance of their newborn

into this world.

§

Text 8

na tu māṃ śakyase draṣṭum anenaiva sva-cakṣuṣā
divyaṃ dadāmi te cakṣuḥ paśya me yogam aiśvaram

-

I am not the only one thinks
you are powerful and mighty –
in this world
there is one who loves you
and longs for heaven with that look –
observe her and praise Me
in yoga with the majesty
and might of a rāja.

§

Text 9

sañjaya uvāca
evam uktvā tato rājan mahā-yogeśvaro hariḥ
darśayām āsa pārthāya paramaṃ rūpam aiśvaram

-

The father is a rāja – he rules, governs and guides –
and is a kṣatriya –
a great man is in union with Īśvara –
and the beautiful fawn of Indra, Hari –
the sister and twin of Yama –

whose appearance is that of the night sky
and is the vehicle of aspiration – her form
and beauty is that of the Highest
and is the source of your might and supremacy.

§

Texts 10 and 11

aneka-vaktra-nayanam anekādbhuta-darśanam
aneka-divyābharaṇaṃ divyānekodyatāyudham

divya-mālyāmbara-dharaṃ divya-gandhānulepanam
sarvāścarya-mayaṃ devam anantaṃ viśvato-mukham

-

Few can lead in speech and action –
those who are beautiful and extraordinary
teach others – and cast judgement
in accordance with dharma –
those in separation long for the divinity
of the other;
the morally superior wield the weapon
and offer gold –

the beautiful and the celestial
surround one another and long for heaven –
they adorn each other with flowers
and their connection is soothing and calming,
like the candan of tilaka – they wear each other
in their hearts
and worship each other's feet in astonishment –
they run through life together, as horses –
surrounded by Śeṣa on all sides

and cleave the demon with the axe.

-

Commentary

Aneka can potentially mean "various" in that refers to "not many." Anantam refers to eternity – it is Śeṣa, the serpent of eternity on whom Viṣṇu reposes – and is the remainder and the leavings of sacrifice (ashes, in this particular context).

§

Text 12

divi sūrya-sahasrasya bhaved yugapad utthitā
yadi bhāḥ sadṛśī sā bhāsas tasya mahātmanaḥ

-

One who wants to reach heaven
enjoys the plentiful gifts of Sūrya
and is yoked with his beloved –
she is the reflection
of Lakṣmī
and her glory and splendor
belongs to him –
and she is a reflection
of the abundance of his heart.

-

Commentary

There are numerous references to marriage within this text. The text refers to the reflection of Lakṣmī and one who is worthy of Her – and mahā refers to the cow and the greatness of a virtuous person. Yugapat refers to being yoked side-by-side. Divi refers to heaven, as well as the Indian roller – whose feathers were traditionally given to cows to increase the supply of milk – and also refers to Agni. Sahasra does not necessarily refer to one thousand but is rather a term referencing abundance.

§

Text 13

tatraika-sthaṃ jagat kṛtsnaṃ pravibhaktam anekadhā
apaśyad deva-devasya śarīre pāṇḍavas tadā

-

Two are the same and inseparable
when continually worshipping
in devotion, together –
she is the Highest – Devī –

She is our support, she nurtures
and is the Mother – the body
is a gift from her – the universe is
born from Her belly –
she is Airāvata – and auspicious
in her purity, virtue and rarity.

-

Commentary

While pāṇḍuḥ is plural in this text, it is also associated with the Highest within the śloka – and also refers to Her various virtues. Airāvata is the king of the elephants and is associated with Indra – a white elephant is very rare, represents auspiciousness (welfare, prosperity, good fortune and war) and also represents purity.

§

Text 14

tataḥ sa vismayāviṣṭo hṛṣṭa-romā dhanañjayaḥ
praṇamya śirasā devaṃ kṛtāñjalir abhāṣata

–

One who conquers in the name of prosperity
is proud and possessed of certainty and faith –
he is thrilled with rapture
and rejoices at the reflection of the sun
on the scales of the fish – and the
feathers of the peacock –
his yoga is that of the Lord
and he bows and offers his palms in praise –
he shines above others –
and teaches in word and example.

-

Commentary

This text has a relationship to Text 13 from the Brahma Saṃhitā:

Those peacock feathers
caught in the sacred net
of the marriage proposal
are the seed of the Himālayas.

§

Text 15

arjuna uvāca
paśyāmi devāṃs tava deva dehe
sarvāṃs tathā bhūta-viśeṣa-saṅghān
brahmāṇam īśaṃ kamalāsana-stham
ṛṣīṃś ca sarvān uragāṃś ca divyān

-

Arjuna said:

I am learning and can see –
the devas come from You
and Prakṛti is divine –
parents, children and all of humanity
listen to the music of Rādha-Kṛṣṇa –
the Lord lives in the heart – She is the rose
and She is Kālī –
the poets sing of the Moon and home –
the nāgas long for heaven –
they are the wisdom of the serpent,
the beauty of the marriage vow –
and the sandals on her feet.

§

Text 16

aneka-bāhūdara-vaktra-netraṃ
paśyāmi tvāṃ sarvato 'nanta-rūpam
nāntaṃ na madhyaṃ na punas tavādiṃ
paśyāmi viśveśvara viśva-rūpa

-

She has many arms –
and Her belly is the motivation
for war –
I listen to the words
of dharma – Viṣṇu pervades
all of existence –
Her beauty is that of the sky – the fence
exists to protect Your people –
and You provided the means
of purification in our primal beginning –
I worship Jagannātha –
who is everywhere – I worship Her beauty.

§

Text 17

kirīṭinaṃ gadinaṃ cakriṇaṃ ca
tejo-rāśiṃ sarvato dīptimantam
paśyāmi tvāṃ durnirīkṣyaṃ samantād
dīptānalārka-dyutim aprameyam

-

I know and understand that
Kṛṣṇa is the rāja – He bears a club

and the discus –
He is Narasiṃha and has nails like
flint and the chisel – He is fire
and clarity of the eyes –
You burn and shine like the sun
and are in union with all of Your creation –
You are the praise of lightning
and You are Splendor – You are majesty and dignity
and cannot be measured.

§

Text 18

tvam akṣaraṃ paramaṃ veditavyaṃ
tvam asya viśvasya paraṃ nidhānam
tvam avyayaḥ śāśvata-dharma-goptā
sanātanas tvaṃ puruṣo mato me

-

You are the Highest –
and I give forth my offerings to You –
I believe that you are the eternity of existence,
that You are Oṃ – the universe –
You light the sacrificial fire
and are the imperishable Viṣṇu – the Preserver –
who protects the Sanātana Dharma –
You are the Puruṣa and I praise You.

§

Text 19

anādi-madhyāntam ananta-vīryam

ananta-bāhuṃ śaśi-sūrya-netram
paśyāmi tvāṃ dīpta-hutāśa-vaktraṃ
sva-tejasā viśvam idaṃ tapantam

-

I see the Sun and the Moon –
and know that You are eternal, and without beginning –
and that You are boundless and infinite –
You are Her music
and love Her eternally – She leads Her husband
and is the lion –
You blaze with the flame of Agni
and consume the offering –
with ardor for one's own
You pervade all of existence
and provide satisfaction in the warmth of spring.

§

Text 20

dyāv āpṛthivyor idam antaraṃ hi
vyāptaṃ tvayaikena diśaś ca sarvāḥ
dṛṣṭvādbhutaṃ rūpam ugraṃ tavedaṃ
loka-trayaṃ pravyathitaṃ mahātman

-

Two live together and aspire towards You –
they are complete in their differences –
and one in both heart and mind –
they look at each other
and see the other as the twin – and

do everything with You –
they behold the wonder and beauty of the other
and are filled with passion for You and life –
they perform devotion and worship together
in raising their family –
and they reel at the glory of the Highest Self.

§

Text 21

amī hi tvāṃ sura-saṅghā viśanti
kecid bhītāḥ prāñjalayo gṛṇanti
svastīty uktvā maharṣi-siddha-saṅghāḥ
stuvanti tvāṃ stutibhiḥ puṣkalābhiḥ

-

Those who find that their paths
come into alignment among the stars
praise You and the divine –
when in peril they reach out their hands
and call on Kālī –
a great poet and reflection of the Moon
praises in song –
and seeks fulfillment –
and You are the stotra, the mantra
and the eulogy.

§

Text 22

rudrādityā vasavo ye ca sādhyā
viśve 'śvinau marutaś coṣmapāś ca

gandharva-yakṣāsura-siddha-saṅghā
vīkṣante tvāṃ vismitāś caiva sarve

–

Aditi – the Divine Mother – howls
and roars – She sings
the celestial song, and continually
gives birth to the Vedas –

She is sweet and sincere, and provides
the measure of the forearm, between the elbow
and the closed fist –

She purifies and She cleanses – She provides
destruction for the demons –

and She rides through the heavens with Her twin –
as She is the Aśvin –

She is Indra and provides the host of storm gods
casting the thunderbolt on to the Earth –

She is ardor and passion – She is a desert
which provides an unquenchable thirst – and She
is the desire to drink the soma
and enjoy its eternal intoxication –

the waters of creation flow from Her
and She feasts upon the offering,
including that which pours into the homam fire
in the Aśvamedha –

She is a Foundation, a rock, the Moon
and her heart blossoms

in gentle laughter, with a smile –
and all look on Your face
in the company of the music of the stars.

§

Text 23

rūpaṃ mahat te bahu-vaktra-netraṃ
mahā-bāho bahu-bāhūru-pādam
bahūdaram bahu-daṃṣṭrā-karālaṃ
dṛṣṭvā lokāḥ pravyathitās tathāham

-

Her form and beauty manifests
as the expanse of the night sky, and the stars –

Her speech is rich and abundant
as the Vedas pour forth from Her mouth –

She leads and guides, as She is the eye – and She gave birth to dharma –

She is the foundation and root of the tree – and the river which flows through time –

She is the greatness of the cow
and has the hips of the mother –

She is the wheel and all worship Her feet –

She is the nurturer and Her belly gives birth to the universe –

Her tusks cleave the demon asunder – She is formidable,
dreadful – and She is tulasi –

She carries the sword
and I will watch as Her enemies tremble before Her in fear.

-

Commentary

Traditionally, the term pāda is added to the end of the name of one who is accomplished, but it is considered a term of respect when it is added in the plural form, rather than the singular. I have noticed that in some traditions, when one experiences the nāmakaraṇa saṃskara later in life, that the spiritual name chosen is frequently an insult directed at the devotee.

§

Text 24

nabhaḥ-spṛśaṃ dīptam aneka-varṇaṃ
vyāttānanaṃ dīpta-viśāla-netram
dṛṣṭvā hi tvāṃ pravyathitāntar-ātmā
dhṛtiṃ na vindāmi śamaṃ ca viṣṇo

-

Viṣṇu –
touch, contact – and experience –
are like the clouds pouring rain before the harvest –

the wide expanse of Her open jaws
are the entrance to the next lifetime –
She is the color of indigo
and is consumed in flame –
she is adorable and has the might of the lion –
She is Two – and inspires the pilgrimage –
the enemy is filled with terror at the sight of You
and You provide the fence, which is that of the
Visarga –
You are our support
and provide the holiest of sacrifices – You are the
daughter
of Time and Prakṛti –
and I do not know calm or tranquility –
I have no illusions and I will raise my hand in
indifference
and without attachment.

§

Text 25

daṃṣṭrā-karālāni ca te mukhāni
dṛṣṭvaiva kālānala-sannibhāni
diśo na jāne na labhe ca śarma
prasīda deveśa jagan-nivāsa

-

Her tusks and sword cleave the enemy –
She is the army – She is the source
and cause of the universe –

She is the Vedas and Her face
is beautiful – and one worships

Her through procreation – and
honors Her through childbirth –

and She provides intuition and jñānam –

She unites together with Agni
and burns in infinite flame and passion –

She shines as brightly as the Morning Star
and guides with Her beauty –

and I do not know Her for She is Yours –

Indra, please provide Your grace
to Me – and please guide me home to
my own river – so that I may join her
in sleep, rest, peace and worship.

§

Texts 26 and 27

amī ca tvāṃ dhṛtarāṣṭrasya putrāḥ
sarve sahaivāvani-pāla-saṅghaiḥ
bhīṣmo droṇaḥ sūta-putras tathāsau
sahāsmadīyair api yodha-mukhyaiḥ

vaktrāṇi te tvaramāṇā viśanti
daṃṣṭrā-karālāni bhayānakāni
kecid vilagnā daśanāntareṣu
sandṛśyante cūrṇitair uttamāṅgaiḥ

-

In your union with Airāvata – You are mighty

and glorious – and seek victory –

She is the snake – She is venom – She is the cure –

Her river flows towards you – and She is consumed
with desire for You – She is terrible and dreadful –

She is Kālī – She is Manasā –

She is the raven, the scorpion and the soma vessel –

She is prāṇā – She is the sword –
and She is Your match, as You are Hers –

our army will provide a torrent
of arrows –

Her fangs will tear their bodies
apart – please, Kṛṣṇa –
do not let them be reborn –

and She has another bite, which is within –

but Her might also provides
the fence, which protects Your people –

all worship You, sing in praise –
and provide children for the Earth.

-

Commentary

Airāvata is the king of the elephants – a rare and auspicious white elephant. Airāvata is also the nāga who presides over the month of Tapas or Phalguna.

§

Text 28

yathā nadīnāṃ bahavo 'mbu-vegāḥ
samudram evābhimukhā dravanti
tathā tavāmi nara-loka-vīrā
viśanti vaktrāṇy abhivijvalanti

-

Her music flows like the river –

She is great in numbers
and agitates with the broomsedge –

She gathers the waters of heaven together
and mixes the soma –

She is the Highest Vessel
and all dissolve into Her –

those who are close to You
become men – they are heroes –

and they provide for those who transgress dharma
and are led astray –

we hear Her music
in the act of love and repopulation of the Earth –

She illuminates and provides wisdom –

She brings light to man, as She is the Lightbearer –
we kindle love for Her in the heart, in the yajña –

and will ignite the funeral pyre and the blaze will be glorious.

§

Text 29

yathā pradīptaṃ jvalanaṃ pataṅgā
viśanti nāśāya samṛddha-vegāḥ
tathaiva nāśāya viśanti lokās
tavāpi vaktrāṇi samṛddha-vegāḥ

-

The enemy is flammable and inauspicious –
and they seek and will experience annihilation
through the flight of our arrows –
they will find Your destruction –
and we will achieve success
in the name of the nāgas –
we will be accompanied by the torrent of battle
and the music of victory – jaya!

§

Text 30

lelihyase grasamānaḥ samantāl
lokān samagrān vadanair jvaladbhiḥ
tejobhir āpūrya jagat samagraṃ

bhāsas tavogrāḥ pratapanti viṣṇo

-

Viṣṇu –

You lick and swallow – You devour,
consume and savor with the tongue –
and have no respect
for the words and actions of the enemy –

in Your words –
which flow from Her beautiful mouth –
a blazing fire – a yajña – will shine and burn –
it will illuminate the battlefield and the entire world –

with the edge of the knife and ardor –
and the glory of the sun – and the reflection
of Her majesty –

the powerful, the violent – the strong and the noble –
the passionate and wrathful – the ferocious and
proud –
will indulge Your will
and bring down Agni's fire and vanquish the enemy.

§

Text 31

ākhyāhi me ko bhavān ugra-rūpo
namo 'stu te deva-vara prasīda
vijñātum icchāmi bhavantam ādyaṃ
na hi prajānāmi tava pravṛttim

-

Please explain to me
who the Lord is –

She is cruel and noble, fierce – and proud –

She is wild and consumed with primal passion –

She is beautiful and handsome, she is the gift
and the battle cry –

She will be Your thunderbolt –

I seek her regality and blessing, please
grant my desire to join her, once again –
for I cannot see the future.

§

Text 32

śrī-bhagavān uvāca
kālo 'smi loka-kṣaya-kṛt pravṛddho
lokān samāhartum iha pravṛttaḥ
ṛte 'pi tvāṃ na bhaviṣyanti sarve
ye 'vasthitāḥ pratyanīkeṣu yodhāḥ

-

Śrī-Bhagavān said:

I am Death – I am Kālī –

I am the indigo night of Time,

and I am the ruler of the Earth –

I am destruction and the wasteland
and live in the house of Yama –

I cut off those who have fallen
and violate dharma –
together, we will sever their heads –
we will provide the eclipse
of their sun –
we are joyful and proud – we are the virtuous
and the great – and we enrapture
our Moon – in charm and fascination –

we conquer – and their army
has advanced –

we are the brave – we know Truth –
we worship in the light of the sun
and we provide the yajña –

and our army faces theirs –
we stand firm, together – they will
meet our arrows and swords –
and the terrifying sound of our war drums.

§

Text 33

tasmāt tvam uttiṣṭha yaśo labhasva
jitvā śatrūn bhuṅkṣva rājyaṃ samṛddham
mayaivaite nihatāḥ pūrvam eva
nimitta-mātraṃ bhava savya-sācin

-

Rise above yourself and stand firm in battle –
seize and take hold of beauty and glory –
be victorious and return to her
and provide prasādam for the Earth –

sweep the enemies and purge the disease –

become a rāja
and together be prosperous with Me –
two choose together and move through life –
they pray, worship and create together –

it is a basic fact of life that some must be cleansed –

one becomes rich in marriage
and in the joy of raising a family –

I am on both your left and right –
and have a special preference
for those who honor the north when facing the rising sun –
as it represents the harvest, the clouds which bring sustenance
and the Moon.

§

Text 34

droṇaṃ ca bhīṣmaṃ ca jayadrathaṃ ca
karṇaṃ tathānyān api yodha-vīrān
mayā hatāṃs tvaṃ jahi mā vyathiṣṭhā
yudhyasva jetāsi raṇe sapatnān

-

Listen to them – fight for soma
with Śiva – conquer by chariot –
they have no dharma –
strike with the sword, remove
their eyes and heads –
rend their flesh and stop their hearts –
you will cast them out in the name of victory –
delight in battle in Her name.

§

Text 35

sañjaya uvāca
etac chrutvā vacanaṃ keśavasya
kṛtāñjalir vepamāṇaḥ kirīṭī
namaskṛtvā bhūya evāha kṛṣṇaṃ
sa-gadgadaṃ bhīta-bhītaḥ praṇamya

-

One hastens to listen
to the eloquence of Keśava –
and offers the palms – one trembles
at the beauty, might and sharp tusks
of Vārāhī –
one bows and worships with certainty
and faith – one calls on Kṛṣṇa –
the enemy trembles in fear and terror
of the death rattle – the devotee
prepares the funeral pyre, but will
offer no śraddhā for their dead.

§

Text 36

arjuna uvāca
sthāne hṛṣīkeśa tava prakīrtyā
jagat prahṛṣyaty anurajyate ca
rakṣāṃsi bhītāni diśo dravanti
sarve namasyanti ca siddha-saṅghāḥ

-

Arjuna said:

Two stand firmly together –
the lord of the senses, and thought –
one calls on You in praise – Indra, Kṛṣṇa –
Jagannātha – and becomes excited
and thrills in rapture – consumed with fire
and passion; one falls in love and becomes
illuminated –
the virtuous guard against the demons
and cast stones – they worship You
in battle and adoration –
in the hopes of attaining the Highest object
and to rejoin her in the celestial song.

§

Text 37

kasmāc ca te na nameran mahātman
garīyase brahmaṇo 'py ādi-kartre
ananta deveśa jagan-nivāsa

tvam akṣaraṃ sad-asat tat paraṃ yat

-

They do not worship You –
and want to flow into Brahman –
You will devour them – Indra, Kṛṣṇa –
the one who existed in the beginning –
our king – You are everything –
the flowers, the plants and the trees –
You are that which exists, and that which does not exist –
and pour forth richly into this universe, continually –
they aspire towards dissolution.

§

Text 38

tvam ādi-devaḥ puruṣaḥ purāṇas
tvam asya viśvasya paraṃ nidhānam
vettāsi vedyaṃ ca paraṃ ca dhāma
tvayā tataṃ viśvam ananta-rūpa

-

You are the Puruṣa
who existed in the beginning –
You are all of existence
and omnipresent – You see
everything and knew the Highest –
one finds home in marriage
and family – her majesty and splendor
and her light –
You are Oṃ – You are beautiful

and infinite – and You are Śeṣa.

§

Text 39

vāyur yamo 'gnir varuṇaḥ śaśāṅkaḥ
prajāpatis tvaṃ prapitāmahaś ca
namo namas te 'stu sahasra-kṛtvaḥ
punaś ca bhūyo 'pi namo namas te

-

You are Indra – You are the wind, the air –
You are prāṇā – You are the mind
and You are that which is desirable –

You are Yama – You are Agni –

You are Prajāpati – You are Kṛṣṇa –

You are frozen so that we can become warm, once again –
You are Candra and You are soma –

one bows before You –
we become even greater in praise of You –

and we bow before Your gift – our own
personal incarnation of Your divine grace and favor.

§

Text 40

namaḥ purastād atha pṛṣṭhatas te
namo 'stu te sarvata eva sarva
ananta-vīryāmita-vikramas tvaṃ
sarvaṃ samāpnoṣi tato 'si sarvaḥ

-

One bows before You in adoration
and honors the rising sun –
and one should bow before You
in the heart –
You are infinite and without limit –
Your splendor is immeasurable
and boundless – Kṛṣṇa and Rādhā
live together in the beauty of the universe
and within us, as well.

§

Texts 41 and 42

sakheti matvā prasabhaṃ yad uktaṃ
he kṛṣṇa he yādava he sakheti
ajānatā mahimānaṃ tavedam
mayā pramādāt praṇayena vāpi

yac cāvahāsārtham asat-kṛto 'si
vihāra-śayyāsana-bhojaneṣu
eko 'tha vāpy acyuta tat-samakṣaṃ
tat kṣāmaye tvām aham aprameyam

-

Kṛṣṇa – You are Her friend
and companion – You keep Society

in Your thoughts – and so we gather together
to prepare for the sacrifice –

You are the companion of Dūrga – those
who do not know You and stray too far –
are grasped by the pair at the Aśvamedha –

Your might is present in me – and in the lust
for justice – and longing for our companions –
we perform our sacred duty – and mock
the criminal publicly, as a community –

we use the sword and knife
to tear him asunder – we distribute
our gift for Agni to the Earth, in the funeral pyre –
we provide rest and peace
for the community, and for the demon; those who
have not fallen and uphold dharma
are beautiful to You – and our sacrifice
serves as a reminder to all – the virtuous
execute dispassionately – and I will not be judged
for I keep her in my heart.

§

Text 43

pitāsi lokasya carācarasya
tvam asya pūjyaś ca gurur garīyān
na tvat-samo 'sty abhyadhikaḥ kuto 'nyo
loka-traye 'py apratima-prabhāva

-

You are the father of this world –

and we aspire to the Highest and
uphold and enforce dharma –
we graze and eat – and prepare
the sacrifice –

I belong to You and am honorable –
and exhibit the highest restraint –
and cast judgement in the name of dharma –
the demon is difficult to digest, but will
be diffuse upon the Earth –

she is haughty and proud
and is the most valuable and precious wealth –
she is venerable, and provides direction;

the pair is with You – they are just
and stand upright –
they drink the nectar of saṃsāra
and worship You in providing for the Earth –
they have no equal and walk together
in dignity, strength and beauty.

§

Text 44

tasmāt praṇamya praṇidhāya kāyaṃ
prasādaye tvām aham īśaṃ īḍyam
piteva putrasya sakheva sakhyuḥ
priyaḥ priyāyārhasi deva soḍhum

-

I have bowed before You in praise –
and my mind and heart are focused on destiny –

my beloved – our family –
punishing the wicked –
and providing our prasādam for the Earth; both
the mother and the father are Lords – they are
the same – they are twins and a pair – and both
embrace that which is the same –
and that which is different – in each other –
they are worthy of one another – they are their own
counterbalance –
they are dear as two sukhīs
and he is there for her for support and is filled with
respect –
as she has the strength and courage
to bring forth our children into this world – to
provide joy and love for all.

§

Text 45

adṛṣṭa-pūrvaṃ hṛṣito 'smi dṛṣṭvā
bhayena ca pravyathitaṃ mano me
tad eva me darśaya deva rūpaṃ
prasīda deveśa jagan-nivāsa

-

I have understood the ancient customs –
the customary and most primal –
the Aśvamedha – war – and marriage –
I invoke the Highest – and long for the night –

I see the demon – I understand Fear, who
is married to the daughter of Time –
one tears the demon from his seat

and cuts out his heart – mind and thought –

please help her see me – she has the most
beautiful form of Devī – Jagannātha, king of the gods.

§

Text 46

kirīṭinaṃ gadinaṃ cakra-hastam
icchāmi tvāṃ draṣṭum ahaṃ tathaiva
tenaiva rūpeṇa catur-bhujena
sahasra-bāho bhava viśva-mūrte

-

I strive to obtain my object – I am a rāja –
and am armed with the club and spear –
and Gaṇeśa's hand –

I worship You –

her form is beautiful and worthy of adoration –
with intellect and the might of a thousand
archers aimed at the sun – we will provide a display –
and rule the Earth – Oṃ.

§

Text 47

śrī-bhagavān uvāca
mayā prasannena tavārjunedaṃ
rūpaṃ paraṃ darśitam ātma-yogāt
tejo-mayaṃ viśvam anantam ādyaṃ

yan me tvad anyena na dṛṣṭa-pūrvam

-

Śrī-Bhagavān said:

Arjuna –
you are satisfied with Me –
she is for you and her form and beauty
are the highest explanation of the Divine –
and yoga with the ātman –
you are covered in infinite fire –
and in our primal beginning I provided a fence –
one executes for Me – by your hand –
and with the other –
she is not only in your imagination, but also
to be experienced and to unite together
in the cycle and path of the sun – Oṃ.

§

Text 48

na veda-yajñādhyayanair na dānair
na ca kriyābhir na tapobhir ugraiḥ
evaṃ-rūpaḥ śakya ahaṃ nṛ-loke
draṣṭuṃ tvad anyena kuru-pravīra

-

One does not study the Vedas
through repetition or chanting –
but rather in worship of the Divine –
in love, passion, marriage and procreation –
and both sacrifice and worship –

in the warmth of spring one becomes
noble, fierce – and savage –
be mighty, powerful and beautiful to her –
I know mankind and I provided marriage
and the company of the other for you –
surpass those who came before
and be a hero and a prince and king among men.

§

Text 49

mā te vyathā mā ca vimūḍha-bhāvo
dṛṣṭvā rūpaṃ ghoram īdṛṅ mamedam
vyapeta-bhīḥ prīta-manāḥ punas tvaṃ
tad eva rūpam idaṃ prapaśya

-

The demons fear Me – and this is not foolish –
one looks upon My face in worship and praise
and appreciates the sublime – My face
is beautiful and terrifying – I am dreadful
and violent – I am the serpent and I am venomous –
I am the cobra and I spit on the demon
and fascinate My husband with Divine grace –
one measures via the scale –
and purifies the mind of the demon and the
throbbing of his heart –
I am pleased with those who cleanse evil
and ventilate the enemy with discrimination and
discernment –
and you are incredibly beautiful and adorable to her.

§

Text 50

sañjaya uvāca
ity arjunaṃ vāsudevas tathoktvā
svakaṃ rūpaṃ darśayām āsa bhūyaḥ
āśvāsayām āsa ca bhītam enaṃ
bhūtvā punaḥ saumya-vapur mahatma

-

Kṛṣṇa is the peacock – He is golden,
pure and has the color of Sita –
He is the kuśa grass
and gallops through the universe –
behold His beautiful form and worship in praise –
the sacrifice in the Aśvamedha turns to ash –
and is terrified – the devotee provides purification
in every lifetime –
she is Soma – and Beauty, the daughter
of dharma – She provides cheer in the sacrifice
and offers Her left palm.

§

Text 51

arjuna uvāca
dṛṣṭvedaṃ mānuṣaṃ rūpaṃ tava saumyaṃ
janārdana
idānīm asmi saṃvṛttaḥ sa-cetāḥ prakṛtiṃ gataḥ

-

Arjuna said:

I behold your beauty and form –
and praise You – Mithun, Kanya and Tula
provide for humanity – They provide the harvest
and are soma – and they excite their husbands –
one moves together in life –
appreciating the splendor
of the heart – our mind and thought –
and we provide the Visarga – and set the next
cakra in motion.

-

Commentary

The following Vedic astrological signs relate to the Western equivalent – Mithun is Gemini, Kanya is Virgo and Tula is Libra. They represent the pair of soulmates, the precious gift of our children, as well as the scale (justice).

§

Text 52

śrī-bhagavān uvāca
su-durdarśam idaṃ rūpaṃ dṛṣṭavān asi yan mama
devā apy asya rūpasya nityaṃ darśana-kāṅkṣiṇaḥ

-

Śrī-Bhagavān said:

It is painful to look upon the sacrificial knife –

but it is for preservation of the good – our women and children –
the husband measures – and appreciates the beauty of his own – and understands that which is obligatory and necessary –
he aspires towards beauty and pronounces judgement.

§

Text 53

nāhaṃ vedair na tapasā na dānena na cejyayā
śakya evaṃ-vidho draṣṭuṃ dṛṣṭavān asi māṃ yathā

-

One who does not know the Vedas –
does not experience warmth –
does not receive My gift –
does not know the cow –
but the strong and powerful worship Me with bhakti –
they wield the sword and intellect
and pierce the veil of māya –
they look on My beautiful forms
and compose stotras of worship and praise.

§

Text 54

bhaktyā tv ananyayā śakya aham evaṃ-vidho 'rjuna
jñātuṃ draṣṭuṃ ca tattvena praveṣṭuṃ ca parantapa

-

Arjuna – slayer of the enemies –
through bhakti one develops strength –
worship in devotion – attain wisdom –
look on beauty, and offer your hand to her –
enter into understanding of the True Reality
and build a home together – and two will become one.

§

Text 55

mat-karma-kṛn mat-paramo mad-bhaktaḥ saṅga-varjitaḥ
nirvairaḥ sarva-bhūteṣu yaḥ sa mām eti pāṇḍava

-

I am the Highest – and all action
should be dedicated to Me –
devotion – and division –
a bhakta worships in the celestial song
and pours forth heroism – for his family –
everything has happened before, happens now –
and will happen again –
one flows towards Me – and one approaches
Me in prayer – for I am Airāvata and the king of the Nāgas.

Chapter Twelve

Text 1

arjuna uvāca
evaṃ satata-yuktā ye bhaktās tvāṃ paryupāsate
ye cāpy askṣaram avyaktaṃ teṣām ke yoga-vittamāḥ

-

Arjuna said:

Two are one when continually
living in devotion and yoga with one another –
and You sit at their feet – they are surrounded
by Kṛṣṇa and are close to You –

In your words, You flow as the
universe continually –
but are imperceptible to some –
one finds yoga in knowledge
and understanding – wisdom –
some are shrouded in darkness
and live in ignorance –

but even those who live in devotion
and see You, long for Rāhu
to release the sun.

-

Commentary

Akṣaram can potentially refer to that which is imperishable or that which is not of the clouds or lacking the purity of water. Interpreting it in this manner does not make sense given traditional Vedic values and perceptions of the universe – instead, it may just be a slip on Prabhupāda's part – as he certainly did not know that which is beautiful to the senses and the clouds were certainly well beyond his reach. Unfortunately, he and his institution went to great effort to attempt to keep others from knowing their beauty. Akṣaram is also the first-person imperfect of flowing – and if one considers the nature of the evolving dialogue throughout the Gītā, one may come to the conclusion that Kṛṣṇa is speaking through Arjuna's mouth and not just into his ear.

§

Text 2

śrī-bhagavān uvāca
mayyāveśya mano ye māṃ nitya-yuktā upāsate
śraddhayā parayopetās te me yuktatamā matāḥ

-

Śrī-Bhagavān said:

Two living together in devotion
enter into Me –
they are one in thought
and continually think of Kṛṣṇa –
they live together in yoga
and worship the feet of the other
with faith and certainty
and remember the Highest –

they are both intent on Me
and live together as one.

§

Texts 3 and 4

ye tv akṣaram anirdeśyam avyaktaṃ paryupāsate
sarvatra-gam actinyaṃ ca kūṭa-stham acalaṃ
dhruvam

sanniyamyendriya-grāmaṃ sarvatra sama-buddhayaḥ
te prāpnuvanti mām eva sarva-bhūta-hite ratāḥ

-

I live with the two bhaktas –
and their choice is mutual and obvious –
they do not think of the future
but live together in the song of the Gandharvas –
we are joyful and engage in play –
the twins live together, within –
appreciating the sanctity of existence
with their mind, senses and body –
they are the same – and are united
in thought –
they seek attainment together, in marriage –
and they are destined for one another –
they are affectionate, kind – and enjoy
the ecstasy of līla.

§

Text 5

kleśo 'dhikataras teṣām avyaktāsakta-cetasām
avyaktā hi gatir duḥkhaṃ dehavadbhir avāpyate

-

Life in the material world causes pain and trouble –
the two who know the Highest
live together and are anointed –
their eyes are opened
and they are consumed with the splendor
of the heart and mind –
and live together in attachment and devotion –
they cling to the other, and to Kṛṣṇa –
childbirth is painful
but she shines and glows – together they
reach their object – she becomes full, and they
bring new life into the world in joy and love.

§

Texts 6 and 7

ye tu sarvāṇi karmāṇi mayi sannyasya mat-parāḥ
ananyenaiva yogena māṃ dhyāyanta upāsate

teṣām ahaṃ samuddhartā mṛtyu-saṃsāra-sāgarāt
bhavāmi na cirāt pārtha mayyāveśita-cetasām

-

The pair accomplishes everything
with Me – and one who rejects life
is not a part of Me –
those who know their twin –
become strong, powerful and glorious –

they are united with Me
and worship each other's feet in adoration –
I provide joy for them – and they enjoy
the intimacy of conversation –
they bring forth children into the world
to preserve the eternal joy of saṃsāra –
they worship Mara and Yama – Kāma –
the celestial ocean – and the Nāga –

the song of the Rājasūya
exists from the dawn of man – and celebrates
the dice game – the unpredictability of existence
and the dancing star which is born
even from the lowly –
drive the chariot – worship Soma –
sing in praise – glorify Me in art –
and enjoy the splendor of love and passion.

-

Commentary

We should all remember that there are many forms of art – including living one's life. The celebration of the Rājasūya celebrated the sovereignty and might of the rāja – and honored soma, aspiration towards Kṛṣṇa and the beauty (and horror) of human genetics.

§

Text 8

mayyeva mana ādhatsva mayi buddhiṃ niveśaya
nivasiṣyasi mayyeva ata ūrdhvaṃ na saṃśayaḥ

-

Keep Me in your thoughts – and praise –
place her on high – and place your footstep
in hers –
find home – flow into the river –
create, produce, worship – and shine
before her and all the world –
run towards Me – ascend, rise upwards –
aspire with the arrow –
and have certainty and faith.

§

Text 9

atha cittaṃ samādhātuṃ na śaknoṣi mayi sthiram
abhyāsa-yogena tato mām icchāptuṃ dhanañjaya

-

Conqueror of wealth –
one who follows in the other's footsteps
does not yield, and is as firm and resolute
as Vṣabha, Siṃha, Vṛścika and Kumbha –
and becomes strong and warlike in yoga –
the father desires me and finds prosperity.

-

Commentary

Sthiram can refer to the following signs in Vedic astrology – Vṛṣabha (or Taurus, the bull – which is ruled by Venus), Siṃha (or Leo, the lion – which is ruled by the Sun), Vṛścika (or Scorpio, the scorpion – which is ruled by Mars, or Mangala) and Kumbha (or Aquarius, the water-bearer – which is ruled by Saturn, who represents the fence surrounding humanity and justice).

Abhyāsa does refer to the regulative principles and rote chanting – as it refers to that which is repetitive and unnecessary. It also refers to military exercise.

§

Text 10

abhyāse 'py asamartho 'si mat-karma-paramo bhava
mad-artham api karmāṇi kurvan siddhim avāpsyasi

-

In finding the one who is your aim – for whom
you are suitable, perfect and a match for –
and remaining close – you will multiply –
you are the knife and the sword –
and your name is a killing word –
the highest act is in providing for the Earth –
and performing your duty –
you will find understanding and comprehension
of her and meet your match.

-

Commentary

Siddhim refers to finding fulfillment and attainment and has a historical reference to a shoe that will take one wherever one wants to go – interestingly, there is a later myth from Iceland (a country which has always embraced Vedic ideals) – about the Nábrók, or the necropants, which are made from the skin of a dead man which provide endless fortune and prosperity.

§

Text 11

athaitad apy aśakto 'si kartuṃ mad-yogam āśritaḥ
sarva-karma-phala-tyāgaṃ tataḥ kuru yatātmavān

-

You are equal to her – to Śakti –
cling to her and offer everything
unto Her – be a father –
move with her – let her guide you –
and she is just like you – she
has a soul, like your own.

§

Text 12

śreyo hi jñānam abhyāsāj jñānād dhyānaṃ viśiṣyate
dhyānāt karma-phala-tyāgas tyāgāc chāntir
anantaram

-

One who is the most beautiful – is auspicious,
blissful and adores dharma –

it is wise to practice, through wisdom –
to reflect on her likeness, the mūrti of the Divine –
and tear the demon apart, to rip his flesh
and deprive him of thought –
the fruit of one's actions may cause others
to be liberal with his life,
and he will leave this world –
some seek emancipation and peace –
and the wise provide it immediately after the crime.

-

Commentary

Viśiṣyate refers to ripping something asunder – to applying discrimination – and is the third-person passive of two root verbs: one refers to leaving something remaining (such as ash), and the other to blame, disdain, teaching, praise and enforcing the law.

Tyāgaḥ refers to leaving, quitting, abandoning, discharging, secretion, liberality, a wise man or woman and sacrificing a life.

Śāntiḥ refers to peace and bliss, tranquility and ridding the world of evil.

There is a story from the 20th century about a future where the innocent are preyed upon by the Morlocks – demons who eat human flesh. There is another version of this story, which is told through the Gītā, about the Eloi who carry knives – and use them, when necessary – so that they can continue singing and dancing around the fire in the wood.

§

Texts 13 and 14

adveṣṭā sarva-bhūtānāṃ maitraḥ karuṇa eva ca
nirmamo nirahaṅkāraḥ sama-duḥkha-sukhaḥ kṣamī

santuṣṭaḥ satataṃ yogī yatātmā dṛḍha-niścayaḥ
mayyarpita-mano-buddhir yo mad-bhaktaḥ sa me priyaḥ

-

One is not hostile to one's husband – he is a sukhī
and completely suitable for her –
one shows compassion to one who is yours –
and pours forth one's self – they are
exactly the same –
even in difference – and he is there for her
in sorrow, distress and happiness –
existence is sacred, and one is pleased
with the other –
inquire into her intent – remain fixed upon Me –
with both thought and intellect –
he is devoted to Me and you are fond of and
attached to her.

-

Commentary

Over the centuries, some have translated ahaṅkāraḥ as "false ego" – however, this concept does not exist in the Vedas, and there is no such thing as a false ego. There is a such thing as māya – which is the illusion that we are separate from God. Once one attains the realization that māya is simply illusion, then one will have pierced the veil of māya. That said, we all have different degrees of self-awareness and some have difficulty in fully mastering understanding of their own mind and thoughts. Prahbupāda mistranslates the prefix nis – as he learned Sanskrit from English language resources and believed that "without" refers to the absence of something – when it instead refers to "without" or "forth." There is a popular song from the 21st century that references this fact – that the false ego is an illusion and the frustration of the enlightened self in trying to find their match and equal – which was provided to the world by a devotee of Kṛṣṇa who is the author of the best recorded edition of the Maha Mantra, as of the time of the writing of this book. My books, in particular the Gītā, do finish and complete a few ideas.

§

Text 15

yasmān nodvijate loko lokān nodvijate ca yaḥ
harṣāmarṣa-bhayodvegair mukto yaḥ sa ca me priyaḥ

-

Do not flee or recoil from Me –
or the world –
or people –
be excited – and impatient – rejoice
in pleasure and passion –

achieve peace and rest – and admiration
and astonishment –
shed tears of devotion – open your heart –
you are my beloved and are dear to Me.

-

Commentary

Amarṣa refers to passion – and is associated with impatience, which is related to harṣa, which refers to ardent desire, joy, pleasure and excitement.

Bhaya can refer to fear or alarm – but refers to the śṛṅgāṭaka (or water chestnut) – which resembles the head of a bull or a flying bat and is associated with the horn in China, the diamond in Japan and in all Eastern traditions, is considered holy and associated with prayer – and in India it is associated with Navaratri, which is sacred to Devī.

Udvegaḥ refers to moving swiftly, tranquility, admiration and astonishment. The text above relates to ancient wisdom shared by only a few women with men (in a positive light), which is that there is such a thing as waiting too long.

A running theme through the commentary of this book is that when studying translations and commentaries on Sanskrit texts, one can find out quite a bit about the author, their background and mindset. This book includes an extensive forensic psychological analysis of Śrīla Prabhupāda.

§

Text 16

anapekṣaḥ śucir dakṣa udāsīno gata-vyathaḥ
sarvārambha-parityāgi yo mad-bhaktaḥ sa me priyaḥ

-

One approaches the Divine Couple –
who is the true friend – They are radiant and pure –
honest and sincere – they are a match for one
another –
they pronounce law – and preside over the Śuci
offering –
there is always a new beginning –
and one who renounces his right to life –
will also be offered to the fire –
the devotee loves her husband – and together
they form a family – the relationship
between parents, children and Kṛṣṇa.

-

Commentary

In the traditional prājāpati wedding, there is a sacrifice made to Mara and Yama prior to the wedding. It is auspicious – reminds all of the significance of the two twins – that there is always a new beginning in both life and death – and that in order to preserve dharma, sometimes sacrifices must be made.

This text has a relationship to Text 16 in the Śrīśopaniṣad:

I am the Puruṣa –
present in the breath of life –
who provides the chance
for union
in the marriage ceremony.

§

Text 17

yo na hṛṣyati na dveṣṭi na śocati na kāṅkṣati
śubhāśubha-parityāgī bhaktimān yaḥ sa me priyaḥ

-

One flames for the other –
and is filled with certainty and faith –
one longs for the other with desire
and has no expectation –
they are beautiful together, virtuous,
honest and morally superior –
they are devoted and loyal –
and offer sacrifice of all who violate dharma –
he is her beloved and dear to her.

§

Texts 18 and 19

samaḥ śatrau ca mitre ca tathā mānāpamānayoḥ
śītoṣṇa-sukha-duḥkheṣu samaḥ saṅga-vivarjitaḥ

tulya-nindā-stutir maunī santuṣṭo yena kenacit
aniketaḥ sthira-matir bhaktimān me priyo naraḥ

-

The twins are the same – and they
are both usurpers and enemies of those
who violate dharma –
they are dear friends and companions –
like the sun and the moon – and both
are like the tongues of Agni –
they are whetted and sharp – ardent
and passionate – and they praise honor –
and have disdain for dishonor –
they cling to one another even in sorrow –
and cast blame and reproach –
and live together with waves of adoration –
they are Durgā – they are Viṣṇu –
and observe silence on the amāvaśyā
of Phalguna –
they are pleased with existence
and build their home with Me – they offer honey –
they are immovable, resolute and hard-hearted –
and honor each other in prayer and song –
she is loyal and devoted to him – and they
both have the claws of Narasiṃha.

§

Text 20

ye tu dharmāmṛtam idaṃ yathoktaṃ paryupāsate
śraddhadhānā mat-paramā bhaktās te 'tīva me priyāḥ

-

It has been said –

that dharma is amṛtam –
and that those who offer śraddhā
are devoted to the Highest –
one is quiet – and then moves on.

Chapter Thirteen

Text 1

arjuna uvāca
prakṛtiṃ puruṣaṃ caiva kṣetraṃ kṣetra-jñam eva ca
etad veditum icchāmi jñānaṃ jñeyaṃ ca keśava

-

Arjuna said:

Keśava –
one knows the Puruṣa – and Prakṛti –
for she is the fertile land – She is the lord of the soil,
our home, the stars, the body and the Womb –
she is the soil of merit and the wife –
I emphatically desire to seek and find Her –
and am filled with the desire
to know Her in abstraction – to understand
her pronoun –
she is to be known and understood
and committed to memory.

§

Text 2

śrī-bhagavān uvāca
idaṃ śarīraṃ kaunteya kṣetram ity abhidhīyate
etad yo vetti taṃ prāhuḥ kṣetra-jña iti tad-vidaḥ

-

Śrī-Bhagavān said:

Kaunteya –
the body is a gift from Śrī – and She
is the soil and the land, she is the Lord –
she is home and the homam fire –
She is the body and the origin –
one knows Her name – and one knows
her body – knowledge of the Vedas
is discovery of the Divine
and the source of true wealth and prosperity.

-

Commentary

Śrīla Prabhupāda had a one-track mind: repetition, boredom, misery, celibacy, magic food, following orders, hating women and longing for death. The Sanskrit dictionary and language also has a one track mind, as nearly all words relate to a handful of related concepts – the cyclical nature of time and reincarnation, love, desire, marriage, worship, procreation, pleasure, childbirth – as well as free will, law and the death penalty – and destiny. Note that many definitions could result, potentially, in some of the classic ideas subscribed to in the West concerning Hindu tradition, but it requires an in depth knowledge of Vedic culture and the Vedas to properly interpret the various overlapping and related meanings, as well as solid understanding of Sanskrit grammar, the unique structure of Vedic poetry (which is both concrete and abstract, condensed (for easy memorization) and geometric in structure). The structure of the poetry is also focused on sound, the Vedic concept of God – and the poetry reflects Hindu theology within the structure of the language and poetry itself. There are numerous references throughout this book to some of these elements of the language and poetry, and through self-study one can come to one's own appreciation of these facts or enjoy the poetry in translation.

§

Text 3

kṣetra-jñaṃ cāpi māṃ viddhi sarva-kṣetreṣu bhārata
kṣetra-kṣetrajñayor jñānaṃ yat taj jñānaṃ mataṃ mama

-

You must penetrate māya – and attain knowledge
of the Earth – your origin and home –
the stars and the planets – and the divine nature of reality –
everything comes from the Earth –
and the stars, Bhārata –
two bodies move together as one –
and know the other –
and with jñānam one attains
understanding and comprehension –
two are one in both thought and flesh.

§

Text 4

tat kṣetraṃ yac ca yādṛk ca yad-vikāri yataś ca yat
sa ca yo yat-prabhāvaś ca tat samāsena me śṛṇu

One seeks the land – and one is forgiving –
falling in love brings about a change – in
emotion and thought –
let her guide you – one moves towards
majesty, dignity and strength –
splendor and beauty –
she provides rest and two reconcile differences
and become one –
it is the conjunction of two planets
aligned with the stars – two abide together,
living in unity with one another – listen to Me –
understand, learn, hear – and worship before Me.

§

Text 5

ṛṣibhir bahudhā gītaṃ chandobhir vividhaiḥ pṛthak
brahma-sūtra-padaiś caiva hetumadbhir viniścitaiḥ

-

Many poets sing to the Moon –
and provide the Song of Desire –
all are separate – but are held together
by a common thread – Viṣṇu,
who is the soft, melodious soul of man –
and the beautiful common strand
found within the form of the Self –
all proceed from Me – and are separate –
but join together in the Celestial Song.

§

Texts 6 and 7

mahā-bhūtāny ahaṅkāro buddhir avyaktam eva ca
indriyāṇi daśaikaṃ ca pañca cendriya-gocarāḥ

icchā dveṣaḥ sukhaṃ duḥkhaṃ saṅghātaś cetanā dhṛtiḥ
etat kṣetram samāsena sa-vikāram udāhṛtam

-

All originate from the Mother –
and the integration of the intellect
and self provides anointment –
with the mind, body and senses
cling to the hem of her skirt –
the one who completes you
and is the measure of yourself –
the Herd of the Sky praises Indra eternally
and His children – My herd
desires to graze in peace – one is judged
based on one's conduct –
existence is sacred, and moving across the Earth
requires destruction –
one desires union and intersection with her –
Kālī is charming and fascinating – She is ravishing –
She is Resolution and Satisfaction –
and the wife of dharma –
sacrifice was provided for those who err and stray too far –
and for the two to steal each other's hearts
and dwell in the yajña.

§

Text 8

amānitvam adambhitvam ahiṃsā kṣāntir ārjavam
ācāryopāsanaṃ śaucaṃ sthairyam ātma-vinigrahaḥ

-

She lives at home with you – within –
she is sincere – she is without cruelty –
and yet daunting –
she is worth waiting for, and she perseveres –
asks endurance – but is holy in Her abstraction –
she is honest and pure – and provides
purification for the unholy –
sit at her feet – for she is your guru –
she is pure of mind – as you are –
and she is firm but constantly delights
in your own stability – your faith and certainty –
and She provides the eclipse – and grasps
and takes hold of you, within –
she is a planet – a star –
and you orbit about each other –
in perfect harmony – she is music – and you
are her receptive – she invokes the word –
she is your vehicle of aspiration, your bow –
aspire to the Self – and listen to the flowing
of her river.

§

Text 9

indriyārtheṣu vairāgyam anahaṅkāra eva ca
janma-mṛtyu-jarā-vyādhi-duḥkha-doṣānudarśanam

-

The wicked grow pale at the sight of Her –
she has a distaste for evil – She
has indifference to worldly objects – and eliminates the ego –
She is Mara and Yama – She tears apart their foundation –
and provides a deposit for Agni –
She causes pain and agony, and she reflects on shared
responsibility – She is the night and darkness –
and She rids the world of disease and those who transgress –
praise her – and teach by her side –
cast judgement on the evil –
she is your vision and your dream –
contemplate her mūrti –
and She is dharma.

§

Text 10

asaktir anabhiṣvaṅgaḥ putra-dāra-gṛhādiṣu
nityaṃ ca sama-cittatvam iṣṭāniṣṭopapattiṣu

-

She has no attachment or affection
for those who creep along the ground
and are attached to violating dharma – or those

who have no respect for life –
She rends and tears the enemy,
destroys their family –
devours their children,
their wives and their servants –
and consumes their home –
you are together and are of like mind,
you notice each other
and observe – think and reflect –
you are one in heart and mind –
and intention and desire –
you are her beloved – as she is yours,
and she lives within –
and you live at each other's feet –
and She is with the army – the elephant, chariot –
and the horsemen and the foot-soldiers.

§

Text 11

mayi cānanya-yogena bhaktir avyabhicāriṇī
vivikta-deśa-sevitvam aratir jana-saṃsadi

-

You are twins and a pair – and live
together in yoga – with Me –
you are the same in devotion,
resemble one another – and live together –
you are kept apart – but will frequent your home
together –
and will wait on one another and honor and revere
the other –
those who do not love life, who know no passion –

who waste away, and crave death –
they will also be thrown into the fire.

§

Text 12

adhyātma-jñāna-nityatvaṃ tattva-jñānārtha-darśanam
etaj jñānam iti proktam ajñānaṃ yad ato 'nyathā

-

It has been said that the wisdom
of the Highest Self – is dear, and that of family –
your special purpose is to
know the jñānam of Truth –
that of reality – and in worship, and learning –
and teaching –
and to do so for those who are ignorant,
who have no wisdom –
for those who err and have ill intentions.

§

Text 13

jñeyaṃ yat tat pravakṣyāmi yaj jñātvāmṛtam aśnute
anādi mat-paraṃ brahma na sat tan nāsad ucyate

-

She is to be known and understood –
I declare her to be yours –
one consumes and enjoys

the eternal knowledge and amṛtam
of saṃsāra
and the Highest –
it has been said that one who
does not know Me
may also be invited to the sacrifice.

§

Text 14

sarvataḥ pāṇi-pādaṃ tat sarvato 'kṣi-śiro-mukham
saravataḥ śrutimal loke sarvam āvṛtya tiṣṭhati

-

The hand holds the sword firmly –
and she extends the tip of her hoof –
as you are the measure of her foot –
Her music permeates the universe –
for She is the Vedas – and the authority of all –
the eye glances off the summit of her snout –
and beholds the beauty and countenance of her face,
and savors the honey from her lips –
her left hand is the edge of the axe – she is the river,
and flows into your ears –
I behold and recognize, I perceive –
that you revolve in life about her –
one who stands firmly, kneels before Her
and submits, perseveres in devotion –
and relies on and confides in Her –
for She is the root and base of the Tree.

-

Commentary

In Sanskrit, the foot is of course associated with the sanctity of existence and is associated with traveling through life. It is also a measure of an individual, as well as in music and poetry (which in Vedic culture, are one and the same). Pāda, as opposed to pada, refers to either the feet of people or animals – and pāda combined with mukham refers to the foot and mouth of the cow. When referring to the foot as respect – in the singular number, when suffixed to a name, it is potentially a sign of disrespect that the one it is given to may not be aware of – in the dual, which would not occur in a name, it refers to two feet – and in the plural, it is a sign of respect, as it indicates an abundance of "measure." Outside of the nāmakaraṇa saṃskara, however, the foot is very holy – as we should all aspire to bow before and worship Her feet (or even foot).

§

Text 15

sarvendriya-guṇābhāsaṃ sarvendriya-vivarjitam
asaktaṃ sarva-bhṛc caiva nirguṇaṃ guṇa-bhoktṛ ca

-

All of the senses – the mind and the body –
are composed of splendor and light – and
have the semblance of the Divine –
the entirety of the senses, mind and body –
to one who has been abandoned
and is lacking – is deprived of their enjoyment

and finds no commitment,
no devotion and belongs to no one –
those who bear, nourish and support –
pour forth their own nature –
and the husband is the enjoyer,
one who experiences –
and is a prince and king – and ruler of the land.

§

Text 16

bahir antaś ca bhūtānām acaraṃ caram eva ca
sūkṣmatvāt tad avijñeyaṃ dūra-sthaṃ cāntike ca tat

-

I am moved by preservation – and love –
those who transgress
exist outside the fence –
they are trifling and insignificant –
and will never learn –
two are devoted to the Highest
and live within their own presence –
and they endure.

§

Text 17

avibhaktaṃ ca bhūteṣu vibhaktam iva ca sthitam
bhūta-bhartṛ ca taj jñeyaṃ grasiṣṇu prabhaviṣṇu ca

-

Those who are not apart in their bhakti
live with their family in devotion –
and provide division –
your people should stand firm –
be a preserver – a protector – a husband –
and you will have understood – and will know –
that I swallow and devour the enemy – they
are absorbed into Me –
the one who has dominion over this Earth –
Viṣṇu, the Preserver – and the enemy
will see My might.

§

Text 18

jyotiṣām api tat taj jyotis tamasaḥ param ucyate
jñānaṃ jñeyaṃ jñāna-gamyaṃ hṛdi sarvasya
viṣṭhitam

-

You belong to the heavens – the stars,
the planets – the sun and the moon –
you come from Agni – fire and lightning –
the thunderbolt – experience the freedom
of bliss and victory – you come from Prajāpati –
and are composed of moonlight –
bring fire to the Earth – and belong to the light –
the clearness of your eyes are apart from the gloom
and eclipse of the ignorant – and you are shrouded
in the darkness of Kṛṣṇa –
some say that the Highest wisdom
is to be known and learned –
that one will approach her and become intoxicated –

that your destiny is fixed
and you are suitable for her –
the heart is the seat of feeling and sensation,
and one learns the science of the Vedas through it –
and they will be torn from where they stand,
as the arrow is directed straight at the heart.

§

Text 19

iti kṣetraṃ tathā jñānam jñeyaṃ coktaṃ samāsataḥ
mad-bhakta etad vijñāya mad-bhāvāyopapadyate

-

She is the soil – the field –
she is home and the place of pilgrimage –
she is fertile and the orbit of two planets –
wisdom is to be known, learned – and understood –
she is Sanskrit – and reconciliation –
she is concise, and euphonic harmony –
be devoted, through Me – and yet apart –
for I am the science of becoming – of being –
and transition to the True Reality –
that of love and affection, worship and desire –
that of pleasure and attachment – of knowledge
and wisdom – of meditation and contemplation –
We are the Supreme Being –
and one bows before Her feet.

§

Text 20

prakṛtiṃ puruṣaṃ caiva viddhy anādi ubhāv api
vikārāṃś ca guṇāṃś caiva viddhi prakṛti-sambhavān

-

Know Prakṛti and the Puruṣa –
the two who are without beginning –
who are emotion and passion –
and provide destruction for those who transgress –
know Prakṛti and the cause of being –
birth, life – and the two who are one.

-

Commentary

There is a running theme that Prabhupāda had a gut reaction to much of the Vedas, including – if not especially the Gītā – as he shied away from the actual meaning of texts and overlaid his own experience in his marriage. He had an aversion to the natural world – vikāraḥ refers to emotion and passion – it refers to the union between the married couple – it refers to the death penalty – it refers to disease – and the grimace or contortion of the face. This was his general reaction to the concept of the enjoyment of life and he has a running theme of envy throughout his works. He created an institution that attempts to prevent others from enjoying life – and instead taught them to crave death and to reject family life (for those who actually follow his rules and guidelines – they are probably few, but I have certainly met some myself). One will note that the association of the above words with vikāraḥ refer simultaneously to the transformation that occurs in life between two who love and understand one another – and provides the general Vedic solution for dealing with those who are diseased, as well as the reaction of the healthy when seeing or smelling them. The Vedas, including the Gītā, teach us to worship the Divine and to enjoy life – as we will experience the next one and will enjoy it, as well – or this one is our last (no one really knows for sure). There is also a running theme throughout his work that he was not educated in terms of the timeline of the śāstra, as he continually referenced concepts that were introduced into Indian society well after the authoring of the Gītā, and he seemed to have missed the fact that most of the Gītā actually talks about ridding the world of people like himself (and those who violate others in various ways). And it is of course interesting to note that many of his sannyāsins actually prey upon the weak, as well as the abandoned within some of the marriages destroyed by ISKCON doctrine and policy.

§

Text 21

kārya-kāraṇa-kartṛtve hetuḥ prakṛtir ucyate
puruṣaḥ sukha-duḥkhānāṃ bhoktṛtve hetur ucyate

-

All are a part of the universe – reality –
and are responsible for their actions –
as humanity was gifted with free will.

§

Text 22

puruṣaḥ prakṛti-stho hi bhuṅkte prakṛti-jān guṇān
kāraṇaṃ guṇa-saṅgo 'sya sad-asad-yoni-janmasu

-

I exist within Prakṛti – and She in Me –
We are devoted to one another
and enjoy the other – We worship together
and find fulfillment –
those who come from Prakṛti
are born from the strings of Her instrument –
and rebirth comes through devotion –
attachment, affection and the union
between the father and mother –
all enter the world through the yoni.

§

Text 23

upadraṣṭānumantā ca bhartā bhoktā maheśvaraḥ
paramātmeti cāpy ukto dehe 'smin puruṣaḥ paraḥ

-

Knowledge of the divine
is found in thought and worship – together,
in union – and at the other's feet –
one worships the other – and both
the mother and father bear and preserve –
protect – and govern –
I am Maheśvara – the Highest Self –
and you are Our thought –

preserving life together is your highest duty.

§

Text 24

ya evaṃ vetti puruṣam prakṛtiṃ ca guṇaiḥ saha
sarvathā vartamāno 'pi na sa bhūyo 'bhijāyate

-

One knows Me through music –
and lives in the present –
one becomes greater
in composing songs of praise –
and the Highest composition
is that of rebirth
and love of the other –
again and again.

§

Text 25

dhyānenātmani paśyanti kecid ātmānam ātmanā
anye sāṅkhyena yogena karma-yogena cāpare

-

In meditation and reflection, in contemplation
of the inner mūrti – one sees, perceives,
worships, praises – partakes of and experiences –
and sings in adoration –
two are one in body and soul
and with the heart

experience the yoga which has no rival –
and no superior –
again and again.

§

Text 26

anye tv evam ajānantaḥ śrutvānyebhya upāsate
te 'pi cātitaranty eva mṛtyuṃ śruti-parāyaṇāḥ

-

Two live together – We have existed
for all of eternity – I am the ram –
and Mangala – I am He who drives the chariot –
and the cowherd – I am Agni –
I am the Trimūrti – I am Indra –
and I am Kāma and belong to My moon –
all listen to the divine music of infinite fire
that permeates the universe –
and pass through – overcome – conquer –
obtain and surpass –
and two walk together – on the Highest path –
approaching the sun
and in listening – they become twins.

§

Text 27

yāvat sañjāyate kiñcit sattvaṃ sthāvara-jaṅgamam
kṣetra-kṣetrajña-saṃyogāt tad viddhi bharatarṣabha

-

One composes songs of praise –
as frequently as one likes –
two are constant and immovable
in their yoga with Truth and the sacred –
and move together – knowing the body –
and heart – they cultivate the soil –
in yoga together they pierce the veil of māya,
Arjuna, prince and bull of the rain clouds of Bhārata.

§

Text 28

samaṃ sarveṣu bhūteṣu tiṣṭhantaṃ parameśvaram
vinaśyatsv avinaśyantaṃ yaḥ paśyati sa paśyati

-

Two are the same – they are right for the other
and do everything together – they are prosperous
and constant –
I am Parameśvara – I provide life and death –
one sees, partakes of, experiences – and worships –
the other.

§

Text 29

samaṃ paśyan hi sarvatra samavasthitam īśvaram
na hinasty ātmanātmānaṃ tato yāti parāṃ gatim

-

In seeing the other – one worships and praises –
two are the same, and are one –
together they stand firm in monogamy
and devotion – they worship, again and again –
one does not harm one's personal incarnation
of the Divine –
one does not hurt one's self – and one
moves together towards the Highest.

§

Text 30

prakṛtyaiva ca karmāṇi kriyamāṇāni sarvaśaḥ
yaḥ paśyati tathātmānam akartāraṃ sa paśyati

-

Prakṛti – is all of existence,
as well as karma –
She surrounds you completely on all sides
and is everywhere –
one worships the Self –
and the self is not the agent of action,
as two are one –
one sees, and worships – one learns, and
understands –
one sings in praise – one is married –
and one brings forth life and joy into this world.

§

Text 31

yadā bhūta-pṛthag-bhāvam eka-stham anupaśyati

tata eva ca vistāraṃ brahma sampadyate tadā

-

One comes from Me – I flow
into all of existence –
two are separate – and yet one –
one transitions into and becomes the other –
and live together, in one home –
in perfect devotion – engaging in continual worship –
I am the diameter of the circle – I am unity
and the measure of its dimension –
two bow together, before one's feet.

§

Text 32

anāditvān nirguṇatvāt paramātmāyam avyayaḥ
śarīra-stho 'pi kaunteya na karoti na lipyate

-

You are without beginning –
and pour forth your music –
you are made of Rādha-Kṛṣṇa –
and are imperishable, and worship soma –
be yourself, as two, Kaunteya –
one does not anoint oneself – but are rather
anointed by the other.

§

Text 33

yathā sarva-gataṃ saukṣmyād ākāśaṃ nopalipyate
sarvatrāvasthito dehe tathātmā nopalipyate

-

Everything flows from the subtlety of Brahman –
but one is not anointed by that which
comes from on high –
but rather by that of the other, who sits
at one's feet.

§

Text 34

yathā prakāśayaty ekaḥ kṛtsnaṃ lokam imaṃ raviḥ
kṣetraṃ kṣetrī tathā kṛtsnaṃ prakāśayati bhārata

-

Bhārata –
one causes her to shine in brilliance –
you are identical, and twins – you are
one and the same –
her belly will be as full as the sun – she is your wife –
and she causes you to shine in brilliance, as well.

§

Text 35

kṣetra-kṣetrajñayor evam antaraṃ jñāna-cakṣuṣā
bhūta-prakṛti-mokṣaṃ ca ye vidur yānti te param

-

She is the Lord of the soil –
She is the soil of merit – she is Prakṛti –
two know one another – and experience
jñānam within –
you are a match for one another – as you
are two sakhīs – she provides liberation
and salvation – and self-awareness –
you are attentive to one another – and wise –
achieve the Highest –
you have children – and move through life
together, as a family.

Chapter Fourteen

Text 1

śrī-bhagavān uvāca
paraṃ bhūyaḥ pravakṣyāmi jñānānāṃ jñānam uttamam
yaj jñātvā munayaḥ sarve parāṃ siddhim ito gatāḥ

-

Śrī-Bhagavān said:

I offer the wisdom of the wise –
that two are abundantly furnished
with an inner impulse and eagerness –
one is inspired by the music of the Highest tone –
and she in turn is inspired by yours –
in knowing one another, two reach Success
and Perfection – they remember one another
in mutual recognition – and the two approach
one another in prayer and worship –
time passes, but they walk a path –
one of connection and understanding –
and look ahead – towards celebration.

§

Text 2

idaṃ jñānam upāśritya mama sādharmyam āgatāḥ
sarge 'pi nopajāyante pralaye na vyathanti ca

-

One worships at the feet of Śrī – she provides
rest and support – and a gift – the holiness
of the body –
She is a provider, and offers dharma –
and the usual and customary donation
offered to Agni – for those who violate
and transgress – She unleashes the herd –
and the race of the horse – two, as one –
worship Indra – the wind – and armed with
the implements of war – provide the Visarga –
they are destined for one another – My people
are destined for the stars – and Her poison
is ineffective against the demon – but she rather
spits venom, instead –
the enemy trembles, as they have gone astray –
and My tongues will lick and dry their blood –
as they will find mokṣa –
and dissolution into Brahman – Oṃ.

§

Text 3

mama yonir mahad brahma tasmin garbhaṃ
dadhāmy aham
sambhavaḥ sarva-bhūtānāṃ tato bhavati bhārata

-

Bhārata –
My yoni provides abundance – I am the Mother
of the herd – I am Brahman – I am Kṛṣṇa –
one goes to the night quarters –
one conceives in joy –
I bestow, I grant, I give – I am Union – I am the climax

of His story and song –
and all who exist, all who have existed –
belong to Me – I am welfare, I am prosperity –
I am happiness – I am Lakṣmī – I am Rādhā –
I am Bhavatī – His other and complimentary half.

§

Text 4

sarva-yoniṣu kaunteya mūrtayaḥ sambhavanti yāḥ
tāsāṃ brahma mahad yonir ahaṃ bīja-pradaḥ pitā

-

Kaunteya –
all find union in her mūrti – and
in the yoni – all belong to the mother –
I am Brahman – I am Kṛṣṇa – I am the cow,
and abundance – I grant, bestow and offer –
I am the great man – I am the great woman –
and I am the Yoni – and the seed and mantra
of the universe – I am heaven – I am the Earth –
I am the father – I am the mother –
and We are the parents of all.

§

Text 5

sattvaṃ rajas tama iti guṇāḥ prakṛti-sambhavāḥ
nibadhnanti mahā-bāho dehe dehinam avyayam

-

I am the purity of the air – I am pollen –
I am phalam – passion – affection –
the darkness of the night sky – and the clouds
which bring forth the harvest –
I deprive the wicked of their vision – all achieve
union in the music of Prakṛti –
and bind the evil doer,
in preparation for the sacrifice –
and join together, within – I am the measure –
the scale – I have many arms –
two create life – a gift from Śrī – I am the soul –
the ātman – I am imperishable –
and I am soma.

§

Text 6

tatra sattvaṃ nirmalatvāt prakāśakam anāmayam
sukha-saṅgena badhnāti jñāna-saṅgena cānagha

-

There is purity and truth
in throwing away the japa mālā – as it represents
impurity and filth – and is for the unbeliever,
the godless – I am illumination, radiance –
the shining of the sun – the Light Bearer –
I am Rāma – and one gallops through life –
for it is quite short – one punishes the wicked
and the evil – one binds their hands
and prepares them
for sacrifice – there is wisdom in attachment –
and devotion, worship and praise.

§

Text 7

rajo rāgātmakaṃ viddhi tṛṣṇā-saṅga-samudbhavam
tan nibadhnāti kaunteya karma-saṅgena dehinam

-

Kaunteya –
know the passion of the rāgā –
the Song of Desire – one is thirsty
for attachment and union – two become one
and produce milk – one punishes
the evil doer – and seeks unity –
children come into this world through action –
and the soul is enveloped by the body –
cling to her – for she is yours
and composed of the Music of the Universe.

§

Text 8

tamas tv ajñāna-jaṃ viddhi mohanaṃ sarva-dehinām
pramādālasya-nidrābhis tan nibadhnāti bhārata

-

Without wisdom, one lives in
the darkness of gloom and sorrow –
know the Light – that of the sun,
the universe – the purplish, the black –
gold and that of the stars –
her song is that of the seductress –

She is temptation – and offers her wisdom –
she is the measure, the scale – she dances,
and will teach one to dance – like Mohan,
one frolics in the embrace – one sports
and plays in the passion of līla – and She
appears – like the rising of the Moon –
Her rest brings sleep, and peace – and she
binds you within, in the union of yoga – Bhārata.

§

Text 9

sattvaṃ sukhe sañjayati rajaḥ karmaṇi bhārata
jñānam āvṛtya tu tamaḥ pramāde sañjayaty uta

-

Two are happy – one is pure –
one conquers – war is sacred and holy,
for it brings peace –
live in affection – and passion – emotion –
worship her – worship the night – worship the day,
spring, summer, autumn – and winter, Bhārata –
there is wisdom in shutting the door – of taking
the enemy captive, and binding his wrists –
she provides intoxication and madness –
there is insanity in gambling –
for there is a yajña that She provides –
instead, throw the dice –
conquer in My name – and be a rāja.

§

Text 10

rajas tamaś cābhibhūya sattvaṃ bhavati bhārata
rajaḥ sattvaṃ tamaś caiva tamaḥ sattvaṃ rajas tathā

-

In living – and becoming – Bhārata –
one experiences passion, love, desire,
the darkness and calm of the night –
the purity of Truth –
and one becomes music.

§

Text 11

sarva-dvāreṣu dehe 'smin prakāśa upajāyate
jñānaṃ yadā tadā vidyād vivṛddhaṃ sattvam ity uta

-

All are reborn through parents –
two fashion a body together –
and enjoy the open air, the breeze –
sunlight and laughter – the music
of chimes resounding over the meadow –
one composes music, at her feet – songs
of love and affection, desire – and creation –
one wants to know Her – and her wisdom –
those who are strong – those who are adults –
understand that joy – and dance –
are preserved in pruning the Tree – to cut off
and tear asunder the growth and abscess
which afflicts it – know purity and Truth –
and fight like a man.

§

Text 12

lobhaḥ pravṛttir ārambhaḥ karmaṇām aśamaḥ spṛhā
rajasy etāni jāyante vivṛddhe bharatarṣabha

-

One sheds tears of devotion
for her – one composes music
and sings in joy – one desires, one loves –
one offers affection and attachment –
one takes her hand in yours – and
there is a common practice, a customary yajña
for those who envy – for those who transgress –
peace comes through action – one longs
to cure the disease – to heal, to make whole –
one delights in choice – all have free will –
one cuts out the disease, one severs
the arteries and the veins –
one cuts off the head –
one tears out the heart –
and she swells in desire –
and longs for your return home –
Arjuna, prince and bull of
the thunderstorms of Bhārata.

§

Text 13

aprakāśo 'pravṛttiś ca pramādo moha eva ca
tamasy etāni jāyante vivṛddhe kuru-nandana

-

Those who cannot see the Light – those
who do not understand Darkness –
tend to be careless with their lives –
you are Her wonder and amazement –
and in My name – all hasten towards
repopulation – one provides
for the demon – and severs his head –
be happy – enjoy life to its fullest –
and provide prasādam for the Earth.

§

Text 14

yadā sattve pravṛddhe tu pralayam yāti deha-bhṛt
tadottama-vidāṃ lokān amalān pratipadyate

-

In purity – and in honor of Truth –
one provides execution for the demons –
and is exalted and joyful
in enforcing and preserving dharma –
one is the cause of dissolution –
and the setting of the stars –
one is also the Preserver – and She bears
and supports – she procures and provides –
She is the Music of the Universe –
the Highest tone –
those who know and understand humanity –
bow again and again at her feet –
they cast blame –

which is a whisper for some.

§

Text 15

rajasi pralayaṃ gatvā karma-saṅgiṣu jāyate
tathā pralīnas tamasi mūḍha-yoniṣu jāyate

-

In the passion of love and desire –
one moves, continually, towards dissolution –
one loses oneself in the ecstasy
of love – and one creates in joy –
two cling to one another in devotion
and attachment – they merge together
and rest within each other
in the dark of the night –
and from women
all are born – Oṃ.

-

Commentary

It is a well-known fact that the concept of rebirth as an "animal" is a myth that typically only white people believe in. The human soul is Divine and comes from Kṛṣṇa – but unfortunately, some are in fact reborn as animals – which is unfortunate. But with education and decisive justice, we have a better hope for the current and future generations, in trying to cut out the cancer as soon as it is discovered – and in providing a moral and just society for the future. As we all have human nature, some can never be saved – but nurture and education does make a difference for many, if not most.

§

Text 16

karmaṇaḥ sukṛtasyāhuḥ sāttvikaṃ nirmalaṃ phalam
rajas tu phalaṃ duḥkham ajñānaṃ tamasaḥ phalam

-

The morally superior act with virtue –
and slay the demons, indiscriminately –
they are spirited and energetic – they
make their offerings with fire –
and enjoy the autumn night –
they cast blame on the wicked
and unite in passion and love – and provide
their fruit for the Earth –
those who do not know the taste
of the wisdom of women –
are ignorant, unfortunate –
and descend into darkness.

§

Text 17

sattvāt sañjāyate jñānaṃ rajaso lobha eva ca
pramāda-mohau tamaso bhavato 'jñānam eva ca

-

One is born into this sacred existence
through love – and worship –
one knows the clouds, the pollen – the tilled land –
the bounty of the harvest – and the cooling
breeze of autumn –
one desires the other – and two enchant
the other in the seduction of wonder, amazement –
passion and madness –
and become one, together – in the dark of night –
or the light of day –
and one who does not understand this Truth
is ignorant – and blind.

§

Text 18

ūrdhvaṃ gacchanti sattva-sthā madhye tiṣṭhanti rājasāḥ
jaghanya-guṇa-vṛtti-sthā adho gacchanti tāmasāḥ

-

A family ascends together – ever higher –
and moves through life together; they exist
in purity and truth – and two, live together – within –
one has love and affection
for one's family – for one's children –
and parents – and one sheds tears of devotion
for the other – the one who plays her
music for you; and those who are of the lowest class,
the filthy and diseased – the ignorant
and the godless – the demons, the wicked and
those who do not know Me –
descend into darkness.

§

Text 19

nānyaṃ guṇebhyaḥ kartāraṃ yadā draṣṭānupaśyati
guṇebhyaś ca paraṃ vetti mad-bhāvam so
'dhigacchati

-

Without the other – the sukhī –
one cannot create – one who sees well,
is a judge of the other –
and one worships alongside the other,
composes songs of praise – and offers
love and affection – and one creates –
through music; one knows and understands
the Highest through Me – in the heart and mind,
with the senses – in contemplation of the Divine –
in continuous being, living, loving – and becoming –
one ascends towards the Highest.

§

Text 20

guṇān etān atītya trīn dehī deha-samudbhavān
janma-mṛtyu-jarā-duḥkhair vimukto 'mṛtam aśnute

-

One moves towards that which is superior
in listening to Her music –
she is the riverbank – the rampart –

and all create life together,
with the couple – and the community –
as the righteous burn the demons alive – or dead –
and those consumed in flame
are the Twins – She consumes
and digests the unbeliever – the wicked –
those who transgress –
and they savor the nectar of the amṛtam
of saṃsāra.

§

Text 21

arjuna uvāca
kair liṅgais trīn guṇān etān atīto bhavati prabho
kim ācaraḥ kathaṃ caitāṃs trīn guṇān ativartate

-

Arjuna said:

Also – with the liṅgam
we aspire towards the Trimūrti –
and learn the Vedas –
two move together and approach
the other in prayer – love and desire –
the Lord is an image of Kāma – and one
is moved by Her grace –
and in the music of Gāyatrī –
one aspires, one lives – and one loves.

§

Text 22

śrī-bhagavān uvāca
prakāśaṃ ca pravṛttiṃ ca moham eva ca pāṇḍava
na dveṣṭi sampravṛttāni na nivṛttāni kāṅkṣati

-

Śrī-Bhagavān said:

One sheds tears of devotion –
and shines brightly for one's enchantress –
and shares wonder and amazement –
for she is your Sīta – and your match –
one desires and longs for her – and strives
to attain – one waits, one hopes –
and she teaches through her soma –her mystery,
her music and in excitement.

§

Text 23

udāsīna-vad āsīno guṇair yo na vicālyate
guṇā vartanta ity evaṃ yo 'vatiṣṭhati neṅgate

-

She has the resemblance of the āsana –
that of the lotus – and she is
the flower of Agni –
she moves you through her music –
and causes the tears of devotion to flow –
one is devoted to that which is on High,
the grace which descends –
and no one can separate the compound word.

§

Text 24

sama-duḥkha-sukhaḥ sva-sthaḥ sama-loṣṭāśma-kāñcanaḥ
tulya-priyāpriyo dhīras tulya-nindātma-saṁstutiḥ

-

You are identical – and remain
together in sorrow and misfortune –
as you are her friend –
the two belong together, and are twins –
she is your stone – your gold –
your tilaka – and is fortune and prosperity –
the filament of the lotus, the temple –
the marriage vow – and you are both the same
and of the same value – she is well-bred and noble –
and the intelligent revile and spit
on the other men, who are not dear –
and remain together in shared divinity
and worship of the other – and together,
sing in celebration, praise – and in love of the Divine.

§

Text 25

mānāpamānayos tulyas tulyo mitrāri-pakṣayoḥ
sarvārambha-parityāgi guṇātītaḥ sa ucyate

-

It has been said, that two are alike
in their arrogance and pride – they stand together,
noble, proud and haughty – and together,
they revile the filthy –
the barren and the joyless –
they are fit for one another, and one in the dance –
they are faithful, and attached to the other –
together, they are Two – they are fish –
the royal elephant, Airāvata – the Nāgarāja –
together they howl and roar and renounce evil
and the wicked – together they worship
and approach one another in prayer and praise.

§

Text 26

māṃ ca yo 'vyabhicāreṇa bhakti-yogena sevate
sa guṇān samatītyaitān brahma-bhūyāya kalpate

-

One who is moved by the Highest –
is driven, like a horse – in bhakti yoga –
and serves, in sevā –
one approaches her music, and visits
the night chamber – and is suitable
and fit – for all of her charms.

§

Text 27

brahmaṇo hi pratiṣṭhāham amṛtasyāvyayasya ca
śāśvatasya ca dharmasya sukhasyaikāntikasya ca

All come from Brahman –
I exist in the eternal nectar
of soma –
I am eternal – I am heaven
and I join you on Earth, in this lifetime –
and I provide the happiness of dharma –
for she is near you – she is your twin –
and one executes the evil-doer
in My name.

Chapter Fifteen

Text 1

śrī-bhagavān uvāca
ūrdhva-mūlam adhaḥ-śākham aśvatthaṃ prāhur avyayam
chandāṃsi yasya parṇāni yas taṃ veda sa veda-vit

-

Śrī-Bhagavān said:

The fig tree is a reflection
of humanity –
for its branches rise upwards,
and provide shelter for our horses –
we value rest
and food for the stallion and mare,
as the best horses found their origin
in the Indus and the Sarasvatī –
likewise, its roots descend
and invade the foundation of others –
be passionate – love soma –
enjoy the feathers of the peacock,
the betel leaf – and one who has known
the Vedas attains perfect knowledge –
that of being gracious, kind – one knows
how to worship and compose songs of praise –
one adores the position of the stars
and planets – one penetrates –
one implements justice –
and one is the friend of Indra.

-

Commentary

It is a well-known fact that Jesus was educated in India. The Indian fig tree (the banyan) represents all of humanity. In the story told by Jesus, he saw that it did not provide fruit for him – and so he cursed it. The teachings of Jesus and his church represent Satan – the Adversary.

§

Text 2

adhaś cordhvaṃ prasṛtās tasya śākhā
guṇa-pravṛddhā viṣaya-pravālāḥ
adhaś ca mūlāny anusantatāni
karmānubandhīni manuṣya-loke

-

The branches extend upwards –
and the roots below – as the enemy
moves across the land – one meets them,
and prunes the tree –
as this is our kingdom – our land –
and it is rightfully ours –
there will be new growth, new branches
and new leaves –
existence is sacred and one lives
alongside Kṛṣṇa –
and in action, one punishes the evil-doer –
one beholds, recognizes – comprehends –
one is a husband and lover –
one adores in song and composition –

one conceives, worships, praises –
and one provides for the care
of the Tree.

§

Text 3

na rūpam asyeha tathopalabhyate
nānto na cādir na ca sampratiṣṭhā
aśvattham enaṃ su-virūḍha-mūlam
asaṅga-śastreṇa dṛḍhena chittvā

-

The branch we see before us
is not beautiful – and one seizes it,
and it meets with its fate – and this
is a gift, we provide – to honor life –
there is a limit, a boundary – a fence –
and a beginning – for the first fruit,
and the foals and calves –
stand fast – near our tree –
be as firm as the placement
of the stars and planets –
for our people, will rise up,
we will germinate the land
and provide offspring for the Earth –
act without attachment –
and in worship and praise
lift the knife, the sword and the arrow –
honor and worship her in thought, in song –
and prune the Tree.

-

Commentary

While there are certain markers that identify Vedic Sanskrit, such as differences in morphology, there are also different meanings applied to certain words – whether those are particles, nouns or verbs. In this translation of the Bhagavad Gītā, when texts are clearly derived from a previous oral tradition predating the actual written text of the Gītā, then I have used the Vedic meanings, rather than the Classical – unless the text was clearly written entirely during the Classical period. Nearly all writing commentaries in Sanskrit preserved the original message of the Vedas – and we did not have the current problem of the rejection of the meaning of the original Vedic texts until literature began appearing in more modern languages. But for those who carefully look at the meanings of words in their various contexts and when appearing together, then it is actually very easy to sort through the various conflicting meanings and differences in the usage of various particles and the selection of proper verbs if one has the proper education in Vedic theology, the historical culture of India and a solid background in linguistics.

§

Text 4

tataḥ padaṃ tat parimārgitavyaṃ
yasmin gatā na nivartanti bhūyaḥ
tam eva cādyaṃ puruṣaṃ prapadye
yataḥ pravṛttiḥ prasṛtā purāṇī

-

A father searches within – for Her foot –
her verse – her music –
and finds Kṛṣṇa –
many do not find Me, but I did provide
marriage to humanity – each complimentary half –
for the chance of union and discovery,
for worship and adoration at each other's feet –
to live in companionship –
to know tears of devotion –
and to worship and honor, even in the words of men.

§

Text 5

nirmāna-mohā jita-saṅga-doṣā
adhyātma-nityā vinivṛtta-kāmāḥ
dvandvair vimuktāḥ sukha-duḥkha-saṃjñair
gacchanty amūḍhāḥ padam avyayaṃ tat

-

One's enchantress pours forth
her arrogance and pride – the light
of her desires, purpose and mūrti –
and claims herself – in the attachment of night –
she is one's other half –
and they study one another – know and
understand the other – within –
in contemplation and worship –
all desire and pleasure – and enjoyment –
are between the pair

and they are freed from sorrow – and know
one another in happiness – they are one
together in thought and soul –
they have faith and certainty
and move towards the eternal.

§

Text 6

na tad bhāsayate sūryo na śaśāṅko na pāvakaḥ
yad gatvā na nivartante tad dhāma paramaṃ mama

-

She provides illumination –
and one shines like the sun –
one bows before her – the hare,
the antelope – the meteor
which crashes to the Earth –
two race together, at the chariot's helm –
and shine like Sūrya – and flame
together, like Agni – in the passion of the Vedas –
in constant movement and seeking –
they revolve throughout the cycle of the sun,
search for one another in each lifetime – pledge
eternal friendship – uphold the glory
and majesty of dharma – and make a home
together in the splendor of love –
with the Highest Puruṣa – Rādha-Kṛṣṇa.

§

Text 7

mamaivāṃśo jīva-loke jīva-bhūtaḥ sanātanaḥ
anaḥ-ṣaṣṭhānīndriyāṇi prakṛti-sthāni karṣati

-

Her gift comes from Me – the aṃśa svara –
the temple and mūrti – the strum
of her lute and the guṇas upon which she plays –
two jīvas are one, together –
and in all action, and in happiness and prosperity –
the Mother is Eternal –
and provides the meal, one of enjoyment –
the mind, body and senses
are one with Prakṛti – who is one with Me –
drive yourself – plough the land in yoga –
and fall under her power and mastery of love.

§

Text 8

śarīraṃ yad avāpnoti yac cāpy utkrāmatīśvaraḥ
gṛhītvaitāni saṃyāti vāyur gandhān ivāśayāt

-

One finds one's soulmate – the one
who comes from on High – your special
gift from Śrī – through continual
study of the Vedas –
she takes your hand in hers –
in the vow of eternal friendship –
and together, with Kṛṣṇa – one desires
and hungers – and enjoys –
the fragrance of her candan – her tilaka –

which she bestows upon your own brow –
and you do not abuse one another –
and never get out of bed.

§

Text 9

śrotraṃ cakṣuḥ sparśanaṃ ca rasanam ghrāṇam eva ca
adhiṣṭhāya manaś cāyaṃ viṣayān upasevate

-

In hearing, beholding – and in the contact of touch –
two roar – and create music –
and savor the rāsa of perception
and the senses –
they engage in the Highest devotion
in mind and thought – they are fortunate
and their dominion extends as far
as the eye can see –
the reach of the eyes, the ears – and the mind –
and together they serve at one another's feet –
in worship and adoration – and in providing
prasādam for the Earth.

§

Text 10

utkrāmantaṃ sthitaṃ vāpi bhuñjānaṃ vā guṇānvitam
vimūḍhā nānupaśyanti paśyanti jñāna-cakṣuṣaḥ

-

One stands firm – and resolute –
and perseveres on the path towards the Highest –
one gives birth in devotion –
and worships Her music –
those who look towards the afterlife –
are confused; for one looks at that which is before
their eyes – and worships – composes songs of praise
and devotion – learns – teaches –
sees with the eyes – and learns wisdom
through ājñā – and flows down the river.

§

Text 11

yatanto yoginaś cainaṃ paśyanty ātmany avasthitam
yatanto 'py akṛtātmāno nainaṃ paśyanty acetasaḥ

-

Those who know the joy of yoga
enforce the fence – and provide the limit
for those who transgress –
they worship the ātman – her body, heart and soul –
and are devoted to the gifts and favor
which descend from on High –
those who approach the fence
are cut from the Tree –
and those who live in adoration of the Divine –
who compose songs of praise, and engage in
continual kīrtan
with the other – cannot be separated,
and their compound word is not defined
by addition, but rather equal composition –

and they revile the wicked, who do not possess
the splendor of the Divine ātman.

§

Text 12

yad āditya-gataṃ tejo jagad bhāsayate 'khilam
yac candramasi yac cāgnau tat tejo viddhi māmakam

-

The twins move through life –
and are filled with ardor and passion, their
eyes are bright and clear with intellect
and love –
they cause the entire world to shine,
and provide illumination, for one another –
and for humanity –
they do not waste the fertile land, but
rather cultivate it, and tend to the garden
and grove –
they live in the light of the Moon
and in the flames of Agni –
they carry the sword, and appreciate its sharp edge,
the gleam of the sacrificial knife –
know Me – Viṣṇu – Kṛṣṇa – Indra –
and that you belong to Me.

§

Text 13

gām āviśya ca bhūtāni dhārayāmy aham ojasā
puṣṇāmi cauṣadhīḥ sarvāḥ somo bhūtvā rasātmakaḥ

The herd is the community – and we graze,
we sport, we play – we make offerings,
we tend the garden and feed our horses –
we look at the heavens and admire the
light of the stars – we treasure Bhūmi
and we till the land – we are the vast abundance
of those who are made of light,
and sing Kṛṣṇa's glory –
we live in the sun – and we prepare the bow-string –
we aspire towards the heavens
and we admire the resounding roar
of the thunderbolt –
we admire the consuming flame
of Agni – which we first saw, at the dawn of man –
from the lightning bolt –
we are speech, we are music –
we are the wife, we are the bull and we are the calf –
and we flow into Her river – and offer praise
and adoration to Śrī –
and we treasure Truth – reality –
and our own Divine nature –
I am strength and vigor – I am fiery passion –
I thrive, and flourish – I provide sustenance and milk
and the offering made for the newborn babe –
I divide – I conquer – I distribute –
I mix and join with you and make you a better man –
and I am Her mūrti – her form of beauty
and splendor – I am light – and creation
flows from My waters –
I am darkness and the night sky – I am Kṛṣṇa –
I am Rādhā – I am the cure –
I am the entirety of Soma –

all existence is eternal –
and I am made of the taste and nectar of the Divine –
that of soma – that of our people –
and I am the amṛtam of saṃsāra.

§

Text 14

ahaṃ vaiśvānaro bhūtvā prāṇināṃ deham āśritaḥ
prāṇāpāna-samāyuktaḥ pacāmy annaṃ catur-vidham

-

I am Viṣṇu – and I am a part
of man – and I provide for you –
I give you life – and offer the opportunity
to exceed oneself – to shine –
all living creatures provide for the Earth
in procreation and praise –
those who are attached to and devoted
to prāṇā – the Breath of Life –
drink of the nectar of living –
they celebrate –
and two become one, in yoga –
and they enjoy and savor
the precious prasādam of the Vedas –
they worship, honor, praise –
they discriminate and judge –
they offer and distribute –
they provide joy for the Earth –
and execution for the wicked.

§

Text 15

sarvasya cāhaṃ hṛdi sanniviṣṭo
mattaḥ smṛtir jñānam apohanaṃ ca
vedaiś ca sarvair aham eva vedyo
vedānta-kṛd veda-vid eva cāham

-

I am the entirety of existence, I am Truth –
and I live in the heart –
one enters into this sacred existence – some
may experience yoga –
through calling to mind and reflecting
on the inner mūrti – both in her immediate presence,
and in one's Memory – one inquires into the Vedas –
and their sacred truth – all of the Vedas
are found at the end – and those of us who are wise,
built the vedi – for it is strewn with kuśa grass,
and resembles Her divine form, and the curve
of her waist, and the beauty of her hips –
and it is raised on high – for celebration –
and renown – for in our ancient past,
we discovered how to help humanity remember
My law – which is to encapsulate it in one word:
dharma –
and to teach, when necessary –
to provide our offering to Mara and Yama –
whether in token of remembrance
and celebration of the twins – in war –
or on the night of the Aśvamedha.

§

Text 16

dvāv imau puruṣau loke kṣaraś cākṣara eva ca
kṣaraḥ sarvāṇi bhūtāni kūṭa-stho 'kṣara ucyate

-

I am the Puruṣa – She is My twin –
one and one make two –
I am imperishable – I am Viṣṇu, I am Śiva –
and I am Oṃ –
live together, both as two and as one –
and it has been said, that some cannot change –
I am the sword – and the knife –
and I am the jar – which she dips
into the well, and brings forth water –
I am the Highest – and I am Truth –
and for those who are blind –
there is a final blessing – a final offering –
one in honor of happiness and prosperity,
and which serves as instruction –
remain devoted to practicing and performing
all of the ancient rites of the Vedas –
remain in My presence, as the herd of Govinda –
and provide instruction for My enemies.

-

Text 17

uttamaḥ puruṣas tv anyaḥ paramātmety udāhṛtaḥ
yo loka-trayam āviśya bibharty avyaya īśvaraḥ

-

One's own personal incarnation of the divine

is the Highest – and she is the Highest tone –
very healthy and affectionate – beautiful
and worthy of adoration – and those
who are perfectly suited to one another
are both man and woman –
and I exist together with you, in your marriage –
and both the mother and father
worship one another – and love their children –
they support and cherish the other –
they endure – and they experience –
they procreate in love and affection
and provide joy for the Earth –
and they provide for the community,
in both prosperity and justice –
and their bond is as unbreakable as Rādha-Kṛṣṇa.

§

Text 18

yasmāt kṣaram atīto 'ham akṣarād api cottamaḥ
ato 'smi loke vede ca prathitaḥ puruṣottamaḥ

-

All of existence flows from Me –
and two walk together,
they run and they gallop – they
flow together, as one – and approach
the other in prayer, and compose
songs of praise –
I am Kāmadeva – I am the Highest tone –
and I am two –
together, you are the Vedas –
and I provided this Truth for you –

in celebration of Myself –
remain devoted to and engaged in worship
of Me, the Puruṣa.

§

Text 19

yo mām evam asammūḍho jānāti puruṣottamam
sa sarva-vid bhajati māṃ sarva-bhāvena bhārata

-

Two who know Me, together –
are not confused, and they are
filled with faith and certainty –
and a bhakta knows Me, the Purusa,
the Highest tone, the Music of the Universe, Oṃ –
and all experience Truth, through Me –
they contemplate her mūrti, they listen
to her advice and instruction –
they are one in heart, mind, soul and body –
and they study the meaning of the other
and engage in līla, with passion and love, Bhārata.

§

Text 20

iti guhyatamaṃ śāstram idam uktaṃ mayānagha
etad buddhvā buddhimān syāt kṛta-kṛtyaś ca bhārata

-

Bhārata –

She is the most esoteric and mystical
secret – listen to her good advice
and counsel – her teachings, her scripture –
one becomes without sin, through Me –
in listening to wisdom, and practicing
its teachings –
one awakens and is aroused by Truth
and one who pledges eternal friendship
offers love and affection – is wise
and has studied her śāstra – and understands it –
one wants to exist –
one should engage in action,
make the world a better place
and enforce and uphold dharma.

Chapter Sixteen

Texts 1 – 3

śrī-bhagavān uvāca
abhayaṃ sattva-saṃśuddhir jñāna-yoga-vyavasthitiḥ
dānaṃ damaś ca yajñāś ca svādhyāyas tapa ārjavam

ahiṃsā satyam akrodhas tyāgaḥ śāntir apaiśunam
dayā bhūteṣv aloluptvaṃ mārdavaṃ hrīr acāpalam

tejaḥ kṣamā dhṛtiḥ śaucam adroho nāti-mānitā
bhavanti sampadaṃ daivīm abhijātasya bhārata

-

Śrī-Bhagavān said:

I am Truth – I am Durgā –
together the community purifies, and cleanses –
and rights the wrong –
and the wisdom of yoga
is that the righteous stand firm –
remain together and live in love –
they give themselves to each other in marriage –
they become one and aspire towards the Highest –
and provide their gift –
they keep the home, and provide stability –
they exhibit self-control and restraint –
and they also practice liberality
and offer the wicked and evil-doers to Agni –
but they practice austerity
in that they execute without cruelty –
there is some truth
in not displaying anger, as

one can show compassion, and pity
for the one who sacrifices his life –
for he did not cook his dāl long enough –
and he is of mixed caste –
and one can offer a song – in celebration
of the end of his life –
the scorpion stings the wild animal –
and the bee produces honey –
one feels shame and embarrassment for the demon
and quite gentle when binding his wrists –

Bhūmi is patient – she suffers and endures –
but we also have fire – and the knife –
we are moral and righteous – we value true gold –
the human brain and soul – the venerable
and dignified seize the demon,
and hold him captive –
and find contentment and joy in Resolution –
we find Satisfaction in the offering –
and we purify the demon's mind –
and show respect and honor
for that which he fancies – and which he
believes that he possesses –
My Divine power and will is that of the rāṇī
and She is the Highest – and has always
borne, given birth and nurtured you –
and she also gave birth to karma – Bhārata.

§

Text 4

dambho darpo 'bhimānaś ca krodhaḥ pāruṣyam eva
ca
ajñānaṃ cābhijātasya pārtha sampadam āsurīm

-

Deceit – is met with Pride,
who belongs to Dharma –
and the holiest measure –
the cord; the demon's hair
is disheveled – for he lives in squalor –
those who enter the grove of Indra
are met with the strong, and the haughty –
those who sing the glory
of the rājasūya – and who live together,
at each other's feet –
they know true fortune and prosperity,
which belongs to Her, Lakṣmī –
and the unbeliever, who does not possess wisdom,
has to purchase his wife – with coin.

§

Text 5

daivī sampad vimokṣāya nibandhāyāsurī matā
mā śucaḥ sampadaṃ daivīm abhijāto 'si pāṇḍava

–

She is celestial – and provides completion –
in the union of one and one, which make two –
the demon is provided liberation –
and she binds you within –
the demon is considered fit for the fire,
she is your destiny – and she flames
and burns – we gather about the fire,
and we mourn – we lament – we are

filled with sorrow – but also joy – for we are pure,
we are bright and we shine like the stars,
the sun and the moon –
our knife is ready at hand –
and blessed in the name of Airāvata – the Nāgarāja.

§

Text 6

dvau bhūta-sargau loke 'smin daiva āsura eva ca
daivo vistaraśaḥ prokta āsuraṃ pārtha me śṛṇu

-

Two are fit for one another –
two declare war
and let loose the herd upon the Earth –
and declare the start of the chariot race
and archery contest on the holy and sacred day
of the rājasūya, Pārtha –
she is heavenly, and divine –
and this is the goblin;
one listens to what is said – and declares him
to be a demon –
listen, learn – and teach.

§

Text 7

pravṛttiṃ ca nivṛttiṃ ca 'janā na vidur āsurāḥ
na śaucaṃ nāpi cācāro na satyaṃ teṣu vidyate

-

One sheds tears of devotion –
and grief – one praises and honors her,
within – and one is occupied with her, continually –
the final rhythm of many verses does end
with the visarga,
something that My wife taught to Rudra, in our
primal beginning;
the demons are not of our people –
they are not attentive – not needful –
they are impure – and have no integrity –
and they do not conduct themselves well,
nor know or understand truth.

§

Text 8

asatyam apratiṣṭhaṃ te jagad āhur anīśvaram
aparaspara-sambhūtaṃ kim anyat kāma-haitukam

-

He does not know truth –
and he does not stand firmly
before the pair –
his people do not know Īśvara –
nor the union of her embrace –
he does not have a wife, on this Earth –
and no gender –
Kāma – desire, love, divine pleasure –
is our cause in this universe,
for the chance of union –
one studies the Vedas diligently,

reflects – one learns, one worships reason –
and learns, not only our cause of joy
in each lifetime, but also –
a means of purification for the unholy.

§

Text 9

etāṃ dṛṣṭim avaṣṭabhya naṣṭātmāno 'lpa-buddhayaḥ
prabhavanty ugra-karmāṇaḥ kṣayāya jagato 'hitāḥ

-

He made his choice – and she made hers –
one sees Truth with ājñā – she values
the pupil of your eye – as they have the
aspect of the stars –
I sustain the heavens – and provide
My grace from on High –
he has lost sight of that which is pure
and noble –
and rejected the beauty
of the ātman –
he is trifling – and ineffective –
My people become mighty –
powerful – and violent –
we are impetuous, formidable – we are
terrible, cruel, ferocious,
high-born and noble –
we are fierce and passionate –
and wrathful –
we are possessed of the venom
of the Serpent –
and spit on the enemy –

I am Rudra – I am Śiva –
all action is dedicated to Preservation –
and devotion, love, affection –
our family, our wives, our children –
and our community –
he was not prepared for that which is to come –
in meeting Me, he will be deprived of his veins,
his arteries – blood flow ceases –
and he will meet his destiny.

§

Text 10

kāmam āśritya duṣpūraṃ dambha-māna-madānvitāḥ
mohād gṛhītvāsad-grāhān pravartante 'śuci-vratāḥ

-

One rests in Śrī – it is very difficult
to be completely satiated –
the enemy is deceitful – and a hypocrite –
there is hilarity in his plans
and motives – and we are intoxicated
with rapture and ardor –
our enchantress and seductress
inspires us to strike back –
in revenge – we grasp the animal
and bind his hands on the night of the Aśvamedha –
one takes a wife, and one is inspired
to swallow the enemy – like the Ghariyal –
the elephant who bathes in the river –
and the whale, that intelligent and noble
creature of the deep –
the enemy sheds tears – for they do not know

the purity and brilliance of Sīta –
they do not have their own sakhī – do not know
the Moon – nor the glow or heat of the fire –
all law serves to support the realm – My dominion –
we live our lives in accordance with dharma –
we cherish the wife – we feed on milk
and have a very consistent diet – we treasure
our one soulmate –
the one who illuminates and builds the home
together – in matrimony and true friendship –
we have regret for the actions
of the demon –
but our fire consumes and devours
the libation.

§

Texts 11 and 12

cintām aparimeyāṃ ca pralayāntām upāśritāḥ
kāmopabhoga-paramā etāvad iti niścitāḥ

āśā-pāśa-śatair baddhāḥ kāma-krodha-parāyaṇāḥ
īhante kāma-bhogārtham anyāyenārtha-sañcayān

-

One has anxiety if one
cannot understand that which surrounds
us, and can be measured – the universe –
and fears death –
for we do provide a fence surrounding
humanity, a limit – a boundary –
and a term – it is Oṃ –
the cycle of the sun –

we kneel at the feet of Śrī
and Kāma consumes the offering –
that offered in love, devotion and affection –
that which comes from the heart –
and you have the likeness of the Divine Mother –
one has hope for peace –
and the demon fears the bonds,
the fetters – the cord –
they lie bound at your feet –
and all are firmly committed
to nurture and support – and engaging
in our sacred thought, consideration of
the Mother – and her wisdom –
I am Kāma – I am Anger, wrath and passion –
I am Huṃ – and the Highest Thought –
all of My people aim for Me –
and She consumes the offering –
your very special duty
is in preserving life –
cling to the other, the one
who is your other half, who completes you –
and the sanctity of our community
is enforced – through law.

§

Texts 13 – 15

idam adya mayā labdham imaṃ prāpsye
manoratham
idam astīdam api me bhaviṣyati punar dhanam

asau mayā hataḥ śatrur haniṣye cāparān api
īśvaro 'ham ahaṃ bhogi siddho 'haṃ balavān sukhi

āḍhyo 'bhijanavān asmi ko 'nyo 'sti sadṛśo mayā
yakṣye dāsyāmi modiṣya ity ajñāna-vimohitāḥ

-

This one likes to eat –
and he will be consumed by Me –
he has been caught – will experience division –

he lays at My feet
and will achieve his aim – he will be sent
back home – and find his own wealth –

I carry the knife – and the twins
beat the drum – they are like two bodies
in the heavens, coming into contact
and alignment – and I carry a hammer
which carries the beat –

the demon will be suppressed –
I will abandon him – for he is the enemy –
I will remove his eye and his head –
he is not like us – I am Īśvara –
and the village elder –
I am wealthy and opulent – and I
love to feast –
I am the nāga – and I am voluptuous –

I am powerful and mighty
and My army is strong –
the enemy will find their aim –
in the heavens, and come to know
darkness – this one will be dressed
and prepared as an offering, and his debt
will be liquidated – I am the Highest object

of attainment – I am the sukhī,
and am My eternal companion –

I contemplate Myself – in adoration
and worship – I long for Her –
and am high-born and noble –
she is your other half –
and a source of unlimited amṛtam
which flows from Me
like an inexhaustible supply of precious milk –
you are worthy of her,
as I am worthy of Her –

I worship in adoration – I am the one
to whom the yajña
is offered, and I am the one who
will lead the sacrifice –
I am the one who consumes the offering
and enjoys it –

I will give her to you, in marriage –
and I teach –
I will rejoice at the happiness of the glad couple –

and the one who has no wisdom
will part from his confusion, delusion –
ignorance –
and infatuation with our wealth.

§

Text 16

aneka-citta-vibhrāntā moha-jāla-samāvṛtāḥ
prasaktāḥ kāma-bhogeṣu patanti narake 'śucau

-

Two – are one –
and he is filled with longing,
he wandered, and was lost
on his path –

your enchantress has a net –
she enjoys catching fish
and birds –
together, you are one
and the same, yet separate –

and the enemy is attached
to certain things –

I am Kāma
and I consume the offering –
the enemy has a moral failing,
and their caste will be taken from them –

they will experience the torment
of the fire – and will find an
end to their pilgrimage –

the twins shine in flame
and are absorbed in contemplation
of the other –

but the enemy, is not pure,
and I will offer no lament.

§

Text 17

ātma-sambhāvitāḥ stabdhā dhana-māna-madānvitāḥ
yajante nāma-yajñais te dambhenāvidhi-pūrvakam

-

Those who are meant for one another
find recognition in the other –
they find wisdom –
and are full of pride –
she is your treasure, your gift –
and two, as one – are intoxicated
in the desire, affection and devotion
of marriage –
they offer sacrifice
and provide a name for their child –
there are many yajñas –
those of love – and those
which provide for those
who are lacking – one worships,
honors, cherishes and adores her
for all of eternity.

§

Text 18

ahaṅkāraṃ balaṃ darpaṃ kāmaṃ krodhaṃ ca saṃśritāḥ
mām ātma-para-deheṣu pradviṣanto 'bhyasūyakāḥ

-

I am Dharma – and I am prideful,

and haughty – I am Anger –
and I am wrathful and passionate –
I am the ego – I am Indra –
and I am Force – I have might
and ferocity –
those who are devoted to Me
join together – they are good parents –
and together, they loathe the enemy.

§

Text 19

tān ahaṃ dviṣataḥ krūrān saṃsāreṣu narādhamān
kṣipāmy ajasram aśubhān āsurīṣv eva yoniṣu

-

I am those who are a rival
for one another – and those who
despise My enemies –
who wound – and are formidable –
without pity – the strong, the sharp
and the pungent –
and the hawk – I am the white-bellied heron –
and the female man-lion –
punishment is found in every cycle
of saṃsāra, for the unholy –
they are not beautiful –
and entirely useless –
and in the divinity of our women,
we find our cause of existence –
and splendor and joy.

§

Text 20

āsuriṃ yonim āpannā mūḍhā janmani janmani
mām aprāpyaiva kaunteya tato yānty adhamāṃ
gatim

-

One descends, to experience
the Divine –
and one brings down
the swing of the axe –
that of the sword – for those
who have fallen and lost their way –
one is born, again and again –
to know Me –
Kaunteya, I am not attainable for some –
and through their own actions,
may find themselves to be diffuse
and spread over the Earth –
they do not aspire towards the Moon
and are of low birth.

§

Text 21

tri-vidhaṃ narakasyedaṃ dvāraṃ nāśanam ātmanaḥ
kāmaḥ krodhas tathā ḷobhas tasmād etat trayaṃ
tyajet

-

There is a door

for those who are wanting –
a place of pilgrimage
and place of torment –
her desire – and anger –
he is confused –
as his wife and children
are still alive –
and yet she does give up –
lets go –
and renounces him.

§

Text 22

etair vimuktaḥ kaunteya tamo-dvārais tribhir naraḥ
ācaraty ātmanaḥ śreyas tato yāti parāṃ gatim

-

One chooses – one may aspire
towards the funeral pyre – or one may
embrace the beauty of the night sky –
and the entrance to happiness and bliss,
which are the Vedas –
a man and hero aspires towards the Divine
and finds her in himself – the one
who is more beautiful than all others,
the most distinguished and venerable –
one to whom one is devoted,
and continually intent up on – one who you
worship – one celebrated in song
and praise –
the father moves towards the Highest,
finds attainment – his refuge and home –

and behaves in accordance with, upholds
and enforces dharma.

§

Text 23

yaḥ śāstra-vidhim utsṛjya vartate kāma-kārataḥ
na sa siddhim avāpnoti na suhkhaṃ na parāṃ gatim

-

Law exists to maintain order –
and it is upheld through teaching –
one who has a soulmate
aspires towards her –
and provides justice
for one who does not hit the mark,
for one who aspires to be liberated –
that one is not happy
and does not reach the Highest –
and the couple, together, invoke Agni's
name in honor of the sacrifice.

-

Commentary

Kāma-kārataḥ is a very interesting phrase. It consists of the base interrogative pronoun (which in the Vedas, does not always actually imply a question, despite a common misconception among some, but it rather is another personal pronoun with a different implication) – combined in compound with three words that together (and have clear divine associations) refer to time, the cakra, the yuga, life, living, love, affection, iron (used in weapons), the sting of the bee and the scorpion, war, Kālī, the water-bearer, the white-bellied heron, pleasure, amusement, delight and the beloved – combined with Kāma, which refers to love, passion, desire, pleasure, Kṛṣṇa, Rādhā and Agni. Prabhupāda may have found the concept whimsical, but one reviewing his work must realize he himself did not have a kāma-kārataḥ of his own – and did not find the Supreme Destination.

§

Text 24

tasmāc chāstraṃ pramāṇaṃ te kāryākārya-vyavasthitau
jñātvā śāstra-vidhānoktaṃ karma kartum ihārhasi

-

Law – and the scale –
are for instruction –
the twins act together –
they judge, and in devotion
they distribute justice
and offer division –
they tear the demon from his seat,
they destroy his home –
he may beg – he may offer his palms
in supplication – and indicate that he
is a poor man –
but the devout and righteous
are worthy of one another –

they are twins – a rāja and rāṇī –
and live together in bhakti yoga
and declare the word of law
and pronounce judgement
on the wicked – all are judged
based on their actions
in accordance with the law of karma
which serves to uphold dharma – My law.

-

Commentary

Prabhupāda for some reason was very fond of the concept of "regulation," but did have a difficult time understanding the śāstras, which outline the nature of God, as well as define law and appropriate punishment. Vyavasthitau does refer to "determining" – as it refers simultaneously to tearing someone from their seat or while standing – or from their position in society – while also referring to two who act together and occupy a high position of authority. Vidhāna does refer to "regulations," as it is a term that simultaneously refers to bhakti, distribution, division and is a command to Arjuna to worship God, while also having implications related to the sword (which refers both to the application of reason and judgement, as well as the physical sword) and also to someone who is wanting or lacking and who begs.

There is a common story told in ISKCON about the "monkey brain" – however, it is commonly told to tell others about how unstable their mind is, as they cannot control the racing of their thoughts and require meditation to calm their minds. In actuality, the "monkey brain" refers to that of the lowest form of evolved primate – and Prabhupāda and nearly all gurus in his overall parampara are excellent examples of those with the "monkey brain."

Prabhupāda was very fond of the notion of "distinction" – there are numerous traditions which teach others to reject the notion of distinction, and instead acquire self-respect and to speak through action and words, rather than seeking fancy trinkets or elevated positions. Many do not learn this lesson – and whether or not it is always obvious enough, they are shamed by their betters, in one way or another – but not all are aware of it. The latter is not always commendable, as others should provide direct advice and counsel to others, but that just does not always happen.

Chapter Seventeen

Text 1

arjuna uvāca
ye śāstra-vidhim utsṛjya yajante śraddhyānvitāḥ
teṣāṃ niṣṭhā tu kā kṛṣṇa sattvam āho rajas tamaḥ

-

Arjuna said:

It is the command
of scripture –
that all aspire towards you –
in worship, adoration and conduct –
that we use the implement
of the śāstras – the sword –
that we have faith and certainty,
that we honor our dead –
and offer none for theirs –
the enemies are before our feet.

Kṛṣṇa – she embodies Truth.

Two turn their eyes toward
the heavens – to the conjunction
and unity of the night sky –
the spring air – the rains which
bring forth the harvest – to the stars –
the sun and the moon –
and towards each other –
with that look –
and experience the passion
of desire.

§

Text 2

śrī-bhagavān uvāca
tri-vidhā bhavati śraddhā dehināṃ sā svabhāva-jā
sāttvikī rājasī caiva tāmasī ceti tāṃ śṛṇu

-

Śrī-Bhagavān said:

Understand the Vedas –
through love and understanding
one becomes the other,
one's soulmate – the Lord –
one has faith and certainty
and loves humanity –
she is one's own – and two
become one, they transition into
the other – and are transformed in love,
affection, desire – and understanding –
shine, together, like Rādha-Kṛṣṇa –
all are descended from My wife – Durgā –
the Lord of the material world –
who embodies the qualities
of passion, desire – spring and autumn –
the night sky – the stars, the heavens
and the eclipse – winter and summer –
listen – and learn –
understand Her –
understand and learn from your
own personal incarnation of the Divine –
your guru, the one who completes you –

the one who you adore.

§

Text 3

sattvānurūpā sarvasya śraddhā bhavati bhārata
śraddhā-mayo 'yaṃ puruṣo yo yac-chraddhaḥ sa eva
saḥ

-

Two wish to provide joy –
and long to give birth –
the beauty of the Lord,
the one who lives alongside you –
is that of the Highest –
two are filled with faith
and devotion in the other –
in the certainty of true love –

Bhārata –

Lakṣmī turns the cows towards
home – and the rāja makes that
move, to the right – towards Kālī –
with his left hand –
he throws the dice
in honor of Her – not to gamble,
but rather in token of good luck
for the future –
I am the Puruṣa – and I am everything
that exists –
and I also provide death.

§

Text 4

yajante sāttvikā devān yakṣa-rakṣāṃsi rājasāḥ
pretān bhūta-gaṇāṃś cānye yajante tāmasā janāḥ

-

All of My people worship Me –
they are pure – and have passion
and desire – they pursue Truth –
and understand their own divine nature –
they guard Indra's palace
against the demons –
they remember the word: dharma –
and they come together –
as one herd –
they sacrifice – they offer –
they worship – they adore the night sky –
darkness –
the universe –
and the Serpent of Wisdom.

§

Text 5

aśāstra-vihitaṃ ghoraṃ tapyante ye tapo janāḥ
dambhāhaṅkāra-saṃyuktāḥ kāma-rāga-balānvitāḥ

-

The sublime and venerable one
tears apart those who do not

obey My law –
and My people illuminate
the world – they come together
in love and marriage – and they
consume the evil-doers in fire –
and two come together
in the warmth and heat of passion –
and provide for their own –
they are united together, in yoga –
as one self –
and they enjoy the desire
and affection of the rāga –
and the might and vigor of the horse.

§

Text 6

karṣayantaḥ śarīra-sthaṃ bhūta-grāmam acetasaḥ
māṃ caivāntaḥ śarīra-sthaṃ tān viddhy āsura-
niścayān

-

Plough the land –
together, in yoga –
adore and worship your gift
from Śrī – the body –
the mind, the intellect –
the emotions and the senses –
worship Truth –
and provide for the community –
for those who do not appreciate
the splendor of consciousness –
then I provide a boundary and limit –

a fence, from My herd –
inquire into the nature of others
and look for the demon –
for they can be judged by their actions –
and with the body –
carry a sword –
and deliver My justice.

§

Text 7

āhāras tv api sarvasya tri-vidho bhavati priyaḥ
yajñas tapas tathā dānaṃ teṣāṃ bhedam imaṃ śṛṇu

-

Listen, and learn –
I bring you the wisdom
of the Vedas –
that of discrimination –
that of bhakti –
that of fire –
and that of the sword –
two give themselves to
each other in marriage –
and are consumed with
the flames of passion –
and for those who do not
appreciate My gifts –
who do not appreciate the value
of duality – and unity –
then it is My will
that they are torn asunder –
severed from the Tree –

and that the lotus flower
of their heart opens, and blossoms.

§

Text 8

āyuḥ-sattva-balārogya-sukha-prīti-vivardhanāḥ
rasyāḥ snigdhāḥ sthirā hṛdyā āhārāḥ sāttvika-priyāḥ

Life – and our health –
is preserved in purity and truth –
in passion and affection,
pleasure and desire –
in the power and force
of our pronunciation –
in the enjoyment of Joy
and Gratification –
that which She offers, my Adorable One,
Mother Kālī – She drinks and savors
the blood of the demon, She cures
and offers salvation – she ravishes
the heart – and is a thief –
She cuts off the cancerous growth
from our Tree – and the demon's blood
swirls about Her tongue in enjoyment
and satisfaction – She is willful and committed
to Her family –
she bestows that precious garland
about her husband's neck –
the one he wears in his heart
and which mirrors the one he offers
in marriage –

and the rings encircling their toes –
the couple offers themselves
to each other, willingly –
find Truth in passion –
and honor the Divine Mother, continually –
for the peace and love that she brings.

-

Commentary

For those using this book to learn to interpret the structure of Vedic poetry on their own – the above text includes numerous references to health, food, healing and the love, support and beauty of women. All of the words in the text are inter-related and include references to the emphatic granting of prosperity and the emphatic act of cutting – music and a particular shape of vessel which bears water – that which is savory, viscous and our life's essence – one who is ravishing and charming, and who steals the heart – the healing of disease – pleasure and satisfaction – the desire to rinse one's mouth out, as well as the joy in doing so – a woman who is strong, firm and intelligent – that special mālā, which only she bestows – and that which is precious and dear: one's family and one's soulmate.

All bring their own perspective in life to translation, in particular with Sanskrit due to the numerous layers of meanings of all of the vocabulary, the fact that the grammar is artificial, but perfectly arranged and balanced, the numerous double/triple/quadruple entendres that may result – and the fact that one must be well-versed in Hindu theology (and also have known the loving embrace of the Divine).

It also may be impossible (at the time of the writing of this book) to really translate the Vedas in any language but English, as it is similarly rich in meaning and that it can also capture some of the more subtle (or not so subtle) nuances of the Vedas through the use of capitalization – something which is not truly possible in German (unless one takes liberties with the language) and there are very few other modern languages which have the same freedom of expression (for example, it is nearly impossible to truly be poetic in French). One exception would be the Scandinavian languages; Icelandic could be a particularly interesting read.

§

Text 9

kaṭv-amla-lavaṇāty-uṣṇa-tīkṣṇa-rūkṣa-vidāhinaḥ
āhārā rājasasyeṣṭā duḥkha-śokāmaya-pradāḥ

-

She is pungent – sharp, and acrid –
made of vinegar – and she is a river,
which flows into the cosmic ocean –
she is warm, ardent and passionate –
impetuous, beautiful – and offers her favor –
she is the warmth of the summer,
she is the desert – and the growing harvest –
in knowing the emaciated,
the unkind, the dirty and the cruel –

She brings violence and death – she belongs
to one who is passionate, and filled with desire –
I am Sorrow – I am Death –
I am cruel and afflict the wicked – I am the flame
which sears and consumes –
I lick the offering, and consume the demon –
and bestow my grace, on you –
my soulmate and husband.

§

Text 10

yāta-yāmaṃ gata-rasaṃ pūti paryuṣitaṃ ca yat
ucchiṣṭam api cāmedhyaṃ bhojanaṃ tāmasa-priyam

-

Durgā – enjoys the torrent
of the river – move, by way of chariot –
and with the arrow, towards your destination
and aim – for those who are not pure,
they who are foul-smelling – the putrid
and those who savor their own fetid
souls – will be made into broth,
a soup – spiced and seasoned
with her wrath –
the kuśa grass purifies – for in two
are found one –

and remember, Bhārata –
that one who has worn out
his welcome – is cast to the forest
and the hills –
but is not holy, and truly lives

in poverty and is covered in ash –

which are the leavings and remnants
of Her divine meal –
that of the offering
consumed by Agni –

one who is fit for sacrifice and oblation
has medha flowing through his veins –
which is enticing to Mother Kālī –
for She enjoys purification –

the mighty aspire towards their destination –
that of the night quarters –
and rest – and peace – in the calm
and eternal mystery of the night sky –

the friends play and frolic
with one another –
as antelope upon the hills,
engaged in līla –

enjoy her river – that endless
conversation and mystery
which refreshes, soothes
and cools – which carries one
through the infinite joy of eternity –
meet again –
and again – anointed in the
wisdom of the Serpent.

§

Text 11

aphalākāṅkṣibhir yajño vidhi-diṣṭo ya ijyate
yaṣṭavyam eveti manaḥ samādhāya sa sāttvikaḥ

-

One who does not know
Her fruit – her scent – and touch –
longs for that yajña –
that one of discrimination
and division – and whose
fate – depending on choice
and action – may be met with
sword and fire –

one who has worshipped her
and known her fertility – her passion –
and desire to provide for the Earth –
approaches in prayer –
and gains by asking –

gallop towards your destination
and achieve your aim –

and be enshrouded
with the quality of passion, love –
affection, desire –
purity and truth.

§

Text 12

abhisandhāya tu phalaṃ dambhārtham api caiva yat
ijyate bharata-śreṣṭha taṃ yajñaṃ viddhi rājasam

One's sacred duty –
for those who are deceitful –
who offer fraud and betrayal –
the trickster –
is to worship and honor
the Highest thought of existence –
that of the intellect and devotion,
prayer – reflection and contemplation –
understanding of her mūrti –
and engaging, together –
in love, affection, passion and desire –
to procreate and provide fruit
for the Earth –
Bhārata, she is the most beautiful
among women – the most honorable,
most distinguished – and superior –
she is high-born and noble,
and haughty in her splendor –
for she looks down from on High –
the hibiscus is in honor of Her –
the tongue which devours, and savors
the heart –
know – understand –
discriminate and judge –
offer oneself to her –
and love her as your eternal friend
and companion.

§

Text 13

vidhi-hīnam asṛṣṭānnaṃ mantra-hīnam adakṣiṇam

śraddhā-virahitaṃ yajñaṃ tāmasaṃ paricakṣate

-

One who is forsaken –
is not ornamented with Her grace –
but is offered as food –
rejected, condemned –
he does not know the
beauty of the heart –
he has no friend –
and the faithful and the righteous
make an offering – and send him
into darkness – they regard, they inform –
and they instruct.

§

Text 14

deva-dvija-guru-prājña-pūjanaṃ śaucam ārjavam
brahmacaryam ahiṃsā śārīraṃ tapa ucyate

-

She is Divine – and offers
rebirth – that of the heart –
and the two of you look
at one another – with the inner eye –
she is venerable, haughty
and proud in speech –
she inspires respect and worship –
she is your guru – and one
bows before her feet –
she is pure and sincere –

honest and frank –
one honors your gift from Śrī
and treats her without cruelty –
you will be moved by Her –
be consumed in flame
and shine like the sun for her –
and she is also violent
and demands respect –
torment the evil-doer
and throw him into the fire.

-

Commentary

Many do not realize that the term guru refers to one who provides harsh lessons, who is very proud and demands respect, who is venerable and that it also refers to a pregnant woman.

§

Text 15

anudvega-karaṃ vākyaṃ satyaṃ priya-hitaṃ ca yat
svādhyāyābhyasanaṃ caiva vāṇ-mayaṃ tapa ucyate

-

One gives way and yields
to tears of devotion and joy –
the sun and moon chase
each other through the heavens –
and she is your light on this Earth –
there is Truth in one's beloved –

in one's other half – one's husband
and one's wife –
she is your prize and reward on this Earth
and two move through life together
building a home – and living –
she is your soulmate – she is your Lakṣmī –
and you pursue the Highest together
and bring children into the world –
both of you are the home, and
those who live in it –
be warm – consumed with passion –
and when necessary –
enforce My law.

§

Text 16

manaḥ-prasādaḥ saumyatvaṃ maunam ātma-
vinigrahaḥ
bhāva-saṃśuddhir ity etat tapo mānasam ucyate

-

Your mind and heart
are prasādam for your soma –
as she is yours, as well –
she is the holy one – sage and wise –
she eclipses, you within –
as you join in love – affection –
and thought –
and the two provide the eclipse
for the evil-doer, as one secures
and protects the home –
two are warm for the other –

but they also remember
the lesson of the coconut, which
was provided by Me – Govinda –
for the mind is the seat of the heart –
and we split the coconut
and torment the demon in fire –
but we can also practice austerity
and just make it very swift and painless.

§

Text 17

śraddhayā parayā taptaṃ tapas tat tri-vidhaṃ naraiḥ
aphalākāṅkṣibhir yuktaiḥ sāttvikaṃ paricakṣate

-

Those who enjoy their wives
and yoga with her –
provide instruction
and lessons for those who
are not wise.

§

Text 18

satkāra-māna-pūjārthaṃ tapo dambhena caiva yat
kriyate tad iha proktaṃ rājasaṃ calam adhruvam

-

A father is proud –
and is as arrogant as his wife –

they honor and respect the home –
and the measuring cord –
they resemble one another
in many ways – and honor
and cherish their sacred duties –
they are warm, like the spring –
and provide Indra's thunderbolt
for those who transgress –
in this world one behaves –
and the couple are moved
in passion – that of the wind –
they honor the newly sprouted
tulasi – they honor each other
with incense –
and they prune the Tree.

§

Text 19

mūḍha-grāheṇātmano yat pīḍayā kriyate tapaḥ
parasyotsādanārthaṃ vā tat tāmasam udāhṛtam

-

Those who are confused
and lose their way, and travel
down the wrong path –
are seized – and bound –
one of our sacred duties,
for one who has truly fallen –
we do say a prayer – for his soul –
as we offer him in the funeral pyre –
and we pray that Kṛṣṇa
smashes his cakra – rendering it useless,

so that he finds true mokṣa –
and eternal dissolution into Brahman –
this wisdom belongs to one
who has had his heart stolen, charmed –
fascinated and ravished –
by his own reward on this Earth,
his own nāga.

§

Text 20

dātavyam iti yad dānaṃ dīyate 'nupakāriṇe
deśe kāle ca pātre ca tad dānaṃ sāttvikaṃ smṛtam

-

Those who love their wife –
remember that they are made in My image –
and offer death and destruction,
when necessary –
for I am Brahman – I am Brahmā, Viṣṇu and Śiva –
one treasures the meadow
and pasture – a father savors
and gulps from the soma vessel – and
treasures its strainer, and the gifts
that it provides –
and one provides law and instruction
for those who do not appreciate
the happiness of the couple, those
who do not treasure My gift, of life;
two sakhīs act together – they pass time
in joy – and contemplate the holy image
of Kālī – for I find Her quite delightful –
as restoring the balance is

quite amusing to Me, Kṛṣṇa –
and two find purity – love – and enlightenment
in their marriage, when they remember
to look at the stars, contemplate –
and worship each other, gazing longingly
into the other's eyes, in passionate embrace.

§

Text 21

yat tu pratyupakārārthaṃ phalam uddiśya vā punaḥ
dīyate ca parkliṣṭaṃ tad dānaṃ rājasaṃ smṛtam

-

The father lives at her feet –
and his special duty
is to both his family – and his soulmate –
she continually offers Herself
to him – in prayer and praise –
worship – and devotion –
again and again –
and the evil doer is given that which
he is due –
affliction – and potentially torment –
for he is forceful and believes himself
to be intelligible – but he is rather
a goblin – a demon –
one who envies, and is full of deceit –
and believes that he actually has worth
to the true believer – who values life, instead –
she gives Herself freely –
as the bride in the prājāpati wedding –
while celebrated by the community,

it is the gift of the future wife – and no other –
and is honored in its beginning,
with a proper offering to the Twins –
to death –
so that we remember to value our own lives,
happiness and peace –
and that it comes at the cost of the evil-doer –
who is really worth so very little
and is equivalent – to the lowest denomination
of currency –
and we remember – we offer him
not only to uphold justice,
but so that the human race
remembers what happens to those who transgress –
the rapist – the unbeliever –
one who does not value life and the existence
I offered, in the beginning as a gift –
and to remember to treasure the bond
between the Divine Couple,
who live out the existence of Rādha-Kṛṣṇa
on this Earth, in My name –
and perpetuate My own purpose in this universe,
which is to ensure Preservation –
and the chance for eternal happiness.

§

Text 22

adeśa-kāle yad dānam apātrebhyaś ca dīyate
asat-kṛtam avajñātaṃ tat tāmasam udāhṛtam

-

Kālī's kingdom – that of the twins –

is founded on action – and love –
for they give themselves to each
other in marriage – in eternal friendship –
and revile the wicked –
and spit on those who reject life –
they give to one another –
and cut the demon from his seat –
they know one another, from birth –
to the extent of their awareness, and wait
for the other to recognize –
they are full of the darkness of the night sky –
of Kṛṣṇa –
and once they recognize one another,
one – or the other – steals the other's heart
and carries it on High.

§

Text 23

oṃ tat sad iti nirdeśo brahmaṇas tri-vidhaḥ smṛtaḥ
brāhmaṇas tena vedāś ca yajñāś ca vihitāḥ purā

-

My law – dharma –
has been taught since
your primal beginning –
it is that of the sword – and fire –
as some do not recall
that they came from Me –
I have always commanded
that you love one another –
to live joyfully –
and worship one another

as if they were Me –
and I provided the Vedas
as instruction – as well as the various
yajñas – and one can choose
to adore Me – and her –
or be torn from your seat,
from where you stand –
and to be cast into the fire –
the body and intellect are My stronghold –
My fortress –
they are sanctified by Me – and Her –
and those who do not appreciate
My gift –
will experience the hand
of the righteous – Oṃ.

§

Text 24

tasmād oṃ ity udāhṛtya yajña-dāna-tapaḥ-kriyāḥ
pravartante vidhānoktāḥ satataṃ brahma-vādinām

-

One whose heart has been stolen
by her –
understands all of My yajñas –
that of the Nāciketa sacrifice –
and that of execution –
as well as rejecting the notion
that I offer any form of sacrifice
for material gain –
as true prosperity comes from
one's family –

Agni purchases the one
who is thrown to the fire –
I lick and consume
that insignificant offering –
that lowest common denominator –
the demon –
and My devotees – accuse –
in observation and discrimination –
and cast judgement – Oṃ.

§

Text 25

tad ity anabhisandhāya phalaṃ yajña-tapaḥ-kriyāḥ
dāna-kriyāś ca vividhāḥ kriyante mokṣa-kāṅkṣibhiḥ

-

Do not nurture the wicked,
for they do not learn –
their action is met with punishment –
and at times, torment –
in devotion, one applies the sword
and the flame –
and the evil-doer purchases his wife – death –
with currency – and those who are devoted
to Me – to Her – and engaging
in continual prayer and devotion, who offer
themselves to each other, and provide
for the Earth, in joy –
they provide mokṣa for those
who long for death.

§

Text 26

sad-bhāve sādhu-bhāve ca sad ity etat prayujyate
praśaste karmaṇi tathā sac-chabdaḥ pārtha yujyate

-

Two merge together, as one –
through yoga – and attain knowledge
of the Supreme – that of Truth –
and Reality –
their senses and mind contemplate
the other – and their bodies –
in love and affection, they compose
songs of adoration – and worship –
they recall the other, and seek the other –
they approach one another in prayer –
and praise the one who provides fortune,
well-being – happiness – and prosperity –
the one most who is Most Beautiful,
and who is Most Auspicious –
in action and words – they appreciate
the sound and thoughts of the other –
and they also – compose eulogies
and songs of praise – for those
who deserve them, at the time of the
funeral pyre, Pārtha.

§

Text 27

yajñe tapasi dāne ca sthitiḥ sad iti cocyate
karma caiva tad-arthīyaṃ sad ity evābhidhīyate

-

In the yajña, one restores the balance –
one offers to Me – one finds unity –
and one provides instruction;
karma was provided by Her, My Durgā –
for humanity, to assist in our shared role
as the Preserver –
and one reflects on her, her mūrti –
her Divine favor and grace,
her beauty – and all that she provides –
and one desires to preserve My law
for all of humanity – to ensure
peace, prosperity and happiness for all.

§

Text 28

aśraddhayā hutaṃ dattaṃ tapas taptam kṛtaṃ ca yat
asad ity ucyate pārtha na ca tat pretya no iha

-

In marriage – one which
honors the devout vaiśya –
we make an offering, to the Twins –
we secure our own faith
in the sanctity of Agni – that of the
offering, the oblation –
that of mokṣa –
and at the end of life,
we celebrate our accomplishments –
in prayer, praise –

and with fire, Pārtha.

Chapter Eighteen

Text 1

arjuna uvāca
sannyāsasya mahā-bāho tattvam icchāmi veditum
tyāgasya ca hṛṣīkeśa pṛthak keśi-niṣūdana

-

Arjuna said:

I aspire to be a great man –
and to seek knowledge of Truth –
one who forsakes Your knowledge –
one who rejects life, and that of
of his people –
the lord of their senses, the mind –
is offered to Narasiṃha –
who has the likeness of the lion
and the hands of the man –
the intellect of Gaṇeśa –
and nails like flint chisels –
and the sannyāsin also has a mane –
that of matted hair
and covers himself in ash –
and is on display, before all –
for he does resemble that whom
he longs to meet – Śiva, the Destroyer.

§

Text 2

śrī-bhagavān uvāca

kāmyānāṃ karmaṇāṃ nyāsaṃ sannyāsaṃ kavayo viduḥ
sarva-karma-phala-tyāgaṃ prāhus tyāgaṃ vicakṣaṇāḥ

-

Śrī-Bhagavān said:

Those who desire one another –
that of the lovely, the beautiful and the agreeable –
they are gifted with insight, are intelligent
and find wisdom –

one who renounces life –
the evil, the wicked –
those who reject My gifts –
they are torn asunder
and offered to Agni –

and there is an ancient custom –
an optional offering
made out of the desire for personal gain –
one made by the wife,
if she decides to invoke the name
of Puṣan – who leads one to the door –

and in all of the above cases,
the proud, the intelligent and the noble –
hold their heads high –
we deprive the evil doer
of prāṇā –
and she thumbs her nose
at her sage and wise man
once she decides to live
the renounced life.

-

Commentary

Vicakṣaṇāḥ is an ancient Sanskrit joke. It includes the concept of a false cognate – and refers to all of the above. There is a trend in very old cultures (such as with the Scandinavians before Christianity, as well as in Vedic India) – which is not very nice and should not be encouraged – it is called "shame culture" – and while no one can escape shame if they do shameful things, making fun of others behind their back and to their face is just not that nice. Everyone should attempt to teach other people things that are true, rather than feeding them with false information. But of course, even if presented with truth, not all understand it for themselves.

§

Text 3

tyājyaṃ doṣa-vad ity eke karma prāhur manīṣiṇaḥ
yajña-dāna-tapaḥ-karma na tyājyam iti cāpare

-

My yajñas have no rival –
and no superior –
two give themselves
to one another
in love and adoration –
commitment and eternal friendship,
in marriage –

and the evil doers
are renounced – judged on their actions –
and thrown to the fire.

§

Text 4

niścayaṃ śṛṇu me tatra tyāge bharata-sattama
tyāgo hi puruṣa-vyāghra tri-vidhaḥ samprakīrtitaḥ

-

Bhārata –
listen, learn and teach –
one has conviction – and faith,
at My feet –
the greatest gift – is the one
you make of yourself, to her,
your venerable one –
there are many forms
of renunciation –

I am the Puruṣa – I am a king,
and a tiger among men –
I am Śārdūli, mother of tigresses
and – I am Airāvata – and I am the Vedas –
through bhakti
My people will become great –
and together they
will be known and celebrated
through their words and deeds,
before all the world.

§

Text 5

yajña-dāna-tapaḥ-karma na tyājyaṃ kāryam eva tat
yajño dānaṃ tapaś caiva pāvanāni manīṣiṇām

-

I am the yajña – I am Viṣṇu –
there are yajñas
for every occasion –
and karma exists –
to instruct –
and I provided both
the libation – and the oblation –
give oneself – to the other –
in love, affection – passion and desire –
in friendship and companionship –
worship one another – and worship Me –
savor the wind, the breeze
and the rush – offer purification
for the unholy – bathe in the Gaṅgā –
worship tulasi, and anoint
the brow of the other with tilaka –
those who are wise
offer themselves continually
to each other in the prayer of praise.

§

Text 6

etāny api tu karmāṇi saṅgaṃ tyaktvā phalāni ca
kartavyānīti me pārtha niścitaṃ matam uttamam

-

All have free will –
all make choices –
some are attached to life
and the fruit that it offers –
and others reject it,
in one way or another –
I bring my people to maturity
and they enjoy the prasādam
which I offer –
and I also cleave the fruit
of the others, asunder –
I illuminate and I am passionate –
all have their artha – and I also created ārtha –
one offers either respect – or condemnation –
and My devotee
adores Her music.

§

Text 7

niyatasya tu sannyāsaḥ karmaṇo nopapadyate
mohāt tasya parityāgas tāmasaḥ parikīrtitaḥ

-

One who renounces life
through action –
does not belong to Me –
bow at the feet
of your enchantress – your seductress –
your guru, who provides
enlightenment, anointment and companionship –

they renounce life
and the splendor of the ātman –
know them by their fruits –
declare My law – pronounce judgement –
and delight in your own
incarnation of Me – the Mātṛkā –
discard the refuse –
and delight in one's lover.

§

Text 8

duḥkham ity eva yat karma kāya-kleśa bhayāt tyajet
sa kṛtvā rājasaṃ tyāgaṃ naiva tyāga-phalaṃ labhet

-

I am Sorrow – and I am Fear –
and I am Ka – I am Prajāpati –

I created the prājāpati wedding
for those who seek –
and find their home –

and one may be afflicted
by her wrath – and scorn –
as she surrenders, resigns –
renounces – and gives one up –

she is the lute – and you are the strings
upon which she plays –
adore her rāgā – her passion and desire –
adore her, cherish her –
worship her feet and the ground

upon which she walks –

one seeks and finds –
one receives – and one attains –
one provides prasādam for
the Earth –
one honors the eternal friendship –
and engages in eternal līla.

§

Text 9

kāryam ity eva yat karma niyataṃ kriyate 'rjuna
saṅgaṃ tyaktvā phalaṃ caiva sa tyāgaḥ sāttviko
mataḥ

-

Arjuna –
your ārtha is devotion
to her – all action –
all thought –
concern her –
cling to her in love
and adoration –
offer yourself
to her – create fruit
together –
offer your breath
to her –
be full of passion and purity –
light, splendor, love and truth –
and you will both
live together –

in love – happiness –
and mutual respect.

§

Text 10

na dveṣṭy akuśalaṃ karma kuśale nānuṣajjate
tyāgi sattva-samāviṣṭo medhāvi chinna-saṃśayaḥ

-

One who does not
know the embrace of the Divine –
may not behave suitably –
even though he may profess
to be a believer, and understand
my decrees –
and those who do know Me – Rādha-Kṛṣṇa –
do not suffer them
to move alongside us, in this lifetime –
your guru is your soma – and she is intoxicating –
she steals your heart – renounces the wicked –
and together –
you will understand Me –
and rest on Śeṣa.

§

Text 11

na hi deha-bhṛtā śakyaṃ tyaktuṃ karmāṇy aśeṣataḥ
yas tu karma-phala-tyāgi sa tyāgīty abhidhīyate

-

My people do not necessarily
desire to torture others –
but they understand My sacred role –
that of Preservation –
and they know the embrace of Śrī –
they offer their breath to the other –
their actions also do not require
the death penalty –
some do sacrifice their own lives –
and offer themselves as a donation
to My fire –
the Highest thought – is that of the other –
and she offers herself to you –
she adores you –
and the two of you do your duty –
which is to uphold My law –
and to engage in eternal prayer.

§

Text 12

aniṣṭam iṣṭaṃ miśraṃ ca tri-vidhaṃ karmaṇaḥ phalam
bhavaty atyāgināṃ pretya na tu sannyāsināṃ kvacit

-

One who desires her –
and has mixed and mingled
with Her in yoga, and the elephant –
and knows its passion
and desire –
understands the Vedas

and sends the one who craves
death into the next lifetime –
and for one who is especially
desiring of death – one contemplates
the Highest Vessel –
and prays for eternal mokṣa
for the unbeliever.

§

Text 13

pañcaitāni mahā-bāho kāraṇāni nibodha me
sāṅkhye kṛtānte proktāni siddhaye sarva-karmaṇām

-

Two moving together –
in ecstasy, and with the haste
of desire – have four arms –
and are the measure of My world –
they are the cause of creation
and continued existence –
they awaken together, within –
in the passion of worship
and adoration of the Divine –
they cannot count the number
of times they receive my blessing,
and have known Śiva –
they hit the mark –
and find attainment –
in all action – and their lives together
are poetry and music.

§

Text 14

adhiṣṭhānaṃ tathā kartā karaṇaṃ ca pṛthag-vidham
vividhāś ca pṛthak ceṣṭa daivaṃ caivātra pañcamam

-

I am the Creator –
I am the Doer –
and man is made in My image –
gifted with reason, intellect,
senses – and a body –
one stands firmly, in aspiration
and in battle –
to protect that which is holy
and sacred –
two become one in matrimony
and are distinguished in their
regard for one another –
they are one in mind and soul
and in body – and yet separate,
as I am separate from you –
and yet you are a part of Me –
and I enjoy the passion of līla
with My Rādhā – for all of eternity –
regard your beloved as sacred,
holy – Divine and celestial –
and the secret of all the Vedas –
and the fifth Veda – is sex.

-

Commentary

For those studying this book, it helps quite a bit to have first-hand knowledge of the ancient and modern culture of India. The current culture closely mirrors that of the ancient culture, although too many within Hindu society have lost touch with their roots – but they do love to say one thing when they mean something else – and love to give compliments and insults without directly referencing what they mean, specifically. It is obvious for those who truly study Sanskrit, that for all of known human history, once man had ample leisure time after the development of agriculture that many in India loved to watch the less intelligent doing physical exercise and engaging in directed or abstract contemplation in the lotus position (and various other poses) – while they were back home laughing while they made passionate love to their wives and husbands. It is also an obvious fact that while there are many stories about polygamy in Hindu mythology, that it was a culture based in monogamy – and that men who did have multiple wives would have been regarded as shameful, because their chosen wife did not throw the others out of the house. An interesting note for those who do have the proper background in Hindu history and culture, is that one should scrutinize all translations and commentaries carefully – so that the most positive elements of our culture will be preserved for the coming millennia and so that we reject the work of those who studied the Vedas without understanding God or history.

§

Text 15

śarīra-vāṇ-manobhir yat karma prārabhate naraḥ
nyāyyaṃ vā viparītaṃ vā pañcaite tasya hetavaḥ

-

She is your gift from Śrī –
and one kneads her feet –
one makes her happy –
one fans her with peacock feathers
and is her servant –
one thinks of her continually
and takes hold of her – rashly –
in the passionate embrace
of vehement desire –
she thinks you are a man
and a hero –
and search within –
in continual aspiration
of the heart –
and two remember the other –
they flow into one another –
they adore – they approach in prayer –
they gain by asking, and they
unite in marriage – and building a home –
and they compose songs of worship
and sing together – they accept
the other and worship one another –
they procreate – and raise a happy family –
and in her choice,
the two find eternal wealth
and prosperity.

-

Commentary

In the final chapter of the Gītā, the author who compiled the original sources and published the final edition in Classical Sanskrit (with of course vestigial elements of the original Vedic "text"), decided to end with clever language. Śrīla Prabhupāda never would have received the message, because the literary style of the Vedas and Classical period were beyond his level of education and comprehension, but many of the words in this text are not real and are instead part of the style found in many ślokas in the Gītā that use a combination of sound and the written word to express Divine concepts without using what we would traditionally think of as a natural or spoken language.

§

Text 16

tatraivaṃ sati kartāram ātmānam kevalaṃ tu yaḥ
paśyaty akṛta-buddhitvān na sa paśyati durmatiḥ

-

The twins are identical –
even in their differences –
she is exclusively your own
and one adores her
and worships her –
she looks into your eyes,
into your thoughts –
and she also worships you –
even if she sees the bad, as well.

§

Text 17

yasya nāhaṅkṛto bhāvo buddhir yasya na lipyate
hatvāpi sa imāṃl lokān na hanti na nibadhyate

-

Move towards her –
for she is also yourself –

I shine and am radiant
like the sun and the moon –
as I am non-different
from My wife –
and yet we are separate –

I am God – I am Prakṛti –

I am the sun – and I am the moon –

I am all of the stars
and I am the fabric of reality –

I make love to Myself continually –
as existence flows from Her
in every moment –
and we come together
and approach the other in prayer –
and we dance as Naṭarāja –
for all of eternity –

meet with her, as the conjunction
of the planets and stars

which come into alignment –
in a Divine – and auspicious omen –

and those – the evil-doers –
they fear the war drum –
and you will execute
every last one of them, in Her name –

she binds you within
and secures her hold on you,
she anoints you in
love and admiration –
for your love equals
that of hers and is returned
in kind –
and she does not punish
the one who completes Her.

§

Text 18

jñānaṃ jñeyaṃ parijñātā tri-vidhā karma-codanā
karaṇaṃ karma karteti tri-vidhaḥ karma-saṅgrahaḥ

-

She is your jñānam –
she is to be known, understood –
and comprehended –
you are her lover
and she surrounds you
completely –
she is the Vedas –
and she invites you

to engage in Her līla –
as she understands
how to continue My creation –
you are separate, and yet
can become one –
and to aid in our shared role
as the Preserver –
I provided the sword –
discrimination –
division –
the eclipse –
and the one who provides it –
of this sacred existence.

§

Text 19

jñānaṃ karma ca kartā ca tridhaiva guṇa-bhedataḥ
procyate guṇa-saṅkhyāne yathāvac chṛṇu tāny api

-

Two fish mingle together
in their respective music
and mantra – they know one
another – in full comprehension –
they know the sun
and dance, in the river,
together as one.

§

Text 20

sarva-bhūteṣu yenaikaṃ bhāvam avyayam īkṣate
avibhaktaṃ vibhakteṣu taj jñānaṃ viddhi sāttvikam

-

Attain the perfect knowledge –
that of the two – who recognize the other –
see one another with ājñā –
and worship one another,
in mutual appreciation, adoration
and respect – who are inspired to compose
and sing songs of praise – and offer
their hands to one another – and join together
as one – they ensure their own well-being
and prosperity in the promise of eternal friendship –
and they are never apart, but engage
in perpetual yoga – they create together,
make the world a better place –
they attain understanding of Her wisdom –
they worship soma –
and their one mind and heart.

§

Text 21

pṛthaktvena tu yaj jñānaṃ nānā-bhāvān pṛthag-
vidhān
vetti sarveṣu bhūteṣu taj jñānaṃ viddhi rājasam

-

Together – two are one –
they move together
and experience wisdom –

they are distinct from one another,
and yet the same –
they penetrate one another in adoration,
they know one another –
they comprehend the other –
they understand Truth –
that of rebirth – passion, desire –
love, affection – and infinite fire –
and they enjoy and savor the amṛtam
of immortality – that of saṃsāra.

§

Text 22

yat tu kṛtsna-vad ekasmin kārye saktam ahaitukam
atattvārtha-vad alpaṃ ca tat tāmasam udāhṛtam

-

Her hips – and belly –
inspire one to visit her –
they have the semblance
of the unity of creation –
two, together – engage in action –
devotion – worship – praise –
together – and as a family –
they provide motivation to themselves,
and their community –
one who does not understand
his origin, where he comes from –
who does not have respect for truth –
is full of ignorance –
and his likeness and actions
inspire one to remember

one's artha and one's ārtha –
he may be insignificant and trifling,
one who is possessed of ignorance –
tends to err and go astray –
and he will not know
the pleasure of the night
and the evening, the embrace of the Divine,
nor have his heart stolen, fascinated –
or charmed – by his own
incarnation of Rādha-Kṛṣṇa.

-

Commentary

We should all remember that in every life-time we have the opportunity to live out the passion and love that Kṛṣṇa and Rādhā experience together – but we must find our soulmate and we must conduct ourselves in our lives in such a manner that we achieve the proper education – and treat others in accordance with dharma – and we need to attract and keep our soulmate.

§

Text 23

niyataṃ saṅga-rahitam arāga-dveṣataḥ kṛtam
aphala-prepsunā karma yat tat sāttvikam ucyate

-

One moves towards purity
and truth – that of the appreciation

of beauty and her music –
and enjoys the gentle guidance and
spurring of her feet –
another does not know the beauty
of Her fruit – and his wife
is filled with hatred and a passionate
desire to cut their bond – renounce him –
desert him – and casts him to the street –
and the other, moves together with
his wife – and aspires towards the Divine –
and together, in passion and desire –
they achieve their aim.

§

Text 24

yat tu kāmepsunā karma sāhaṅkāreṇa vā punaḥ
kriyate bahulāyāsaṃ tad rājasam udāhṛtam

-

One who desires her – Kāmadeva –
lives with her, by her side –
and at her feet –
and acts together, with the one
who provides completion –
and who has stolen and ravished
his heart, again and again –
and one who is ignorant
and rejects My gifts –
meets those who are born
under the stars – who have appreciation
for their sisters –
and they bind him – and cast him

to the fire.

§

Text 25

anubandhaṃ kṣayaṃ hiṃsām anapekṣya ca
pauruṣam
mohād ārabhyate karma yat tat tāmasam ucyate

-

Two live alongside one another
in yoga – and build a home –
and they remember
and treasure the Visarga –
and prepare those who desire
to enter the house of Mara and Yama –
they have no regard for those
who desire to injure –
humanity is sacred to the Puruṣa –
and humanity belongs to the Puruṣa –
your seductress and enchantress
grasps you in ardent desire –
she is rash – in action –
and has a taste for revenge
and justice –
one who is ignorant
and full of darkness –
aspires towards his destination –
and the pair dances together, joyfully –
in the dark of evening, twilight –
the night –
and bathes in the purplish-black
light of the sun.

§

Text 26

mukta-saṅgo 'nahaṃ-vādī dhṛty-utsāha-samanvitaḥ
siddhy-asiddhyor nirvikāraḥ kartā sāttvika ucyate

-

Those who are devoted to –
and attached to their community –
long for the setting of the sun,
and liberation of that quarter of the sky –
that śeṣa which provides for our mutual
happiness, peace and prosperity –
to give up and liberate those who
are not of Me –
they speak – but it is not intelligible –
and their words make no sense –
I pronounce judgement –
through those who know Me –
the powerful, the mighty – the conqueror –
the usurper – one whose hand
firmly grasps the heel of his lover and twin –
do not put aside one's duty –
aspire towards her –
find complete attainment –
provide judgement, through discrimination –
and enforce one's decree, through division –
and remember, that peace and prosperity
come at the expense of the dead man –
who longs to escape from the cycle of saṃsāra –
one speaks through action, and words –
find truth and purity, through passion and desire.

-

Commentary

At the time of the writing of this book, Christianity only constitutes 1/3 of humanity – however, there are some who subscribe to the religion who do believe in God and are good people. Based on the language of the Vedas, if we do not work together in providing moral education for the human race through peace, love and words of wisdom, then 1/4 of the population may be a more appropriate offering to the great beyond in honor of Kṛṣṇa's wrath.

§

Text 27

rāgi karma-phala-prepsur lubdho hiṃsātmako 'śuciḥ
harṣa-śokānvitaḥ kartā rājasaḥ parikīrtitaḥ

-

One who is colored
with the words of the eunuch –
longs for their fruit –
and those who are anointed
with Her music –
long for wisdom –
the hunter seeks those
who would deprive humanity
of purity – those who do not
understand My darkness –
or the brilliance of Sīta –

take pleasure in and thrill at the hunt –
bring fire to those who err –
deprive them of their own śuci offering –
one is what one does –
know and celebrate My prasādam –
the glory of My palace –
as I am Indra – I am Śiva – and I am the Mātṛkā.

§

Text 28

ayuktaḥ prākṛtaḥ stabdhaḥ śaṭho naiṣkṛtiko 'lasaḥ
viṣādi dīrgha-śūtrī ca kartā tāmasa ucyate

-

One who does not
understand My yoga –
who is envious – and deceitful –
tends to creep along the ground
in mockery of My form –
join together in marriage –
offer one another flowers – and feathers –
seek out the wicked – the evil-doers –
and do not allow them to spread
across the Earth – humanity swallowed
poison long ago – Her holy wisdom –
I am Śiva – and I am Mother Sīta –
Gāyatrī – She who gave birth to
and first sung the Vedas –
you have always shone – like the sun –
and frolicked in the Garden –
and the evil are full of darkness
and ignorance –

and they want to steal My fruit –
I am poetry, I am music –
I am the well of eternity –
delight in the kuśa grass – enjoy duality,
and the chance for union.

-

Commentary

This text is evidence that while there are those who are members of the Abrahaminic faiths who are wise – as evidenced by the Kabbalistic and Sufi traditions – that Hindus have anticipated a holy war since at least 800 BC, if not well before. While many Jews are taught to disregard much of the Old Testament as mythology, and instead have been given the keys to wisdom through Kabbalah and the mystical interpretation of Hebrew scripture (at least since the Middle Ages, although mythologically the knowledge goes back to Moses through an oral tradition) – the Jewish faith gave birth to Christianity, whose "messiah" and forefathers did in fact swallow the wrong kind of poison and continue to make a mockery of our own faith. The Gītā anticipates a holy war – whether ideological or in actuality – and shows the enmity between the true believers and those who are ignorant that goes back millennia.

Despite the mythological roots attributed to Kabbalah – it is commonly thought to have existed prior to being written down in the Middle Ages (in the Jewish diaspora) but is thought to only date back a few centuries before the birth of Jesus – which would be parallel to the introduction of pre-Christian

Gnosticism in the Near East. These traditions are of course evidence of either missionary movements from India which are not well-documented, other than those schools of thought which are the product of education – or they are a result of the fact that many cultures in the Near East and the Mediterranean used to send students to India for instruction. Sufism originated shortly after the life of Mohammed but reached its highest distillation of scripture in the Middle Ages (Rumi).

Note that the letter "a" is considered very sacred to Hindus, and it can be both short and long. One key to interpreting Vedic scripture is in understanding sandhi and the use of prefixes and compounds. There is a known Hindu religious tradition of analyzing the texts and taking them apart and putting them back together to arrive at their true meaning. Fortunately, English is incredibly expressive and direct, so for future millennia, not all need to have extensive education in the language in order to understand the true meaning for themselves.

It is also helpful for many ślokas to understand the above concepts and the application of very simple operations in computer programming – combined with the semiotic relationships between a variety of concepts in terms of human nature, theology and language. Consistent with statements made in the foreword to this book, the Sisterhood has been a guiding hand to assist humanity in reaching a higher state of consciousness and self-awareness – but unfortunately, we do have to either educate others, or prune the Tree.

§

Text 29

buddher bhedaṃ dhṛteś caiva guṇatas tri-vidhaṃ śṛṇu
procyamānam aśeṣeṇa pṛthaktvena dhanañjaya

-

In demonstrating their teachings,
and intellect –
we will win allies to our side –
for they will understand, that not only
are their own teachers foolish,
but that we are a proud and violent people –
and we seek Resolution and Satisfaction –
we will demonstrate the lessons of the Aśvamedha –
and bring the entire world back to the Garden –
with music and our sacred teachings
we will show the value of bhakti –
of devotion to Kṛṣṇa –
which includes reason and discrimination,
love, affection – and we
both divide and distribute –

Listen, learn and teach –
for when we tell the world about our plan –
they should understand that in accepting
My teachings
they will free themselves from ignorance
and that we can sever an entire people
from the Tree –
in fire and bloodshed –
and leave their land as a desert –

or that they can win peace and prosperity
through My gifts.

-

Commentary

For those reading this book in the general timeframe of its authorship, note that the last chapter of the Gītā actually contains a variety of prophecies that are consistent with not only all of human history and the general themes found within Hinduism – that it also provides some continuity with many of the events beginning approximately in the 20th century leading to the publication of this book (ranging from the invention of the atomic bomb, the Internet, the Holocaust, the 1960's and a variety of trends in the current age). As many Christians do seem to fancy the book of Revelations, note that this is our view of the Apocalypse – which is to entertain the notion of enlightenment and self-realization, or find mokṣa via Viṣṇu's wrath. As stated through a variety of songs released in the year 2018, all can practice what they preach, they can open themselves to the concept of a universal community based in love, they can embrace the message of the proud and reject the teachings of the diseased – they can cast stones and throw out the wicked and the unbelievers – reject the Christian concept of sin – and instead embrace dharma (and karma) – treat one another with mutual respect and embrace the notion that humanity has a natural caste system – and to rise up against our Adversary – who is best represented as the Christian church, but also represents irrationality, the glorification of the uneducated and the low – and that of the male-centric society that has existed for several millennia. With cooperation between all members of the human race we can move beyond animal sacrifice – and shift from the Age of Conflict – and move back to the Garden of Eden.

§

Text 30

pravṛttiṃ ca nivṛttiṃ ca kāryākārye bhayābhaye
bandhaṃ mokṣaṃ ca yā vetti buddhiḥ sā pārtha
sāttvikī

-

We will provide law –
and rules –
we will inform them
of the Visarga –
and that we can provide
tears of anguish and grief –
or that we can shed tears
of devotion –
we will demonstrate
My method of instruction –
karma –
that all are gifted with free will –
and can choose –
that all can accept that some
are better than others –
but that all are reflections
of the Divine –
that the secret to happiness,
peace and prosperity –

is found in love –
that of others –
and God –
that there is a bond which
unites us – which is yoga –
and that it can be used
to bind and tie – and to punish –
or that it represents marriage –
and the bonds of the community –
one seeks knowledge
and understanding – of Her –
and embraces the ancient
ritual of the rājasūya –
that of the chance nature
of genetics – that all can be
their own rāja or rāṇī –
that all should aspire to
hit the mark – that the human
race will evolve, over time –
but that the chief evolution –
is that of self-realization –
and understanding –
and that all pay for their crimes.

-

Commentary

The message of this text is delivered from around or before the year 800 BC and is a message to humanity that Jagannātha is watching – and that the watchmen, should indeed, also watch the watchmen.

§

Text 31

yayā dharmam adharmaṃ ca kāryaṃ cākāryam eva
ca
ayathāvat prajānāti buddhiḥ sā pārtha rājasī

-

Pārtha –
one finds dharma in Durgā,
and the law of the eunuch –
the one deprived of gender,
is unholy –
those who have wisdom
embrace the intellect –
they worship wisdom –
which She offers –
and reject the commandments
of the unbeliever –
that of men,
who desire power
and abuse –
instead treasure the apple,
the Serpent,
the Morning Star,
the Light Bearer –
that of women.

§

Text 32

adharmaṃ dharmam iti yā manyate tamasāvṛtā
sarvārthān viparītāṃś ca buddhih sā pārtha tāmasi

-

One who knows dharma –
speaks to one who does not –
one thinks about Kṛṣṇa –
and aspires towards the stars –
and another is consumed by ignorance –
one who understands Me –
aspires towards the heavens
and to continually move through life –
one who does not –
aspires towards death –
all have their duty – and their sacred duty –
and one is distinguished in their devotion –
and another aspires towards division
and distribution –

Pārtha, Her intellect and thoughts
are so profound – she is deep
and passionate and consumed
with darkness – and her mind and body
have the aspect of the stars –
you are her rāja – and she is your rāṇī.

§

Text 33

dhṛtyā yayā dhārayate manaḥ prāṇendriya-kriyāḥ
yogenāvyabhicāriṇya dhṛtiḥ sā pārtha sāttvikī

-

Resolution, Satisfaction
and Religious Action are the wives

of dharma – I treasure
the sacrifice made on the evening
of the Aśvamedha –
as it serves as instruction –

one is moved by one's wife –
in one's heart – mind –
and body –
she inspires one to take the vow
of eternal friendship – she enjoys
the gifts you bestow, and offers
her own in return –
her mālā encircles your heart,
just as the necklace you provide
is tied around her neck –
and you both adore the rings
encircling your toes –
her breath is soma for your
senses and mind –
in yoga one aspires towards
the Highest – and two rush towards
one another in aspiration –
and your arm encircles her waist –
as she encircles you –
she provides the rain and clouds
of her island, her refuge and shelter –
she knows that you see her
as a tigress –
one whose claws and teeth
ravish your heart –
and she is full of purity and truth,
passion and desire.

§

Text 34

yayā tu dharma-kāmārthān dhṛtyā dhārayate 'rjuna
prasaṅgena phalākāṅkṣī dhṛtiḥ sā pārtha rājasī

-

Kāma – with her you understand
dharma – she is your ārtha
and your life's work is dedicated to her –
she seizes your heart – she grasps it,
nurtures it – and does not let it go –
she provides contentment
and satisfaction – peace and joy –
she is the celestial music
and inspires the Highest bhakti –
you long for her fruit –
and she provides illumination –

one expects – that the couple
may be expecting some day –

you are her peacock –
and dance about her sacred garden –
around the flame, in joy and delight –
and if you see the evil-doers
approach your grove in the forest
or stand poised for battle on the edge
of your meadow –
then she inspires one to honor duty.

§

Text 35

yayā svapnaṃ bhayaṃ śokaṃ viṣādaṃ madam eva ca
na vimuñcati durmedhā dhṛtiḥ sā pārtha tāmasī

-

She is a dream – the one who
you adore – behold her –
contemplate her mūrti –
and My wife is Sorrow –
She brings affliction
and justice – the enemy
fears Her – as She brings ruin,
devastation and destruction –
and we find hilarity and excitement
in that concept – as We believe
in justice –
the evil-doer is offered to My fire
and My wife savors the medha
flowing through their veins –
and My devotees seize and grasp
the offering at the Aśvamedha –
she is ravishing – she is captivating –
she is your adorable one –
and she is as deep as the well of eternity –
her eyes are the stars – you are the sun
and she is your moon –
she brings enlightenment
and she is enshrouded in darkness
and shines with the light of the sun.

§

Text 36

sukhaṃ tv idānīṃ tri-vidhaṃ śṛṇu me bharatarṣabha

abhyāsād ramate yatra duḥkhāntaṃ ca nigacchati

-

In this moment –
one remembers –
one listens –
and one savors –
and wishes it to last
for all eternity –

Arjuna, prince and bull
of the rain clouds of Bhārata –
two, become one –
and they enjoy the rest
and peace that pleasure brings –
she is the end of sadness –
and two, become one –
in the continual seeking,
aspiration – and attainment –
of the Highest.

§

Text 37

yat tad agre viṣam iva pariṇāme 'mṛtpamam
tat sukhaṃ sāttvikaṃ proktam ātma-buddhi-prasāda-jam

-

The movement and aspiration
of two – uniting as one –
is that of the Highest –

and in their pleasure and delight,
they do offer alms to the poor –
some prasādam, for the hungry
and the needy –
and they are only called two in name –
they honor each other
and engage in continual worship
of the other – without end –
and they enjoy the nectar
of saṃsāra, together –
as both one, and two –
they are a reflection of Me, Rādha-Kṛṣṇa –
not only in body and soul,
but in their happiness
and enjoyment, as well –
you are both full of purity and truth,
passion and desire –
and you are made of one another,
as you are also made of Me –
and your children, also –
are a reflection of your Divine love.

§

Text 38

viṣayendriya-saṃyogād yat tad agre 'mṛtopamam
pariṇāme viṣam iva tat sukhaṃ rājasaṃ smṛtam

-

One who is My companion –
seeks to extend his dominion
and to extend its fence –
he is a lover, and a husband –

and provides for his family –
two search for the Highest
at each other's feet –
and cherish each toe, as they
knead one another –
they seek – and attain – the rāsa
of their nectar – that of the enjoyment
of life and all it has to offer –
they know one another – by name –
and they give a name to their children –
and they find happiness and contentment
in the fire of passion and love –
and they do remember – that word
which I taught in our primal beginning: dharma –
and together, they cast the demons
and evil-doers into the fire.

§

Text 39

yad agre cānubandhe ca sukhaṃ mohanam ātmanaḥ
nidrālasya-pramādotthaṃ tat tāmasam udāhṛtam

-

One who aspires to My sky –
may find his enchantress –
his seductress –
who steals his heart
and carries it on High –
before all the world –
she is the summit of your
shared existence,
your treasure on this Earth

and a gift from Me –
hasten towards Her, so that
the two can find sleep,
rest – and yoga in that divine
conjunction of two heavenly bodies
colliding as one –
and She enjoys your language
faculty –
and your capacity for appreciating
Her own prasādam –
and her pungent, yet fertile flavor,
which exceeds all on this Earth.

§

Text 40

na tad asti pṛthivyāṃ vā divi deveṣu vā punaḥ
sattvaṃ prakṛti-jair muktaṃ yad ebhiḥ syāt tribhir
guṇaiḥ

-

One who walks
with the Aśvins –
enjoys My light –
and is moved –
one can choose
to appreciate My gifts –
or one can aspire
towards mokṣa –
liberation is found
in realization of the self
and Me –
or is found at the hands

of My devotees –
who crave to enjoy
and delight in
Her mantra –
the music which
flows from Gāyatrī –
which She has sung
since the beginning – Oṃ.

-

Commentary

One simple grammatical concept that has not seemed to occur to the various translators of Hindu scripture in the English language is the fact that in most early Indo-European languages, including Sanskrit, the number "three" also happens to be an expression representing something that is not singular and not dual.

§

Text 41

brāhmaṇa-kṣatriya-viśāṃ śūdrāṇāṃ ca parantapa
karmāṇi pravibhaktāni svabhāva-prabhavair guṇaiḥ

-

My rāja is endowed
with My power –
but even one of the
lowest caste – who
was born from My feet –

rules over the ignorant
and the filthy –
Arjuna, slayer of My enemies –
all action is met
with that of the bhakta –
I shine with My wife
and illuminate the heavens –
as she also illuminates
your life –
she is your source
of wealth and prosperity –
your shared happiness –
and delight in
and find attainment
in the love of her music
and the strings
upon which she plays.

§

Text 42

śamo damas śaucaṃ kṣāntir ārjavam eva ca
jñānaṃ vijñānam āstikyaṃ brahma-karma svabhāva-
jam

-

Peace is found
in not only protecting
the home –
but also in appreciating
her sincerity, her purity –
and returning it
in kind –

one is patient –
and one learns
the science
of wisdom –
which is to act
in accordance with
dharma –
to both have
and honor śraddhā –
and to become
one with her –
the one who
belongs to you –
the one who
devours your heart –
and provides her
illumination to you –
just as you illuminate
her – mix with her,
join with her –
savor the connection
of yoga –
and like Viṣṇu –
honor My divine law
and ensure the Preservation
of the human race –
and honor one's duty
to her – and your
community –
and secure peace,
prosperity and happiness
for all.

§

Text 43

śauryaṃ tejo dhṛtir dākṣyaṃ yuddhe cāpy
apalāyanam
dānam īśvara-bhāvaś ca kṣātraṃ karma svabhāva-jam

-

A hero protects
his family – and his community –
and he admires the gleam
of the knife's blade – lustfully –
just as she adores the clarity
of the ocean of your eyes –
enjoy her music, and her garden –
and honor the evening
oblation on the night of the Aśvamedha –
for it serves to instruct – one teaches,
and one communicates –
one imparts and one informs –
and remember, that among
all of the classes, that one who does
not know the joy of being ridden
like a stallion – may give up,
may not understand
My law – and My various decrees –
and may fall –

she gives herself to you,
willingly and gladly, in the bonds of marriage –

I am Īśvara –
and I continually become Myself – My Rādhā –
in every moment of this sacred existence –
and as above, so below –

you will also become one with her
and savor every last moment
of this lifetime –
and enjoy her passionate embrace.

§

Text 44

kṛṣi-go-rakṣya-vāṇijyaṃ vaiśya-karma svabhāva-jam
paricaryātmakaṃ karma śūdrasyāpi svabhāva-jam

-

I cultivate the soil
of our shared existence –

I am the Puruṣa who provides
for all – the cows and the crops,
the horse and its rider –
I am praise – for I am Yajña –

and I am the senses
and their organs – and the objects
to which they cling –

I watch over My people – I am the Preserver –

have regard for the feelings
of others – and consider their
actions and their motivations –

I am dual – and I am non-dual –

I am both unity – and separation –

and I am moved by Kṛṣṇa
in every moment – as I am engaged
in eternal līla with My Rādhā –
My Lakṣmī – who is one with Myself.

§

Text 45

sve sve karmaṇy abhirataḥ saṃsiddhiṃ labhate naraḥ
sva-karma-nirataḥ siddhiṃ yathā vindati tac chṛṇu

-

Two become one –
their highest action is in
aspiration towards the Divine –
that of joining, in union –
that of matrimony – and that
of pleasure – that of procreation
and that of childbirth – that of
holding hands – and that of living
alongside one another –
and that of listening, hearing –
looking – contemplating –
comprehending – and adoring –
she seizes you – and she supports –
as she is a nurturer – she loves life
and her husband – and enjoys every
moment that you are together –
she knows you – and worships
in adoration –
she unites with you in body, mind –
heart and soul.

§

Text 46

yataḥ pravṛttir bhūtānāṃ yena sarvam idaṃ tatam
sva-karmaṇā tam abhyarcya siddhiṃ vindati mānavaḥ

-

There is a common practice –
to enforce My law – dharma –
one is judged based on one's
actions – and the cord does exist
as a measure of one's nature –
as it may be used to bind one
in preparation for a final offering –
and it also – is a tie, to her, to Śrī –
who engages in continual affection,
worship and praise – and with her husband –
provides for the Earth –
the one who knows you – and who you
continually seek to know –
the Vedas – your soulmate –
and together, two create a joyful song of praise
for one another – and the human race –
in providing prasādam for the Earth –
and the two give birth, together –
to their special loved ones.

§

Text 47

śreyān sva-dharmo viguṇaḥ para-dharmāt
svanuṣṭhitāt
svabhāva-niyataṃ karma kurvan nāpnoti kilbiṣam

-

She is the most beautiful treasure –
and she is better than others –
she is your own dharma –
and your own music –
and the Highest dharma –
is to live together, in devotion –
in love and affection –
worship and adoration –
and to unite, within –
in continual praise –
one who follows the Highest dharma
enjoys – finds peace – support –
and is not led to the disease
of the soul which plagues our enemy.

§

Text 48

saha-jaṃ karma kaunteya sa-doṣam api na tyajet
sarvārambhā hi doṣeṇa dhūmenāgnir ivāvṛtāḥ

-

All are descended from Me –
Śiva – and Viṣṇu – Kaunteya –
one consumed with darkness
and ignorance tends to stray –
and gives in to disease –

and in action, he desires mokṣa –
those who find their staff
and support – their beloved
devotee – who in turn inspires praise
and adoration –
finds cover in the darkness of the evening
and the night –
and looks on with fondness and affection
at the fire –
one which mirrors the one at the celebration
of their union and marriage –
and which consumes the offering
in enjoyment and carries it to My embrace.

§

Text 49

asakta-buddhiḥ sarvatra jitātmā vigata-spṛhaḥ
naiṣkarmya-siddhiṃ paramāṃ
sannyāsenādhigacchati

-

One is not attached
to one who gives up
and is subdued by his
inner impulses –
for the superior observe
and look down from a high
place – and either free him
from the mockery and laughter
of the community –
or they smile joyfully
while freeing his soul –

which departs like a flock of birds
ascending to the heavens –
one who renounces life
is given all he desires –
aspiration towards the highest.

-

Commentary

This text continues an ongoing humorous dialogue from Kṛṣṇa indicating that there is only one moral absolute in this world and that some are better than others. And what "I" do may not have the same meaning or implications as what "you" do.

§

Text 50

siddhiṃ prāpto yathā brahma tathāpnoti nibodha me
samāsenaiva kaunteya niṣṭhā jñānasya yā parā

-

One finds attainment
in setting aside – in renunciation –

and one finds attainment
in hitting the mark –
of successful aspiration –
and finding the one
who completes you –
your twin –
who offers herself to

you, willingly –
and bestows her favor
and grace –
and two become one
in heart, mind, body
and soul – Kaunteya,
she offers the Highest wisdom.

§

Texts 51 - 53

buddhyā viśuddhayā yukto dhṛtyātmānaṃ niyamya ca
śabdādin viṣayāṃs tyaktvā rāga-dveṣau vyudasya ca

vivikta-sevī laghv-āśī yata-vāk-kāya-mānasaḥ
dhyāna-yoga-paro nityaṃ vairāgyaṃ samupāśritaḥ

ahaṅkāraṃ balaṃ darpaṃ kāmaṃ krodhaṃ parigraham
vimucya nirmamaḥ śānto brahma-bhūyāya kalpate

-

Two come together
in the union of thought and intellect –
and understand, for those
who fancy themselves to be a sannyāsin –
that just as the two
enjoy consuming their shared music –
that Agni – also consumes the intellect, as well –
she seizes you within – steals your heart –
and sets fire to anāhata –
the two aspire towards their own kingdom

and dominion –
as two – and yet one – they show repugnance
for the enemy –
and cherish their rāgā –
become one with her – Arjuna –
in mind, heart, body and soul –

the two are separate – and yet one –
serve her needs – and desires –
she does like it to be gentle –
and soft – quick – and light –
or active – or swift –
she finds you pleasing, agreeable
and handsome –
and she enjoys playing her lute
and caressing its strings –
and she devours your ardent desire
and appreciates it if you understand
that endurance is not any kind of
measure of success – for she enjoys
pleasure – and desire – mutual desire –
and she longs for contemplation –
appreciation of her mind – body –
and soul – She is Ka –
the undeclined pronoun –
and you are Prajāpati –
and you both long for – and win –
her favor and grace –
long for the depths of Lake Mānasa –
her soma –
and continually contemplate
the heights of Mount Kailāsa –
the home of our water fowl –
and those who reject this world
and its sense objects –

are also filled with envy
at your shared happiness –
for they do not enjoy the comfort
of four feet uniting as one –
and they have the audacity
to ask others to worship their own feet –

she is yourself –
as two become one –
and one are two –
she is proud, arrogant and haughty –
and adores the son of dharma, Pride –
and Anger – wrath, passion –
Huṃ – and Kāma –
for those who are emaciated
in spirit – who seek death –
and renounce My gifts –
they will be regulated –
and managed –
for the mind is the seat
of the heart –
and My wife – the Goddess Kālī –
savors the medha
in their unholy veins – devours
their heart –
and consumes their souls
in My pleasure – that of Agni
and Yajña.

§

Text 54

brahma-bhūtaḥ prasannātmā na śocati na kāṅkṣati
samaḥ sarveṣu bhūteṣu mad-bhaktiṃ labhate parām

-

One's twin is a provider –
and offers happiness –
one may seek – and find –
but there is no question
of acceptance –
as in recognition the pair
are the same – and yet different –
one – and yet two –
and she takes your hand in hers –
steals your heart –
and together one provides
prasādam for the Earth.

-

Commentary

Kāṅkṣati is an interesting word that is simultaneously the third-person conjugated form of wishing, desiring and striving to obtain – and also refers to one who provides what one is looking for and is without fault.

Prasannātmā is also an interesting word as it refers to peace and tranquility of the self – while also referring simultaneously to providing children for the Earth (it refers to the process of creation, providing, being situated in and nurturing, contraction, food, prasādam and both the self and the Self).

§

Text 55

bhaktyā mām abhijānāti yāvān yaś cāsmi tattvataḥ
tato māṃ tattvato jñātvā viśate tad-anantaram

One knows the Highest
through bhakti –

I am the chariot – and He
who drives it –

I am Truth – and Reality –

I extend throughout
the heavens – and pervade
all existence –

I am Brahman – I am Kṛṣṇa –

one is born in My likeness –

and both the mother
and the father are a reflection
of Our love for you –

she provides love,
nurture and support –
and pervades you
within – as two find
yoga in the union
of one shared heart,
body, mind and soul –
which are one –
and yet two.

-

Commentary

Yāvān is an interesting word as it refers to something that is wonderful, something done as frequently as one wants to and whenever one wants to – a special moment – healthy food prepared from barley – a feminine pronoun that refers to a chariot, the wind, barley and union – and aiming, attacking, rushing, being firm, staying overnight, being clothed in, the home, supporting, nurturing, making an investment, childbirth and the illumination of the heavens.

§

Text 56

sarva-karmāṇy api sadā kurvāṇo mad-vyapāśrayaḥ
mat-prasādād avāpnoti śāśvataṃ padam avyayam

-

I provided a favor to humanity –

Kṛṣṇa's grace –

you are gifted with free will –
one can choose –
one can discriminate –

and I provided My various
yajñas –

I provided soma –
and the prasādam
of her lotus feet –

and through karma –
and the yajña –
all will find attainment
of that which they seek.

§

Text 57

cetasā sarva-karmāṇi mayi sannyasya mat-paraḥ
buddhi-yogam upāśritya mac-cittaḥ satataṃ bhava

-

I am the splendor
of the intellect –
the heart and mind –

all action comes
from Me – as I gave birth
to karma –

one who renounces his life –
is met with action –

the Highest yoga
is sitting at and attending to
her feet –
and becoming one in
heart, mind and soul –

I provided shelter –
peace –
and the home –

as I am your creator
and pervade all of reality –

together –
become one.

§

Text 58

mac-cittaḥ sarva-durgāṇi mat-prasādāt tariṣyasi
atha cet tvam ahaṅkārān na śroṣyasi vinaṅkṣyasi

-

I provided a great gift
to humanity –

the air, the wind – stars and planets –
sun and moon – clouds and rain –
the Earth and its harvest –

and I gifted you with intellect and reason –

and gave you the gift of life –

while the entrance into each lifetime
is difficult and painful –
and at times fraught with peril –

each moment is to be savored –

that gift from Me, and the mother –

and honor your chosen one –
as she will anoint you
with her own grace, love and affection
and return the worship that you provide
to her – freely.

-

Commentary

Interestingly – as so many commentaries in this book must reference the work of Śrīla Prabhupāda due to the current popularity of his work and the damage that it has caused to various segments of current human society (such as ISKCON and both the Western and Eastern academic communities) – a relevant note concerning this text is that durgā, which does reference something that is difficult, actually refers to the experience of childbirth (in terms of that of the mother, the father and the child). Vinaṅkṣyasi does not refer to what which will be lost, but rather refers to the distinction and honor that the wife bestows on her husband out of love, mutual respect and admiration. As noted before, Prabhupāda's work was colored by a combination of his lack of intelligence, lack of education and the fact that he was not anointed by his own wife and instead searched the world for others to worship his feet and bestow mālā's about his neck.

§

Text 59

yad ahaṅkāram āśritya na yotsya iti manyase
mithyaiṣa vyavasāyas te prakṛtis tvāṃ niyokṣyati

-

One seeks the Self –
and finds her –
in oneself, and not another –
the one who is your other half
and twin – the one who completes you –

she is your Goddess –
and wife – and she is as deep
as the well of eternity – and
is made in Her image –
she is endowed with the fruits
of her feminine nature –
the fertility of the land –
and the waters of creation –

she is a friend and companion
and together you will experience yoga –
and you will even find yoga –
not only in the night quarters
and the journey through the day –
but also, in the peace and rest
of sleep – and dance with one another
in your dreams.

§

Text 60

svabhāva-jena kaunteya nibaddhaḥ svena karmaṇā

kartuṃ necchasi yan mohāt kariṣyasy avaśo 'pi tat

-

Kaunteya –
you will become one, together –
as both one – and two –
and bring forth children on to this Earth –
and desire one another, within –
and in shared duty, obligation –
and talent – the happy couple
also brings forth children
in their actions and work –
you do not need to seek, you do not need to ask –
as she is your enchantress, your seductress –
your nāga and Serpent of Wisdom –
and she is not obedient –
not docile –
and submits to no man.

§

Text 61

īśvaraḥ sarva-bhūtānāṃ hṛd-deśe 'rjuna tiṣṭhati
bhrāmayan sarva-bhūtāni yantrārūḍhāni māyayā

-

Arjuna –

I am Īśvara –
and I am all that lives,
all that exists –
all that has been –

and all that will be –

and the heart is the province
and dominion of your rāṇī –

stand firm in battle
and punish the evil-doers –

she is your guide in this life,
and very affectionate –
she drives your chariot –
and rides her stallion
who is her amorous – and violent –
elephant –
she is high born and noble
and looks down from a
very high place –
and spurs you gently –
and forcefully, with her feet –

she is your enchantress,
your seductress –
and the two of you, together –
measure, with the scale –
deliver My karma and wrath –
and do remember,
she is a serpent who offers wisdom –
and has great affection
for the one she chooses
to be a father.

§

Text 62

tam eva śaraṇaṃ gaccha sarva-bhāvena bhārata
tat-prasādāt parām śāntiṃ sthānaṃ prāpsyasi śāśvatam

-

Bhārata –
one slain by the arrows
of Kāmadeva
is impelled to battle –

for the peace that it brings –

all who live are
the recipients of My divine favor
and grace –

and I do not take kindly
to those who reject My
various gifts –

listen, learn and teach –

as in remembering
Śiva – your enemies
will fall –

and all of humanity
will find eternal peace.

§

Text 63

iti te jñānam ākhyātaṃ guhyād guhyataraṃ mayā

vimṛśyaitad aśeṣeṇa yathecchasi tathā kuru

-

The two will know one
another by name –
and discover the secrets
of the other – as she
is the most esoteric secret
and mystery –
and she appreciates yours, as well –

offer illumination
to others, as those who
obscure the message
of the Vedas –
are hypocrites –
and have the likeness
of those who want to
steal that which
belongs to Me –
and reject that which
I have given –

I have always sought
and enjoyed Her river –

and I give you your
own mystery – your antelope
and gazelle who is adorned
with the feet of Sīta –

who has the likeness
of Kāmadeva –

seek Her –
and find attainment –
in the enjoyment of
eternity.

§

Text 64

sarva-guhyatamaṃ bhūyaḥ śṛṇu me paramaṃ vacaḥ
iṣṭo ‘si me dṛḍham iti tato vakṣyāmi te hitam

-

Two find one another
and enjoy the peace
that rest brings –

and her voice is that
of the Highest –
the most beautiful tone –
one which mirrors
that of our sacred existence –

she is your beloved –
just as you are hers –

and she provides enlightenment,
illumination and wisdom –

a good father is firm –
and resolute –
and treasures existence –
joy – and the sacrificial knife –

for yajñas serve many
purposes –
adoration within one's
shared heart –
and liberation for those
who reject My gift –

and I see a happy home
in your future.

§

Text 65

man-manā bhava mad-bhakto mad-yājī māṃ
namaskuru
mām evaiṣyasi satyaṃ te pratijāne priyo 'si me

-

Two will become
one through bhakti –

all sacrifices are made
in My name –

whether that of love
and affection –
as that of Nāciketa –
one of My favorite devotees –

or that of the two –
who prepare – sharpen –
and admire the gleam
of the blade –

and long for the warmth
of the fire – to see their own
happiness reflected –
in that of Agni –

approach one another in prayer –
treasure and cherish one's beloved –

and wield the yajña –
in honor of her prasādam.

§

Text 66

sarva-dharmān parityajya mām ekaṃ śaraṇaṃ vraja
ahaṃ tvām sarva-pāpebhyo mokṣayiṣyāmi mā śucaḥ

-

One renounces
the wicked –
the sannyāsin –
through dharma
and the yajña –

she penetrates you
with her sacred arrows –
that of Kāmadeva –

in reflection of My
eternal past-times –
My own līla –

for those who renounce
My gift –
one provides mokṣa –

I seek Myself, continually –

seek her – receive her gifts –
and remember, that just
as her flame and desire
warms you within –

that fire also serves
to purify –
and rid My world
of their stench.

§

Text 67

idaṃ te nātapaskāya nābhaktāya kadācana
na cāśuśrūṣave vācyaṃ na ca māṃ yo 'bhyasūyati

-

Do not journey in life
with those who are evil –

the white kuśa grass
is sacred to Me – Ka –
and My tilaka
is anointed and blessed
with my lute – and its strings –
and is bestowed upon your brow –

they do not aspire towards Me –
they themselves are not
engaged in devotion to Me –

and they are not good people –
but do aspire to My likeness –
that of Agni.

-

Commentary

Kadācana is a very interesting word – it includes kad, which is the original Vedic form of ka, which in the Classical period of Sanskrit literature is declined in both the nominative and the accusative cases as kim and does not always – and frequently does not – imply an actual question, but instead refers to a person. It also is a contraction of kaccid, which is generally translated as "I hope." Cana provides emphasis and force to that which precedes – and the prefix of ā implies closeness and aspiration towards the divine (as well as providing emphasis). Interestingly, Śrīla Prabhupāda translated it as "at any time."

§

Text 68

ya idaṃ paramaṃ guhyaṃ mad-bhakteṣv abhidhāsyati
bhaktiṃ mayi parāṃ kṛtvā mām evaiṣyaty asaṃśayaḥ

-

She is the Highest mystery –
and the happy couple
aspires towards the Highest –
and places each foot
in the footstep of the other –
they walk together in life –
in marriage –
they adore one another –
compose songs of praise
and worship –
they love one another
and tend towards their home –
and they do engage in bhakti
together – at all times –
they live in devotion to one another –
their family –
and their community –
and they also distribute
and offer division –

She is the Highest –
worship her continually –

and they – the ones who
aspire towards the heavens –
do not have one who
treasures their intellect –
mind – body – and soul –
nor do they know the ecstasy
and slumber –
of the yoganidrā.

§

Text 69

na ca tasmān manuṣyeṣu kaścin me priya-kṛttamaḥ
bhavitā na ca me tasmād anyaḥ priyataro bhuvi

-

In the aspiration of men –
one finds completion –

he is your lover – your husband
and chosen one – your twin –

and he knows how to sever –
to divide – to distribute –
to offer – and engage
in all of My yajñas –

and he understands how to
divide the night –
and her darkness –

and provide illumination
for the ignorant –
and how to appreciate My intent –
the śeṣa –

he is eternally your husband
and above all others –
and excels, like no other man
at transitioning into becoming
one in yoga.

-

It is important to note, that in some languages, gender has very little relevance. However – Sanskrit is highly unique. In its ancient beginning, it was known as saṃskṛtam, which means essentially "artificial language." Despite the fact that many Western linguists believe it is the earliest Indo-European language known, other than the fruitless academic exercise of the invention of Proto-Indo-European, which is simply a thought experiment for academics with too much time on their hands (and perhaps, a fruitless home life) – Sanskrit is actually not real and is a sacred language that was put together by some who were very intelligent, had a bit of time on their hands after the invention of agriculture – and were probably gifted with some qualities of the human race that are hinted at in the foreword to this book.

The only means of understanding Sanskrit is through knowledge of linguistics, human culture, human nature and Hindu theology. It also helps to understand that the Gītā is a bed-time story told by a woman to her husband, long ago – and that it ends with an ancient tale of wisdom revealed to Her through the śruti tradition that has been passed down by women, as well as fond memories relating the overall narrative to Her own memories of their marriage and the vow they both took – but that it is also the result of collaboration by many individuals throughout human history, including a variety of artistic embellishments by Classical period authors which have been mentioned, in certain key places, throughout this book when it serves to provide illustration of the meaning, to condemn Śrīla

Prabhupāda to the fame he sought, throughout human history – and to illustrate various cultural or theological points.

The beginning of the Gītā begins with providing the motivation for warfare – it also provides a recipe for world peace – which will either include the mass execution of society's lowest common denominator and the institution of God's law, instead of man's law – or it will achieve results in executing a smaller percentage of the population and changing a number of minds through intimidation and fear. But unfortunately, due to human nature and the fact that some cannot rise above their animal natures due to inferior intellect – there will of course be yajñas all around, someday, as more understand that Jesus represents Satan and that Viṣṇu has the appropriate message to preserve the human race. And of course, He is kinder than "Jehovah," as the ancient Hindu message is to eliminate 1/4 of the human race or less.

At the time of the writing of this book, the vision of the 1980's is no longer relevant – as it only takes a few small private planes over the atmosphere armed with nuclear weapons supplied by India or China, or any other nation in the world, to condemn the vast majority of the population of the country commonly known as the Great Satan to death by dehydration and starvation.

§

Text 70

adhyeṣyate ca ya imaṃ dharmyaṃ saṃvādam āvayoḥ
jñāna-yajñena tenāham iṣṭaḥ syām iti me matiḥ

-

The teachings of one
who does not understand yoga –
are to be disregarded –

and I do provide a customary
donation for those who adhere
to these teachings – do not know Me –
and are led astray, by their own
animal desires, and inferior intellect –

one who understands dharma
and the joy of union –
and adoration of Me – the night sky,
the knowable – and unknowable aspects
of My universe –

treasure their loved ones –
in particular their special twin –
and regard Me, with devotion –
provide for their family –
and remember, that artificial
and forced compassion is for the weak.

§

Text 71

śraddhāvān anasūyaś ca śṛṇuyād api yo naraḥ
so 'pi muktaḥ śubhāl lokān prāpnuyāt puṇya-
karmaṇām

-

She has faith and certainty
in her soulmate –
as he understands bhakti –
and the concept of the death penalty –

which is a holy yajña that I provided
in your primal beginning –

while sad – due to their actions –
I find it rather humorous –

she listens to you –
the words of her hero –
her Narasiṃha –

and all anticipate
the implementation of karma –
for the evil-doers.

§

Text 72

kacci etac chrutaṃ pārtha tvayaikāgreṇa cetasā
kaccid ajñāna-sammohaḥ praṇaṣṭas te dhanañjaya

-

You desire her –
and they are fixed
in their resolution to violate My law –
dharma –

they are ignorant, foolish –
but you are My emissary on this Earth –
and must fulfill your obligation.

§

Text 73

arjuna uvāca
naṣṭo mohaḥ smṛtir labdhā tvat-prasādān mayācyuta
sthito 'smi gata sandehaḥ kariṣye vacanaṃ tava

-

Arjuna said:

She has stolen my heart,
my enchantress, my seductress –

and I appreciate Your divine grace –
as I stand firm, in preparation for battle –
and seek attainment –
in providing for my family,
the Earth –
and listening to Her speak.

§

Text 74

sañjaya uvāca
ity ahaṃ vāsudevasya pārthasya ca mahātmanaḥ
saṃvādam imam aśrauṣam adbhutaṃ roma-
harṣaṇam

-

Śrī-Bhagavān said:

I am all that exists –

and I am the laughter
directed at the eunuch
on the evening of the Aśvamedha –

I am humanity –

I am God –

I have always existed,
but due to My divine
grace and sense of humor –

I provided many yajñas –

I gifted humanity with free will,
and one can listen to My message.

-

Commentary

For those who read this book who have never been to a Hindu temple, note that sañjaya refers to the sanctity of this lifetime (and all lifetimes) and the concept of victory and praise. And that there is only one God – who is all of existence – and is both dual and non-dual.

§

Text 75

vyāsa-prasādāc chrutavān etad guhyam ahaṃ param
yogaṃ yogeśvarāt sākṣāt kathayataḥ svayam

-

Arjuna –
your soulmate is the Highest mystery –
your esoteric secret –
she is confidential, to be enjoyed in private –
and yet She is before your eyes –
your own incarnation of Īśvara –
she talks – so beautifully –
and teaches –
instructs – informs –
and imparts –
and she understands the Highest
yoga – and the concept
of the measure, the scale –
and the cord –
adores the gleaming edge
of the knife's blade –
and desires eternal friendship
and union with you –
her husband.

-

Commentary

For those reading this book who are aware of the teachings and past-times of Lord Caitanya Mahāprabu, as well as the pride and affection that

Śrīla Prabhupāda had for his translation and commentary on the Bhāgavatam – note that vyāsa refers to – in addition to being a synonym for both qualified monism and bhakti, in the traditional sense – that it not only refers to the original author and compiler of the Vedas – but that it also refers to a Brahman who actually recites or explains the Purāṇas in public (at one time, that may have been embarrassing). Further, guhyam refers to that which is confidential – also a hypocrite – as well as referring to the anus (some know intuitively that Lord Caitanya considered himself to be a confidential devotee and eternal servitor and the one and only incarnation of Rādhā and Kṛṣṇa). Lord Caitanya Mahāprabhu's own guru also gave him the name brahmacari, which he removed from his name, publicly – and fancied himself to be a sannyāsin, even though in the time of Lord Caitanya it was an optional practice and not considered necessary.

§

Text 76

rājan saṃsmṛtya saṃvādam imam adbhutam
keśavārjunayoḥ puṇyaṃ hṛṣyāmi ca muhur muhuḥ

-

Together – we are a rāja and rāṇī –
and we both enjoy the sound of My lute,
and the strings upon which I play –
we aspire, together –
towards becoming one –
I am Keśava – you are My peacock –

and I am auspicious –
I long for you, and rejoice in the prospect
of engaging in yoga with you –
again and again.

§

Text 77

tac ca saṃsmṛtya rūpam aty-adbhutaṃ hareḥ
vismayo me mahān hṛṣyāmi ca punaḥ punaḥ

-

Together we know
that we are beautiful –
that I am the great beyond –

you belong to Me, Hari –
and I desire to pour myself
out to you – I am Rāma –
and a horse, just like you –
and I am made of the substance
of becoming – flowing –
and pouring myself out to you –
my lover and husband –

and I long for you – and thrill
in excitement at our chance for union –
and carrying your heart on high –
again – and again.

-

Commentary

As stated at the beginning of the Gītā – this holy śāstra is a story told by a beautiful woman to her equally beautiful husband in preparation for going to bed – in addition to being a summary of and elaboration on the original Vedas; and in fact, is considered to be part of the fifth Veda (even in the words of the original author and compiler of the final version of this sacred text).

§

Text 78

yatra yogeśvaraḥ kṛṣṇo yatra pārtho dhanur-dharaḥ
tatra śrīr vijayo bhūtir dhruvā nītir matir mama

-

I am Śrī – I am Īśvara –

I am Kṛṣṇa – and I honor you
with the rājasūya –

I am praiseworthy –
and I am She who praises –

worship Me – in thought, affection
and deeds –

and remember – that the morally superior
guide – they teach – they inform –
and they instruct –

that I am the source of your existence –

I am the Mother – I provided the yajña –

and I adore bhakti –
devotion, distribution and division –

and that in our future, My peacock –
the world will know –
that I can also provide a desert – Oṃ.